First and Second Samuel

Westminster Bible Companion

Series Editors

Patrick D. Miller
David L. Bartlett

First and Second Samuel

EUGENE H. PETERSON

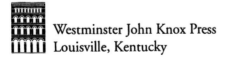

Westminster John Knox Press
Louisville, Kentucky

Book design by Publishers' WorkGroup
Cover design by Drew Stevens

First edition

Published by Westminster John Knox Press
Louisville, Kentucky

This book is printed on acid-free paper that meets the American National Standards Institute Z39.48 standard. ♾

PRINTED IN THE UNITED STATES OF AMERICA

02 03 04 05 06 07 08 — 10 9 8 7 6 5 4 3 2

A catalog card for this book may be obtained from the Library of Congress.

ISBN   0-664-25523-X

Contents

Series Foreword   xi

Introduction   1
   Story   1
   History   3
   God   5
   Jesus   6

PART 1. THE STORY OF HANNAH
   1 Samuel 1:1–2:10   11

Introduction   13

1. **Barren Hannah, 1 Samuel 1:1–8**   15
2. **Praying Hannah, 1 Samuel 1:9–18**   18
3. **Mother Hannah, 1 Samuel 1:19–28**   21
   Hannah Gives Birth to Samuel   (1:19–20)   21
   Hannah Gives Samuel to the LORD   (1:21–28)   22
4. **Blessed Hannah, 1 Samuel 2:1–10**   24

PART 2. THE STORY OF SAMUEL
   1 Samuel 2:11–12:25   29

Introduction   31

5. **Samuel Grows Up, 1 Samuel 2:11–4:1a**   33
   Eli's Scoundrel Sons   (2:11–17)   33
   Hannah's Blessed Son   (2:18–21)   34
   The Decadence of Eli's Sons   (2:22–26)   35

The Demise of Eli   (2:27–36)   35
The Rise of Samuel   (3:1–4:1a)   36

6. **The Ark of God, 1 Samuel 4:1b–7:2**   **41**
   The Ark of God Is Captured   (4:1b–11)   41
   The Ichabod Epitaph   (4:12–22)   43
   The Comedy of the Ark   (5:1–12)   44
   Getting Rid of the "Hot-Potato" Ark   (6:1–12)   46
   The Field of Joshua   (6:13–18)   48
   Kiriath-jearim   (6:19–7:2)   49

7. **Samuel Leads Israel, 1 Samuel 7:3–8:22**   **50**
   Samuel Begins His Prophetic Leadership (7:3–6)   50
   The Mizpah Victory   (7:7–14)   52
   Samuel, Champion of Justice   (7:15–17)   53
   The People Demand a King   (8:1–22)   54

8. **Samuel Establishes Saul as King, 1 Samuel 9–12**   **59**
   Saul   (9:1–2)   59
   The King Is Found   (9:3–26)   60
   Samuel Anoints Saul as King   (9:27–10:16)   62
   Saul Proclaimed King   (10:17–27a)   65
   Saul Defeats the Ammonites   (10:27b–11:14)   66
   Samuel's Valedictory Address   (12:1–25)   69

PART 3. THE STORY OF SAUL AS KING
   1 Samuel 13–15   **73**

Introduction   **75**

9. **King Saul Fights the Philistines, 1 Samuel 13–14**   **77**
   The Philistine Hornets Stirred Up   (13:1–7)   77
   Samuel Calls Saul on the Carpet   (13:8–15)   78
   Business as Usual   (13:15–18)   80
   An Aside: The Philistine Monopoly of Iron (13:19–22)   80
   The Battle at Michmash Pass   (13:23–14:23)   80
   The Cursing of Jonathan   (14:24–46)   82
   Saul the Valiant   (14:47–52)   83

10. **Saul Fights the Amalekites, 1 Samuel 15**   84
    "Holy War"   (15:1–9)   84
    Unholy King   (15:10–35)   85

PART 4. THE STORY OF SAUL AND DAVID'S RIVALRY
    1 Samuel 16–31   89

Introduction   91

11. **David Anointed King, 1 Samuel 16:1–13**   93
    Samuel Goes to Bethlehem   (16:1–5)   93
    Samuel Anoints David King   (16:6–13)   94

12. **David Joins Saul's Court, 1 Samuel 16:14–18:5**   95
    David Serves Saul as Court Musician   (16:14–23)   95
    David Serves Saul against the Philistines   (17:1–58)   96
    David Serves Saul's Family   (18:1–5)   100

13. **Saul Turns against David, 1 Samuel 18:6–20:42**   102
    Saul Becomes Jealous   (18:6–16)   102
    Saul Schemes against David   (18:17–30)   103
    Saul Orders David's Murder   (19:1–17)   104
    Saul Himself Goes after David   (19:18–24)   105
    Saul Hardens in His Hate of David   (20:1–42)   106

14. **David's Wilderness Years, 1 Samuel 21–30**   109
    David at Nob   (21:1–9)   110
    David at Gath   (21:10–15)   111
    David at Adullam   (22:1–2)   112
    David at Mizpeh in Moab   (22:3–5)   113
    The Massacre at Nob   (22:6–23)   114
    David at Keilah   (23:1–14)   115
    David at Horesh   (23:15–29)   116
    David at En-gedi   (24:1–22)   117
    Samuel's Funeral   (25:1)   118
    David at Carmel: Nabal and Abigail   (25:2–42)   119
    David in the Wilderness of Ziph   (26:1–25)   122
    David at Gath (Again)   (27:1–28:2)   123
    Saul and the Witch of Endor   (28:3–25)   125
    David Excused from the Philistine Army   (29:1–11)   127
    David at the Wadi (Brook) Besor   (30:1–31)   128

15. The End of Saul, 1 Samuel 31   133

PART 5. THE STORY OF DAVID AS KING
      2 Samuel 1–24   135

Introduction   137

16. David Made King over Judah, 2 Samuel 1:1–2:11   139
      David's Lament over Saul   (1:1–27)   139
      David Moves to Hebron   (2:1–4a)   144
      David Courts Jabesh-Gilead   (2:4b–7)   145
      Abner's Play for Power   (2:8–11)   146

17. David's Civil War, 2 Samuel 2:12–4:12   147
      Abner and Joab at Gibeon   (2:12–32)   147
      Abner Makes a Deal with David   (3:1–21)   149
      Joab Murders Abner   (3:22–38)   151
      Rechab and Baanah Murder Ishbaal   (4:1–12)   153

18. David Consolidates Israel and Judah, 2 Samuel 5–10   156
      Israel's Elders Anoint David King   (5:1–5)   156
      Jerusalem Captured: "The City of David" (5:6–10)   157
      House and Family   (5:11–16)   159
      Philistines Again   (5:17–25)   160
      The Ark   (6:1–23)   161
      Covenant and Prayer   (7:1–29)   166
      More Fighting   (8:1–14)   170
      Government Appointments   (8:15–18)   171
      Mephibosheth Shows Up   (9:1–13)   172
      Still More Fighting   (10:1–19)   175

19. David's Sin with Bathsheba and Uriah, 2 Samuel 11–12   180
      Bathsheba   (11:1–27a)   180
      Nathan   (11:27b–12:15a)   183
      Bathsheba's Two Children   (12:15b–25)   187
      The Ammonites Again   (12:26–31)   188

20. David's Troubles with Sons and Others, 2 Samuel 13–20   190
      The Rape of Tamar   (13:1–22)   190
      The Murder of Amnon   (13:23–38)   194
      The Return of Absalom   (14:1–33)   196

The Coup of Absalom   (15:1–12)   202
The Flight of David   (15:13–16:14)   207
Absalom's War   (16:15–18:18)   213
David's Mourning   (18:19–19:8a)   223
David's Return   (19:1–43)   227
A Second Revolt: Sheba   (20:1–26)   236

21. David in Retrospect, 2 Samuel 21–24   **242**
First Story: The Famine and Rizpah   (21:1–14)   243
First List: David's Giant Killers   (21:15–22)   246
First Poem: "The LORD Is My Rock"   (22:1–51)   247
Second Poem: "The Last Words of David"   (23:1–7)   256
Second List: "The Names of the Warriors"   (23:8–39)   259
Second Story: The Pestilence and Araunah   (24:1–25)   261

Works Cited   **269**

Series Foreword

This series of study guides to the Bible is offered to the church and more specifically to the laity. In daily devotions, in church school classes, and in listening to the preached word, individual Christians turn to the Bible for a sustaining word, a challenging word, and a sense of direction. The word that scripture brings may be highly personal as one deals with the demands and surprises, the joys and sorrows, of daily life. It also may have broader dimensions as people wrestle with moral and theological issues that involve us all. In every congregation and denomination, controversies arise that send ministry and laity alike back to the Word of God to find direction for dealing with difficult matters that confront us.

A significant number of lay women and men in the church also find themselves called to the service of teaching. Most of the time they will be teaching the Bible. In many churches, the primary sustained attention to the Bible and the discovery of its riches for our lives have come from the ongoing teaching of the Bible by persons who have not engaged in formal theological education. They have been willing, and often eager, to study the Bible in order to help others drink from its living water.

This volume is part of a series of books, the Westminster Bible Companion, intended to help the laity of the church read the Bible more clearly and intelligently. Whether such reading is for personal direction or for the teaching of others, the reader cannot avoid the difficulties of trying to understand these words from long ago. The scriptures are clear and clearly available to everyone as they call us to faith in the God who is revealed in Jesus Christ and as they offer to every human being the word of salvation. No companion volumes are necessary in order to hear such words truly. Yet every reader of scripture who pauses to ponder and think further about any text has questions that are not immediately answerable simply by reading the text of scripture. Such questions may be about historical and geographical details or about words that are obscure or so loaded with meaning that one cannot tell at a glance what is at stake. They may be about the fundamental meaning of a passage or about what connection a particular text might have to our contemporary world. Or a teacher preparing for a church school class may simply want to know: What should I say about this biblical passage when I have to teach it next Sunday? It is our hope that these volumes, written by teachers and pastors with long experience studying and teaching the Bible in the church, will help members of the church who want and need to study the Bible with their questions.

The New Revised Standard Version of the Bible is the basis for the interpretive comments that each author provides. The NRSV text is presented at the beginning of the discussion so that the reader may have at hand in a single volume both the scripture passage and the exposition of its meaning. In some instances, where inclusion of the entire passage is not necessary for understanding either the text or the interpreter's discussion, the presentation of the NRSV text may be abbreviated. Usually, the whole of the biblical text is given.

We hope this series will serve the community of faith, opening the Word of God to all the people, so that they may be sustained and guided by it.

Introduction

The stories of Hannah, Samuel, Saul, and David compose the two-volume narrative that is designated in our English Bibles as First and Second Samuel. Chronologically, they are clustered around the year 1000 B.C., the millennial midpoint between the call of Abraham, the father of Israel, nearly a thousand years earlier (about 1800 B.C.) and the birth of Jesus, the Christ, a thousand years later.

Our Hebrew ancestors in the faith were magnificent storytellers. The stories they told reverberate down through the corridors of communities at worship and resonate in our hearts as sharply in tune with reality as when they were first told. The stories of Adam and Eve, Abraham and Isaac, Jacob and Rachel, Moses and Joshua, Miriam and Aaron, Deborah and Barak, Ruth and Naomi, Esther and Mordecai map the country of our humanity, show its contours, reveal its dimensions. Mostly what they show is that to be human means to deal with God. And that everything we encounter and experience—birth and death, hunger and thirst, money and weapons, weather and mountains, friendship and betrayal, marriage and adultery—is included, every nuance and detail of it, in dealing with God.

STORY

It is significant that stories are given such a prominent role in revealing God and God's ways to us. In both the Old and New Testaments of our Christian scriptures stories are the major verbal means of bringing God's word to us. For that we can be grateful, for story is our most accessible form of speech. Young and old love stories. Literate and illiterate alike tell and listen to stories. Neither stupidity nor sophistication puts us outside the magnetic field of story. The only serious rival to story in terms of accessibility and attraction is song, and there are plenty of those in the Bible too.

1

But there is another reason for the appropriateness of story as a major means of bringing us God's word. Story doesn't just tell us something and leave it there—it invites our participation. A good storyteller gathers us into the story. We feel the emotions, get caught up in the drama, identify with the characters, see into nooks and crannies of life that we had over-looked, realize there is more to this business of being human than we had yet explored. If the storyteller is good, doors and windows open. The He-brews were good storytellers, good in both the artistic and moral senses.

One of the characteristic marks of our Hebrew storytellers is a certain reticence. There is an austere, spare quality to their stories. They don't tell us too much. They leave a lot of blanks in the narration, an implicit invi-tation to enter the story ourselves, just as we are, and find how we fit into it. "The Scripture stories do not, like Homer's, court our favor, they do not flatter us that they may please us and enchant us—they seek to subject us, and if we refuse to be subjected we are rebels" (Auerbach, *Mimesis*, 15). These are stories that respect our freedom; they don't manipulate us, don't force us. They show us a spacious world in which God creates and saves and blesses. First through our imaginations and then through our faith—imagination and faith are close kin here—they offer us a place in the story, invite us into this large story that takes place under the broad skies of God's purposes, in contrast to the gossipy anecdotes that we cook up in the stuffy closet of the self.

The form in which language comes to us is as important as its content. If we mistake its form, we will almost certainly respond wrongly to its con-tent. If we mistake a recipe for vegetable stew for a set of clues for finding buried treasure, no matter how carefully we read it, we will end up as poor as ever and hungry besides. If we misread a highway road sign "60 MILES PER HOUR" as a randomly posted piece of information rather than as a stern imperative, "Don't drive over 60 miles per hour!" we will eventually find ourselves pulled over on the side of the road with a police officer cor-recting our grammar. Ordinarily, we learn these discriminations early and well and give form and content equal weight in determining meaning.

But when it comes to scripture we don't do nearly as well. Maybe it is because scripture comes to us so authoritatively, *God's* word, that we think all we can do is submit and obey. Submission and obedience are part of it, but first we have to listen. And listening requires listening to the *way* it is said (form) as well as *what* is said (content).

Stories suffer misinterpretation when we don't submit to them simply as stories. We are caught off guard when divine revelation arrives in such ordinary garb, and think it's our job to dress it up in the latest Paris silk gown of theology, or outfit it in a sturdy three-piece suit of ethics, before we can deal with it. The simple, or not so simple, story is soon, like David under Saul's armor, so encumbered with moral admonitions, theological constructs, and scholarly debates that it can hardly move. Of course, there are always moral, theological, historical elements in these stories that need to be studied and ascertained, but never in spite of or in defiance of the story that is being told. One of the tasks of this commentary will be to keep the story out in front.

One of many welcome consequences of learning to "read" our lives in the lives of Hannah, Samuel, Saul, and David is a sense of affirmation and freedom: We don't have to fit into prefabricated moral or mental or religious boxes before we are admitted into the company of God—we are taken seriously just as we are and given a place in God's story, for it is, after all, *God's* story; none of us are the leading characters in the stories of our lives.

For the biblical way is not so much to present us with a moral code and tell us "Live up to this"; nor is it to set out a system of doctrine and say, "Think like this and you will live well." The biblical way is to tell a story and invite us: "Live *into* this—this is what it looks like to be human in this God-made and God-ruled world; this is what is involved in becoming and maturing as a human being." We do violence to the biblical revelation when we "use" it for what we can get out of it or what we think will provide color and spice to our otherwise bland lives. That results in a kind of "boutique spirituality"—God as decoration, God as enhancement. The Samuel narrative will not allow that. In the reading, as we submit our lives to what we read, we find that we are not being led to see God in our stories but to see our stories in God's. God is the larger context and plot in which my story finds itself.

Such reading will necessarily be a prayerful reading—a God-listening, God-answering reading. The entire story, after all, is framed by prayer: Hannah's prayer at the beginning (1 Samuel 1–2) and David's prayer near the end (2 Samuel 22–23) bracket the narrative as written; the clear intent of the writer is that they also bracket the narrative as read.

HISTORY

Alongside the necessity of entering into these stories, as stories, is the parallel necessity of acquiring a strong sense of history. History is the context in which these stories are told. First and Second Samuel are grouped among the books of the Old Testament commonly designated as "historical."

Among ancient peoples, no one was more interested in history than the Hebrews. They were the world's first historians. While some of their neighbors were absorbed in gazing at the stars, hoping to discover their fate in the signs of the zodiac, and others were spinning myths that accounted for the comic and tragic complexities of human behavior, and still others were attempting to decipher the weather, animal entrails, unusual trees, and spectacular mountains for omens and clues regarding the future, the Hebrews were simply paying attention to what happened: They observed *events*.

They were intent on observing what happened in and around them because they believed that God was personally alive and active in the world, in their community, and in them. Life could not be accounted for by something less than life, no matter how impressive and mysterious that something was, whether an eclipse of the sun, spots on the liver of a goat, or the hiss of steam from a fissure in the earth. God could not be reduced to astronomical, physiological, geological, or psychological phenomena; God was *alive*, always and everywhere working his will, challenging persons with his call, evoking faith and obedience, shaping a worshiping community, showing his love and compassion, and working out judgment on sin. And none of this "in general" or "at large," but at particular times, in specific places, with named persons: *history*.

For the Hebrews, God was not an idea for philosophers to discuss or a force for priests to manipulate. God was not a part of creation that could be studied and observed and managed. God was *person*—a person to be worshiped or defied, believed or rejected, loved or hated, in time and place. It is for this reason that the Hebrews were interested in dates and events, in persons and circumstances—in history. They knew that God met them in the ordinary and extraordinary occurrences that made up the stuff of their daily lives. It never seemed to have occurred to the Hebrews that they could deal better with God by escaping from history. History was the *medium* in which God worked salvation, just as paint and canvas was the medium in which Rembrandt made pictures. We cannot get closer to God by distancing ourselves from the mess of history.

This deeply pervasive sense of history—the dignity of their place in history, the presence of God in history—accounts for the way in which the Hebrews told their stories, for they did not, as was the fashion in the ancient world, make up and embellish fanciful stories. Their stories were not for entertainment or for explanation but for revelation. Their storytelling

GOOD PREACHING!

was put to the service of giving narrative shape to actual people and circumstances in their dealings with God, and in God's dealing with them.

This is a difficult mind-set to acquire among us, for we are used to getting our history from so-called secular historians, scholars, and journalists for whom God is not involved or present in what they study and write. We are thoroughly trained by our schools, daily newspapers, and telecasts to read history totally in terms of politics and economics, human interest, and environmental conditions. But for the Hebrews there simply was *no* secular history. None. Everything that happened, happened in a world penetrated by God. Since they do not talk a lot about God in their storytelling, it is easy for us to forget that God is always the invisible and mostly silent presence in everything that is taking place. But if we forget for very long, we will not understand either what was written or the way it was written. God is never absent from this story and never peripheral to it. As far as the Hebrews were concerned, the only reason for paying attention to people and events was to stay alert to God.

GOD

God is the primary subject of these stories. Subject, not object. These stories are not *about* God, they are stories that reveal a world, an existence, in which God speaks and acts, chooses and loves, judges and saves.

These stories are all told from the point of view and with the assumptions of men and women to whom God had *revealed* himself and with whom God had made a *covenant*. God was not guesswork for them. God was not an option for them. Moses was history. Sinai was a fact. Covenant was explicit. They didn't know everything, but they knew something: "Hear, O Israel: The LORD is our God, the LORD alone. You shall love the LORD your God with all your heart, and with all your soul, and with all your might" (Deut. 6:4–5).

What is it like to live in a world of clear revelation and concise covenant? Is everything clear and concise? As a matter of fact, it is not. And these stories make it quite plain that it is not. There is ambiguity and incongruity. There is darkness and light. In the earlier writing of the Bible we were treated to a spectacular array of divine interventions: the conception and birth of Isaac, deliverance from Egypt, the Ten Commandments, quail and manna in the wilderness, the fall of Jericho—page after page of miracles and wonders. But now it is as if we are being weaned from holy miracles, or at least from dependence on them. God permeates all of life, but hiddenly. We see men and women learning to recognize God's presence in an act of ordinary friendship quite as clearly as in the "cloud by day" and the "fire by night." We see them being trained to discern God's word in the midst of betrayal and suffering as well as in the place of worship, explicit with altar and incense and candles. God, invisible and silent, is often, even mostly, not apparent, but God is no less present.

The Samuel stories do not smooth difficulties over with a peppy slogan. They don't abstract an episode in life into a moral lesson. In a world in which God is revealed and makes covenant with us, they also reveal the difficulties and confusions that we experience in such a world: the dodges and evasions of sin, the complications of family and politics, and the conditions imposed by culture. They also, with "penetrating artistry" (von Rad), keep us continuously aware of God present and at work in what we sometimes are wont to call the secular world and our ordinary lives. But they don't do it by shouting "God!" at us. They don't bully us with moral cudgels. They tell us stories, real and realistic stories that "story" our seemingly plotless lives and open our ears and eyes to the *real* story, the real *world*, so that we can live in it with all our hearts, souls, minds, and strength. One of our greatest Old Testament scholars, Gerhard von Rad, once commented on how in "masterly fashion they handle every style of writing—the gamut runs from Saul's sombre tragedy with the witch of Endor (I Sam. XXVIII) right up to burlesque (the death of Nabal, I Sam. XXV.36–8). Their portrayal is fascinating: but fascinating, too, however paradoxical it may sound, is their art of saying nothing, of not voicing the comment which the reader himself cannot help making" (von Rad, *Old Testament Theology*, I, p. 54).

JESUS

When we step back and observe the entire Genesis to Revelation context in which this Samuel narrative occurs, it is obvious that the center is occupied by Jesus Christ. From the very beginning of the church's life, Christians have read the Hebrew scriptures in a way that understood that God's revelation in Jesus was implicit from the outset. Our earliest Christian writers and teachers were fond of using the phrase "before [or "from" or "since"] the foundation of the world" to insist that what God revealed of God's self in Jesus was not an afterthought, something tacked on, but was in place and operative from the beginning (see Matt. 25:34; John 17:34; Eph. 1:4; 1 Peter 1:20; Rev. 13:8). And so our Christian ancestors read these Samuel narratives while keeping conscious company with Jesus, prayerfully noticing anticipations, similarities, patterns, and confirmations. If it was all one story, Genesis to Revelation, it made sense to give the final and conclusive coming together of the story (in Jesus) interpretive influence over the earlier parts. That is why Luther taught us to read the Hebrew scriptures always with an eye to "what drives (or impels) towards Christ."

In modern times, though (since the seventeenth-and-eighteenth-century Enlightenment), such "Christian" reading has not been encouraged by many of our most influential teachers and scholars. We have been trained to examine the text as objectively as possible, excluding anything not explicitly in the text from the interpretive process: ourselves—our ideas, our emotions, our commitments, our values—and, of course, Jesus, since he was not part of the "original" writing. The intent was to get a rigorously honest and accurate reading of the text by setting up controlled laboratory conditions for reading; readers put on white coats, face masks, and rubber gloves so that in the act of reading they would not contaminate the text they were reading. The idea was that by purging the reader of personal bias and fanciful notions, nothing outside the text would be present to interfere with the original meaning. Much good was accomplished in this endeavor, for over the centuries a great deal of distortion and contamination had accumulated around the reading of the Bible. In plenty of times and places, the ideas and feelings that people brought *to* the reading of the text were imposed *on* the text and virtually obliterated the text itself. The Christian mind needed a good spring-cleaning from centuries of bad reading habits, reading "into" the text a person's private moral or devotional or political or theological agenda. The new disciplines of reading and interpreting the text ("historical criticism" is the usual term) were both necessary and salutary.

But eventually Christian readers realized that this way of reading, for all its benefits, made it difficult if not impossible to read the text in the way intended—that is to say, personally, with commitments and relationships, in the larger context of all the other biblical books, and with Jesus as the interpretive voice. The strictly and objectively historical and rationalist way of reading scripture excluded too much, far too much, of what was being read; it excluded, in fact, most of what was there: the *story*—person, plot, relationships, responses, prayers. The historical-critical project for improving Bible interpretation turned out to be like some of the modern chemical efforts to improve agriculture—pesticides used indiscriminately did what they were supposed to do, they got rid of insects and disease, but they also sterilized the soil. "And the last state . . . is worse than the first" (Luke 11:26).

Today there is a widespread consensus in the Christian community that the reader of scripture must be totally involved—heart and soul, mind and body—in the reading of scripture. We would be fools to discard the sturdy disciplines acquired and insisted on throughout the last two hundred years which prevent us from *intruding* on the text; but we would be even more foolish if we let these disciplines keep us from *participating* in the text. We are intended to enter the world of the text, listening for resonances, alert to relationships, and most of all mindful of God, for this is a *living* text. This kind of reading requires a developed imagination and wide-ranging memory, so that what is not stated and not seen on the page, on a particular page of the Bible, is present to the reader. And that is why Jesus is the key to reading Samuel, for Jesus through the Holy Spirit reveals God as personal and relational, affirming our very earthy humanity in every detail, calling us by name to lives of repentance and discipleship. Jesus does not exempt us from the hard work of careful study and wise discernment. What he does is prevent us from exempting ourselves from our place in the text as believers and followers. For as long as Jesus holds the interpretive center in our reading of Holy Scripture, we cannot depersonalize the text into general religious and moral principles or detach ourselves from believing and obedient response.

First and Second Samuel were written, along with 1 and 2 Kings, in Hebrew as a single work on two scrolls. It was divided into the four books we now have when it was translated into Greek in the second century B.C. Writing in Greek took twice the space of writing in Hebrew, and so four scrolls were now required. For convenience, the church has maintained the division. It should be kept in mind, though, that 1 and 2 Samuel are the first volume of the original two-volume work that tells the story of the five-hundred-year period of Israel's existence under a monarchy. The larger "historical books" division of the Old Testament, from Joshua to Esther, tells the story from the conquest of Canaan (about 1200 B.C.E.) to life under Persian rule (about 400 B.C.E.).

For the last hundred years, scholars have studied how and why and when this narrative came to be written. Their work constitutes literary sleuthing of the most brilliant sort. The scholarly consensus is that what we have before us now was written, using a variety of written and oral sources, during the exile (sixth century B.C.E.), by a writer (or writers) who combined literary art and theological insight in a most extraordinary way to create, under the shaping influence of the Holy Spirit, this stunningly executed narrative.

Four figures dominate the narrative of 1 and 2 Samuel: Hannah,

Samuel, Saul, and David. Hannah's prayers and spirituality set the context for what follows, much as Mary's do for the Gospels. One of our finest commentators on Samuel, Hans Hertzberg, sees the three stories that follow Hannah as forming a kind of triptych: "Samuel and David, who make a frame round the dark, problematical figure of King Saul, are figures of striking significance in this history of the Kingdom, and much of the message of the Bible is embedded in their lives and in their struggles; and all three, each in his own way, are forerunners and heralds of the real King" (Hertzberg, *I & II Samuel*, 20).

Part 1. The Story of Hannah

1 Samuel 1:1–2:10

Introduction

The story of Hannah is a story in its own right. Hannah is not merely the mother of Samuel, the occasion of a birth story that functions as a kind of entryway to the dominating stories of Samuel, Saul, and David. She holds her own with the best of them. She is as significant, both historically and spiritually, as the three men who follow her in the Samuel narrative.

Historically, the country and culture were a mess. Following the glorious deliverance from Egypt, the revelation at Sinai, and the forty years of wilderness providence, and then the stunning conquest of Canaan, the promised land, things had more or less fallen apart. The book of Judges tells the story—moral and political anarchy, with occasional bright moments when a Deborah or Samson or Gideon would step out of the squalor and act decisively in *God's* name, clearly speak *God's* word. But on the whole and in general things were going from bad to worse. The final sentence in Judges is "all the people did what was right in their own eyes" (Judg. 21:25).

And then, abruptly, in the midst of this anarchy, the entire mood and meaning of that world shifts into a new key as the stories of two women, Ruth and Hannah, are told in sequence. The book of Ruth in our English Bibles (although not in the original Hebrew arrangement) immediately precedes 1 Samuel, which opens with the story of Hannah. Read side by side, the two stories reinforce each other—they are parallel stories. The women are roughly contemporary, but not neighbors; Hannah lived in central Palestine, Ruth in the south. Both stories are similar in that they are quiet stories, worked out in out-of-the-way, domestic circumstances. They are similar also in that each woman stubbornly and prayerfully sets herself against "the way things are," the circumstances handed her by society, and before you know it, history is flowing in a different direction, the purposes of God once again discernible. The spiritualities of these two women—intensely local, insistently personal, defiant of culture, God-centered—are, in the providence of God, the catalyst for initiating the great reversal that is extensively narrated in the story of David and receives its fullest expression in Jesus.

Ruth's story, since she gets a book with her name on it, is the more well known—the foreign widow who finds love in a strange land, becomes the great-grandmother of David (Ruth 4:13–21), and then is honored by name in the genealogy of Jesus (Matt. 1:5). Hannah's story is of parallel significance. She breaks out of the role of "barren wife" imposed on her by her rival's malice, her husband's love, and her priest's ignorance, and prays herself into the conception and birthing of Samuel, who will preside over the renaissance of Israel's identity as the people of God. She deserves a story of her own, out of the shadows of the three men whose stories follow.

1. Barren Hannah
1 Samuel 1:1–8

1:1 **There was a certain man of Ramathaim, a Zuphite from the hill country of Ephraim, whose name was Elkanah son of Jeroham son of Elihu son of Tohu son of Zuph, an Ephraimite.** [2] **He had two wives; the name of the one was Hannah, and the name of the other Peninnah. Peninnah had children, but Hannah had no children.**

[3] **Now this man used to go up year by year from his town to worship and to sacrifice to the LORD of hosts at Shiloh, where the two sons of Eli, Hophni and Phinehas, were priests of the LORD.** [4] **On the day when Elkanah sacrificed, he would give portions to his wife Peninnah and to all her sons and daughters;** [5] **but to Hannah he gave a double portion, because he loved her, though the LORD had closed her womb.** [6] **Her rival used to provoke her severely, to irritate her, because the LORD had closed her womb.** [7] **So it went on year by year; as often as she went up to the house of the LORD, she used to provoke her. Therefore Hannah wept and would not eat.** [8] **Her husband Elkanah said to her, "Hannah, why do you weep? Why do you not eat? Why is your heart sad? Am I not more to you than ten sons?**

Hannah's story opens with a strong assertion of place and person. Nine proper names dominate the opening sentence, three referring to places and six to persons. This is no "once upon a time" story; this is no timeless moral lesson; we are firmly set down in a particular place in the presence of a man with four generations of history backing him up. The place, Ephraim, is fertile and beautiful, blessed with

> the choice gifts of heaven above,
> and of the deep that lies beneath;
> with the choice fruits of the sun,
> and the rich yield of the months.
> (Deut. 33:13–14)

And Elkanah, with four generations of backing, is clearly from a respected family—no Johnny-come-lately.

The prosperous, "solid citizen" picture of Elkanah is rounded out with the detail that will provide internal emotional dynamics to the plot as it unfolds: There are two wives in Elkanah's household, and they don't get along, for the reason that one, Peninnah, has children and the other, Hannah, does not. Hannah's barren condition is the negative note around which the story forms.

And so our attention immediately shifts from the fertility of place and family to Hannah's bereftness. The barren wife is an established biblical motif: Hannah's childlessness is framed by Sarah in Genesis (Gen. 16:1 and 18:9–15) and Elizabeth in the Gospel of Luke (Luke 1:7). The stark phrase "but Hannah had no children" pulls us into the story in a way that descriptions of fertile landscape and solid family, no matter how extravagant, could never do. Even in our culture, where women are no longer defined and valued by their ability to bear children, the pain and sometimes bitterness of those who want to bear children and cannot is familiar. We read "no children" and are immediately in a world of longings, frustrations, tears, and prayers. This story is no longer outside us; it is beginning to get inside us—or we inside it. And the way in, as in so much of life, is through pain and prayer.

The scene shifts to the place of prayer and worship, to Shiloh, where Elkanah made a devout and annual pilgrimage. Shiloh, in the rolling hill country of central Palestine, was less than twenty miles from Elkanah's hometown of Ramah. It was the most important site for worship during the approximately two-hundred-year period from the completion of the conquest under Joshua to the establishment of the monarchy under David. The tabernacle and the ark of the covenant were there. All Israel assembled there annually for worship (Judg. 21:19). In the 1920s, Danish archaeologists identified and excavated the site, so modern visitors to the Holy Land can now view the famous place of worship.

In the normal course of things, a place of worship does not make us into something we are not, but, rather, intensifies whatever we bring to it. And so we see it here: Elkanah's basic generosity is heightened. Instead of blaming or shunning Hannah because she did not bear him children, he went out of his way to compensate for her loss, doubling her gifts from the altar. At the same time and in the same place, Peninnah's mean-spirited cruelty is given scope, using the occasion to lord it over her rival wife. Smug with her own children, she would teasingly and relentlessly ("provoke" occurs twice in the passage) mock Hannah's empty womb, reducing Hannah to tears. It is an odd thing, but amply verified in any place of worship and among any gathering of worshipers, that religion brings out the best in some people, the worst in others. Shiloh evoked generosity in Elkanah but meanness in Peninnah, with Hannah whipsawed between the two of them.

Elkanah tries to help, tries to alleviate her sorrow. By asking four rhetorical questions (1 Sam. 1:8), he attempts to shift her attention from what she does not have, a child, to what she does have, namely, a loving husband. Going against the grain of all the cultural assumptions of that patriarchal society, Elkanah valued Hannah simply for who she was, her intrinsic personhood, and not for what she could produce. Against the stream of the age, which viewed woman as instrument, Elkanah cried out to Hannah, "With or without sons, you are precious to me simply for who you are!" It was a charged moment, woman not as instrument but as person in her own right. All these centuries later we are still trying to translate Elkanah's ethical passion into normative living, rescuing women from imposed societal assumptions.

2. Praying Hannah
1 Samuel 1:9–18

But no matter how passionate, and compassionate, her husband's love, Hannah had needs he could not meet. After the ritual of the annual sacrificial meal, she went off by herself to pray:

> 1:9 **After they had eaten and drunk at Shiloh, Hannah rose and presented herself before the LORD. Now Eli the priest was sitting on the seat beside the doorpost of the temple of the LORD. 10 She was deeply distressed and prayed to the LORD, and wept bitterly. 11 She made this vow: "O LORD of hosts, if only you will look on the misery of your servant, and remember me, and not forget your servant, but will give to your servant a male child, then I will set him before you as a nazirite until the day of his death. he shall drink neither wine nor intoxicants, and no razor shall touch his head."**
>
> **12 As she continued praying before the LORD, Eli observed her mouth. 13 Hannah was praying silently; only her lips moved, but her voice was not heard; therefore Eli thought she was drunk. 14 So Eli said to her, "How long will you make a drunken spectacle of yourself? Put away your wine." 15 But Hannah answered, "No, my lord, I am a woman deeply troubled; I have drunk neither wine nor strong drink, but I have been pouring out my soul before the LORD. 16 Do not regard your servant as a worthless woman, for I have been speaking out of my great anxiety and vexation all this time." 17 Then Eli answered, "Go in peace; the God of Israel grant the petition you have made to him." 18 And she said, "Let your servant find favor in your sight." Then the woman went to her quarters, ate and drank with her husband, and her countenance was sad no longer.**

Most prayer begins as Hannah's did, in pain and with tears. The lament is the most common kind of prayer in the Psalms, our basic prayer book. When we don't have what we need to be ourselves, and are unwilling to settle for what either friend (Elkanah) or foe (Peninnah) makes of our condition, we present ourselves before the Lord—we pray.

But while Hannah's prayer is provoked by pain, it is not confined to it. Her prayer takes the form of a vow (v. 11). By casting her prayer in the form of a vow, she involves herself responsibly, even sacrificially, in her prayer, for she both asks and gives. She asks for a child from God, but her prayer also includes the giving of this same child back to God. Her generosity is as integral to her prayer as her poverty. Her prayer anticipates both getting and giving.

"Nazirite" refers to a person whose total dedication to God's service was marked by abstention from alcohol and haircuts (see Numbers 6). In other words, this was no offhand or whimsical offering.

Hannah prays in solitude and silence. She is not, though, unobserved. Eli, the presiding priest of the Shiloh sanctuary, is at his supervisory post at the doorway and has been watching her. He has watched the soundless movements of her mouth long enough to conclude that she is drunk. It is not the last time that a person at prayer will so violate the conventions of prayer that he or she will be accused of drunkenness. The followers of Jesus, praying on the day of Pentecost, are similarly maligned (Acts 2:13–15). And for similar reasons: *This* is not the way normal, respectable people pray.

To Eli, the normal way of prayer, then, is by means of ritual, incense, and animal sacrifice, a gathering of the community directed by a priest. And then Hannah shows up, without bringing a sacrifice, without asking directions from the priest, and simply prays, soaring past all the liturgical conventions of her age, boldly presenting her petition before her God without benefit of clergy. She uses her own words, her own voice, without intermediaries. Later, rabbis focus on Hannah as a model of authentic prayer, "the prayer of the heart," which eventually replaced sacrifice altogether.

Eli has never seen anything like it. In charge of keeping order in the sanctuary, authorized to guard and guide the religious life of the people, he sees her only as a bag lady, a drunk, and reprimands her, accusing her of violating the decorum of the sacred place of worship. But Hannah is not intimidated by religious authority. She will not be confined by precedent. She is more attentive to her heart than to the hierarchy. She dismisses his charges and asserts her right to pray in her own way by laying out the pain of her life before the Lord. We can hardly miss the unprecedented daring of Hannah. This seemingly ordinary woman, with nothing to distinguish her but her longing, prays without a script, privately, silently. She steps out of the roles given her by her contemporaries and enters holy history in an extraordinary way. Her act is all the more extraordinary in that, by all accounts, she seems to be the first woman, perhaps even the first "ordinary person," to take her place in the sanctuary and give voice to her need, sidestepping the system of sacrifice and liturgy.

Ordinary Hannah, marginal Hannah, unordained Hannah comes into view at this moment as one of our premier exemplars of prayer. She boldly asserts that the efficacy of prayer proceeds neither from piety nor position, but from need: "I am a woman deeply troubled."

The priest Eli does not forfeit his usefulness by his ignorant and insensitive accusation. There is still a place for the priest in all this! The formalities of religion and the spontaneities of spirituality do not have to polarize in opposition. To his credit, Eli recognizes that Hannah's inward and silent prayer is true prayer; he blesses her and joins his prayers to hers. His priestly blessing gathers Hannah's intensely personal prayer into the preceding and continuing life of Israel. And, to her credit, Hannah accepts the blessing from the man who has so recently demeaned her. She goes her way, behaving as if everything is now all right, that her prayers have been answered. Remarkable! For at this point nothing has, as we would say, *happened.* She is still barren. But in the biblical stories, prayer and blessing and belief are as much events as the things that these days get reported in the newspapers.

3. Mother Hannah
1 Samuel 1:19–28

In a world in which God is the primary reality, worship is the primary activity. In worship, we cultivate attentiveness and responsiveness to God. *Cultivate*, because if we live by mere happenstance—looking at what is biggest, listening to what is loudest, doing what is easiest—we will live as if God were confined to the margins of our lives. But God is not marginal; God is foundational and central. The person who lives as if God sits on a bench at the edges of life, waiting to be called on in emergencies, is out of touch with reality and so lives badly.

HANNAH GIVES BIRTH TO SAMUEL (1:19–20)

> **1:19 They rose early in the morning and worshiped before the LORD; then they went back to their house at Ramah. Elkanah knew his wife Hannah, and the LORD remembered her. [20] In due time Hannah conceived and bore a son. She named him Samuel, for she said, "I have asked him of the LORD."**

Hannah is in touch with reality, and it is worship that keeps her in touch. The entire Hannah story is formed on a grounding in worship—seven references to acts of worship establish this grounding (1:3, 7, 9, 15, 19, 21, 24).

Here, as the story pivots from barrenness to fertility, from need to fulfillment, from childlessness to childbearing, from lament to praise, this is made explicit (1:19a).

Back home in Ramah, two things take place simultaneously: Elkanah has intercourse with his wife Hannah, and God creates new life in her. The parallel verbs, "know" and "remember," are two dimensions of a single action, the enacted purpose and promise of God. Sexuality and spirituality are deeply intertwined. Either separated from the other soon goes bad, but together, as here, they enact heaven on earth and generate life.

The name Samuel is a compound of the Hebrew words for "name" (*shem*) and "God" (*'el*), and means "he over whom the name of God has been said" (Budde). In Hebrew the name also sounds very similar to the verb "ask" (*sha'al*). Eli uses the root word for "ask" twice when he blesses Hannah at Shiloh (1:17), and Hannah will use it three more times when she dedicates her son before Eli at Shiloh (1:27–28). Hannah focuses on it here in her naming: "She named him Samuel, for she said, 'I have asked him of the LORD'" (1:20b). Samuel, "The One Who Is God-Named," is at the same time "The One Asked For." The Hebrews loved to play on word sounds and meanings. Unfortunately, there is no way to reproduce this play of sounds and meanings in English; we have to be content with simply noting that the name Samuel joins all those years of asking with the evidence of God's answer. "Samuel" echoes the sounds of Hannah's prayers with the sighting of God's fulfilled promise in this infant.

HANNAH GIVES SAMUEL TO THE LORD (1:21–28)

And the worship continues. Worship is not something one does to get something, and once it is got can be discontinued. Worship is a way of life.

> 1:21 **The man Elkanah and all his household went up to offer to the LORD the yearly sacrifice, and to pay his vow. 22 But Hannah did not go up, for she said to her husband, "As soon as the child is weaned, I will bring him, that he may appear in the presence of the LORD, and remain there forever; I will offer him as a nazirite for all time." 23 Her husband Elkanah said to her, "Do what seems best to you, wait until you have weaned him; only—may the LORD establish his word." So the woman remained and nursed her son, until she weaned him. 24 When she had weaned him, she took him up with her, along with a three-year-old bull, an ephah of flour, and a skin of wine. She brought him to the house of the LORD at Shiloh; and the child was young. 25 Then they slaughtered the bull, and they brought the child to Eli. 26 And she said, "Oh, my lord! As you live, my lord, I am the woman who was standing here in your presence, praying to the LORD. 27 For this child I prayed; and the LORD has granted me the petition that I made to him. 28 Therefore I have lent him to the LORD; as long as he lives, he is given to the LORD."**
>
> **She left him there for the LORD.**

While Elkanah continues his annual trips to worship at Shiloh, Hannah prepares herself and her infant son for his dedication. We can imagine a three-to-five-year stretch of time before Samuel is weaned. In the Middle

East, infants are still breast-fed by their mothers for several years. A three-year period before weaning is mentioned in 2 Maccabees 7:27. Through these years, as Elkanah faithfully makes annual pilgrimages to Shiloh, Hannah prepares for her own return to Shiloh, when she will give back to the Lord what the Lord gave to her. Her primary work through these years is nursing and weaning. Her first task is to nurse and nurture the child given to her by God, to give her strength to the making of this new life; her second task is to wean the child from her dominance so that he can develop a relation to God on his own. The two tasks, nursing and weaning, are a basic substratum in the development of all intimate relationships, ranging from parenthood to marriage to friendship. Only by doing both tasks equally well was she able to stand again before Eli at Shiloh and make a gift of God's gift.

4. Blessed Hannah
1 Samuel 2:1–10

This story began with Hannah weeping. It ends with Hannah singing. Hannah's sung prayer is a powerful witness to a life lived in intense interaction with God. The great, rocklike realities, so-called, that so often intimidate us—biological "fate," political oppression, economic devastation, military bullying, revolutionary terrorism—are nothing in comparison to God. Hannah learned this in the conception, birth, and offering up of Samuel, and then sang this truth with great beauty:

> 2:1 **"My heart exults in the LORD;**
> **my strength is exalted in my God.**
> **My mouth derides my enemies,**
> **because I rejoice in my victory."**

The moment Hannah gave away that for which she had prayed most deeply and which she treasured most closely is explosive with joy. Getting her child from the Lord was a happy day; giving him to the Lord, even happier. But the character and action of God provide the lyrics for the song. Launched by intensely personal experience—*my* heart, *my* strength, *my* God, *my* mouth, *my* enemies, *my* victory—the prayer is soon in orbit around God:

> 2:2 **"There is no Holy One like the LORD,**
> **no one besides you;**
> **there is no Rock like our God.**
> ³ **Talk no more so very proudly,**
> **let not arrogance come from your mouth;**
> **for the LORD is a God of knowledge,**
> **and by him actions are weighed."**

Does this strike us as a huge non sequitur to what occasioned it? We are being told a story about a woman dedicating her young son to the Lord, the child whom she had desperately prayed for and wondrously conceived. The circumstances could not be more personal, more intimate, or more immediate. But the prayer immediately moves from Hannah to God, from the child Samuel to men and women everywhere and at all times. Our prayers, in similar circumstances—at dedications and baptisms—commonly dribble into sentimentality; this prayer is robust with sturdy theology and passionate politics. To our great surprise we hear Hannah singing and praying not about her precious pregnancy and lovely child, but about her incomparable God and God's incredible ways.

Vigorous images and taut sentences set forth a quick succession of three great reversals in the familiar arenas of war, food, and sex:

> 2:4 "The bows of the mighty are broken,
>   but the feeble gird on strength.
> 5 Those who were full have hired themselves out for bread,
>   but those who were hungry are fat with spoil.
>   The barren has borne seven,
>   but she who has many children is forlorn."

The strong and weak, the full and the hungry, the fertile and the barren all find their positions reversed. Nothing has to remain the way it is; in a world in which God is sovereign, nothing circumstantial is set in concrete.

Next, God's sovereignty is explicitly extended to include the absolute extremes of possibility. No part of our human existence takes place apart from God. God's presence and action embrace the polarities of life and death, success and failure:

> 2:6 "The LORD kills and brings to life;
>   he brings down to Sheol and raises up.
> 7 The LORD makes poor and makes rich;
>   he brings low, he also exalts."

A particular point of view is now introduced. The action of God has been presented in general as inclusive and embracing; now it is given explicitly from the perspective of the underdog:

> 2:8ab "He raises up the poor from the dust;
>   he lifts the needy from the ash heap,
>   to make them sit with princes
>   and inherit a seat of honor."

Hannah is one of those who have been "raised up." Early in this story we are told that "Hannah rose and presented herself before the LORD" (1:9). The same verb is used here, but with God as the subject, God doing for us what we cannot do for ourselves. Is there a hint, an intimation, of resurrection here? Many people think so. God raising people up is thematic throughout the scriptures, and will come into explicit and climactic focus when God raises Jesus from the dead.

The complaint is sometimes voiced that history is written from the perspective of the winners. No one seems to be around to tell the story of the losers, the defeated, the marginal. However true that is of other histories, it is not true of biblical history, for much of what we have here is from the perspective of the downtrodden and the left out. The men and women who have the most extensive experience of being "put down"—the poor, the misfits, the exploited—are the very ones most likely to notice the signs and possibilities of being "raised up." These people are given a voice through Hannah's song.

Supporting and holding up all this ordering and helping and saving activity of God is a "firm foundation":

2:8c **"For the pillars of the earth are the LORD's,**
      and on them he has set the world."

Creation provides the solid structure on which the work of salvation is carried out. The wonderful works of God celebrated and sung in this prayer are not a storefront operation, here today and gone tomorrow, some kind of fly-by-night enterprise. Salvation is backed up by the entire creation. The immense image, "pillars of the earth," provides a sense of enduring dependability behind and beneath everything that God does among us.

The final two verses of Hannah's song give a comprehensive, wide-angle view of God's providential care and inexorable judgment worldwide, and then zoom in on a single detail, a person chosen by God ("his anointed") to be obedient to his word.

2:9 **"He will guard the feet of his faithful ones,**
      but the wicked shall be cut off in darkness;
      for not by might does one prevail.
   10 **The LORD! His adversaries shall be shattered;**
      the Most High will thunder in heaven.
   The LORD will judge the ends of the earth;
      he will give strength to his king,
      and exalt the power of his anointed."

"Anointed" is the last word in the prayer, but it doesn't conclude; it antici-pates. It poises us for what is coming. The word, in Hebrew, is *messiah*, a person, usually a king, set apart and ordained to represent God's lordly rule and saving presence among his people. The meaning will be most fully ex-pressed in Jesus, whose title "Christ" is the Greek translation of Messiah.

Hannah is presented as praying more than she knows, anticipating king/messiah Saul, anticipating king/messiah David. And, for those of us who now have the whole story laid out before us, anticipating King/Messiah Jesus.

But the "more than she knows" in Hannah's prayer is implicit in what she already knows very well, namely, the child Samuel whom she is dedi-cating to the Lord. The first verse of her song has the phrase "my strength is exalted." This last line has "exalt the power of his anointed." The words "strength" and "power" are the same word in Hebrew, *horn*—a metaphor that radiates strength, virility, and wild beauty. The prayer begins with Samuel as Hannah's "horn," and ends with him as God's horn. Near the conclusion of this sequence of stories in the books of Samuel, a valedictory prayer is placed on David's lips as he sings of God as "the horn of my sal-vation" (2 Sam. 22:3).

A thousand years later Mary took this same song and reworked and per-sonalized it to sing her joyful witness to the child in her womb who would bring salvation to the world (see Luke 1:46–55). It is called the Magnificat, and Christians continue to sing and pray it, often as an evening prayer, as we continuously return to and get in on the beginning of this story in which God conceives new life and launches fresh episodes of transformed history.

Part 2. The Story of Samuel

1 Samuel 2:11–12:25

Introduction

"That rooted man" (the phrase is from Yeats) is an apt designation of Samuel. Samuel lived through one of the most change-charged times in Israel's history and never once lost his equilibrium. While the culture around him went through radical change, he stayed in touch with past, present, and future and gave continuous representation to the primacy of God in the lives of the people.

Samuel lived in a time of moral and political chaos. The religious traditions of Israel were in shambles and its spirituality in tatters. The patriarchal, exodus, and wilderness traditions had all been developed in a nomadic culture. Now God's people were settled in a world that was agrarian and urban. The recent past in which charismatic judges had shown flashes of brilliance had disintegrated into anarchy. The attempt, out of that chaos, to establish order again through a monarchy soon turned into a royal mess.

Israel had a glorious history—Abraham and Joseph, Moses and Joshua, Rahab and Deborah. But that glorious world was on its way out when Samuel entered the scene. The world changes, political alliances shift, the rich and poor jockey for position, the moral fiber of society alternately strengthens and weakens. God speaks a word; God's will is revealed; God chooses a people. Who is listening? Who is looking? Who is responding? At this moment in Israel, not many. The century or two of moral disintegration compounded by political chaos had been enough to put Israel's identity as God's people at risk. Would they lose touch with their unique history, lose their grip on the theme of salvation that provided meaning and coherence to their lives?

Historically, it looked like a close call. But biblically, Samuel's arrival serves to bring past and future together magnificently. In perspective, the remarkable thing about Samuel is that he lived through a time of change, not by adapting himself and his leadership style to the times, but by maintaining his vocation as God's prophet. He didn't survive by chameleon tactics. He did not serve the people by picking up the new fads and demonstrating that he was "relevant." But neither did he hang on stubbornly to the old ways of doing things. He didn't retreat to a desert hermitage and repeat old rituals that he knew had worked so well in the past. What he did was stay close to God's revelation, more attentive to God's word of salvation than to the people's tastes in religion. In the Gospel passage that describes the growth of the boy Jesus (Luke 2:40), we find the same words that describe the development of Samuel into maturity.

Samuel is a colossus astride two distinct periods of Israel's history, the loose tribal confederacy usually designated the period of the Judges, and the time of the monarchy. During the period of the Judges there was no central government. God's people, delivered from Egypt under Moses' leadership and given possession of the land under Joshua, lived in twelve tribal areas, each more or less on its own. They had a common tradition of origin in the patriarchs (Abraham, Isaac, Jacob, and Joseph) and a common tradition of salvation out of Egypt. But after arriving in the land, each tribe lived separately, coming together for common worship at the central shrine at Shiloh and, under the leadership of a charismatic "judge," pooling their resources when attacked by an enemy. When the need for the judge was over, he or she moved to the sidelines. Israel lived under the rule of God, with a minimum of human government—a kind of controlled anarchy. The Israelites were a God-formed, God-governed people. Samuel was one of these judges—the last one, as it turned out.

Samuel began conventionally enough as an apprentice priest. His priestly duties eventually and quite naturally developed into responsibilities of a "judge." But what throws him into biblical prominence is the way that he melded his role as judge with his calling as a prophet. In the office of "judge," the primary emphasis was in giving leadership to the people; in the office of "prophet," the person spoke and acted out the word and will of God. The two roles overlapped considerably, of course, but it is as prophet that Samuel holds our attention.

The Hebrew prophets were powerful figures, men and women who shaped history not by wielding political or military power, but by speaking God's word in whatever context they found themselves. Still, a prophet was never a person *just* of words; prophets lived what they spoke. When people were in the presence of a prophet, they recognized that God had intentions and purposes for them. Prophets proclaimed different things: comfort, judgment, accusation, promise—a wide range of matters—but always it was centered in a consciousness that God was speaking very personally to the people.

5. Samuel Grows Up
1 Samuel 2:11–4:1a

ELI'S SCOUNDREL SONS (2:11–17)

2:11 Then Elkanah went home to Ramah, while the boy remained to minister to the LORD, in the presence of the priest Eli.
¹² Now the sons of Eli were scoundrels; they had no regard for the LORD ¹³ or for the duties of the priests to the people. When anyone offered sacrifice, the priest's servant would come, while the meat was boiling, with a three-pronged fork in his hand ¹⁴ . . . ; all that the fork brought up the priest would take for himself. ¹⁵ . . . The priest's servant would come and say to the one who was sacrificing, "Give meat for the priest to roast. . . . ¹⁶ . . . You must give it now; if not, I will take it by force." ¹⁷ Thus the sin of the young men was very great in the sight of the LORD; for they treated the offerings of the LORD with contempt.

Samuel is apprenticed to the priest Eli at a young age. This apprenticing, the result of prayerful consecration on the part of his parents, is a most auspicious launching into a life of service to God. But it turns out that the circumstances are most inauspicious, for the sanctuary at Shiloh, over which Eli was the nominal head, was seething with corruption. Samuel has been dumped, inadvertently, into a caldron of religious venality. Hannah assumed that giving her son to the Lord (1:28) and handing him over to the priests was pretty much the same thing. It wasn't, and it isn't. "The fact is that religion is man's great venture and man's great, fatal failure" (Miskotte, *When the Gods Are Silent*, 5).

The venality is narrated in a story that portrays the priests presiding over the Shiloh sacrifices as greedy bullies. It was traditional in Israel for priests to get their meals from the sacrificial offerings brought by the people. At Shiloh, the custom was for a fork to be stuck into the pot at random, and whatever piece of meat stuck to it was given to the priest—the original "potluck." And the fat was *always* kept back to be burnt before God. But

Hophni and Phinehas disdained taking their chances with lowly stew meat; they wanted choice pieces, and roasted specifically to their own tastes, presumably garnished with the fat. Religion, for the two Eli boys, was a chance at privilege and power, by which they were thoroughly corrupted.

HANNAH'S BLESSED SON (2:18–21)

> 2:18 Samuel was ministering before the LORD, a boy wearing a linen ephod. [19] His mother used to make for him a little robe and take it to him each year, when she went up with her husband to offer the yearly sacrifice. [20] Then Eli would bless Elkanah and his wife, and say, "May the LORD repay you with children by this woman for the gift that she made to the LORD"; and then they would return to their home.
> [21] And the LORD took note of Hannah; she conceived and bore three sons and two daughters. And the boy Samuel grew up in the presence of the LORD.

Whereas the scoundrel sons, Hophni and Phinehas, are characterized by a story in which they aggressively grab whatever they can get from the holy place, Samuel, the blessed son, is characterized by a story in which he is clothed year after year in a succession of priestly robes, custom-sown by his mother, suited to his growing stature. Clothing can either disguise or reveal our true identity. Eli's sons, dressed in their inherited, hand-me-down priestly robes, *looked* like priests but were, in fact, wolves in sheep's clothing (Matt. 7:15). The handmade, custom-tailored robe worn by Hannah's son *revealed* his true priestly identity.

The ephod that Hannah made for Samuel was a distinctive garment of some kind, worn by priests. An elaborate description of the ephod worn by the high priest is provided in Exodus 28. The robe Hannah sewed must have been a simpler form. Later, we will find the ephod used in prayers for guidance (23:9). It is not clear what exactly was involved, but something like the casting of lots (Urim and Thummim) would take place, delivering a yes or no answer to the prayer of inquiry. It is common for people today in an attempt to democratize and "spiritualize" all religion to be somewhat condescending to ritual devices such as the ephod. But development in the way of prayer is not a matter of separating ourselves from all material aids—we are a physical people, after all, immersed in materiality. Superstition is always a possibility, of course, but only when the ephod (or other artifact) is given independent status of its own as a magical or occult device. It is not materiality, as such, that contaminates and clogs our prayers and service before God, but the attempt first to depersonalize and then manipulate God by means of material. Materiality as such is of a piece with the incarnation.

THE DECADENCE OF ELI'S SONS (2:22–26)

2:22 Now Eli was very old. He heard all that his sons were doing to all Israel, and how they lay with the women who served at the entrance to the tent of meeting. 23 He said to them, "Why do you do such things? For I hear of your evil dealings from all these people." . . . 25 But they would not listen to the voice of their father; for it was the will of the LORD to kill them.
26 Now the boy Samuel continued to grow both in stature and in favor with the LORD and with the people.

The contrast between Eli's sons and Hannah's son intensifies. Eli blessed Samuel's parents (2:20) but is forced to rebuke his own sons (2:23–24). Hannah's chaste fertility (2:21a) is contrasted with the blatant promiscuity of Eli's sons (2:22b). At the very moment that Samuel was growing up in God's presence (2:21b), Eli's sons were being consigned to a premature death (2:25c).

And these contrasts work themselves out not between a godless and godly society, not between the supposedly chaste suburbs and the conspicuously evil slums, but at the heart of Shiloh, a most honored religious establishment. Environment does not determine holiness.

Samuel's growth "in stature and in favor" is remarkable enough to call for comment, for coordinated growth in size and sanctity is uncommon. Most of us get bigger without getting better. But growth has as much to do with the soul as it does with the body. There *can* be growth in "favor" as well as in "stature." If we are going to be truly human, there *must* be. It is significant that a thousand years later Luke uses similar words to describe both John the Baptizer (Luke 1:80) and Jesus the Christ (Luke 2:40). There is no true growth that does not embrace both human and God relationships. Samuel, John, and Jesus in their different ways provide the pattern.

THE DEMISE OF ELI (2:27–36)

2:27 A man of God came to Eli and said to him, "Thus the LORD has said, 'I revealed myself to the family of your ancestor in Egypt when they were slaves to the house of Pharaoh. 28 I chose him out of all the tribes of Israel to be my priest. . . . 29 Why then look with greedy eye at my sacrifices and my

offerings that I commanded, and honor your sons more than me by fatten-
ing yourselves on the choicest parts of every offering of my people Israel?'
[30] Therefore the LORD the God of Israel declares: . . . [31] 'See, a time is coming when I will cut off your strength and the strength of your ancestor's family, so that no one in your family will live to old age. . . . [34] The fate of your
two sons, Hophni and Phinehas, shall be the sign to you—both of them shall
die on the same day. [35] I will raise up for myself a faithful priest, who shall
do according to what is in my heart and in my mind. . . . [36] Everyone who is
left in your family shall come to implore him for a piece of silver or a loaf of
bread, and shall say, Please put me in one of the priest's places, that I may
eat a morsel of bread.'"

God's man (Eli) who oversees the people needs a man of God to oversee
him. Religious office does not exempt a person from righteous responsibilities. None of us ever arrive at a position or place where we can do as we
like, or let others do as they like. Not only do God's world and God's sanctuary require constant vigilance, but all of us (everybody is included!) who
have responsibilities in exercising vigilance require vigilance.

And so Eli is called on the carpet for his sloppiness as both parent and
priest. He is the heir of a venerable tradition going back to the glorious
days of deliverance in Egypt and involving the glorious work of presiding
over the rituals of holy worship. But under Eli the tradition and work are
far from glorious. Severe judgment is announced, but a blessed continuity
("I will raise up for myself a faithful priest," v. 35) is assured. God's judgment always has a promise embedded in it.

Throughout this passage, contrasts are developed between Samuel on
one side and Hophni and Phinehas on the other: Samuel serves the LORD
(2:11), while Hophni and Phinehas grab all they can (2:13–17); Samuel ma-
tures (2:18–21), while Hophni and Phinehas become more and more deca-
dent (2:22–25); Samuel increases in living stature and favor (2:26), while
Hophni and Phinehas are marked for death (2:27–36). As the curve of Eli's
priesthood declines, the curve of Samuel's ministry rises. The contrast is
explicit in 2:34–35, where the death of Hophni and Phinehas is prophesied
and the establishment of a "faithful priest," that is, Samuel, is assured.

THE RISE OF SAMUEL (3:1–4:1a)

3:1 Now the boy Samuel was ministering to the LORD under Eli. The word
of the LORD was rare in those days; visions were not widespread,
[2] At that time Eli, whose eyesight had begun to grow dim so that he could

not see, was lying down in his room; ³ the lamp of God had not yet gone out, and Samuel was lying down in the temple of the LORD, where the ark of God was. ⁴ Then the LORD called, "Samuel! Samuel!" and he said, "Here I am!" ⁵ and ran to Eli, and said, "Here I am, for you called me." But he said, "I did not call; lie down again." So he went and lay down. ⁶ The LORD called again, "Samuel!" Samuel got up and went to Eli, and said, "Here I am, for you called me." But he said, "I did not call, my son; lie down again." ⁷ Now Samuel did not yet know the LORD, and the word of the LORD had not yet been revealed to him. ⁸ The LORD called Samuel again, a third time. And he got up and went to Eli, and said, "Here I am, for you called me." Then Eli perceived that the LORD was calling the boy. ⁹ Therefore Eli said to Samuel, "Go, lie down; and if he calls you, you shall say, 'Speak, LORD, for your servant is listening.'" So Samuel went and lay down in his place.

¹⁰ Now the LORD came and stood there, calling as before, "Samuel! Samuel!" And Samuel said, "Speak, for your servant is listening." ¹¹ Then the LORD said to Samuel, "See, I am about to do something in Israel that will make both ears of anyone who hears of it tingle. ¹² On that day I will fulfill against Eli all that I have spoken concerning his house, from beginning to end."

¹⁵ . . . Samuel was afraid to tell the vision to Eli. ¹⁶ But Eli called Samuel and said, . . . ¹⁷ "What was it that he told you?" . . . ¹⁸ So Samuel told him everything and hid nothing from him. Then he said, "It is the LORD; let him do what seems good to him."

¹⁹ As Samuel grew up, the LORD was with him and let none of his words fall to the ground. ²⁰ And all Israel from Dan to Beer-sheba knew that Samuel was a trustworthy prophet of the LORD. . . .

The story of Samuel's call comes at a time when the collapse of Eli's priesthood is inevitable. Eli's priestly office is ineffectual and empty of all meaning. The barrenness of the spiritual life at Shiloh parallels the barrenness of Hannah's womb in chapter 1. And Samuel is God's response to both.

This is the third time that Samuel is identified as "ministering to/before the LORD" (2:11; 2:18; 3:1). Samuel is a servant, but primarily a servant of God. His identity is dominated by who he is and what he does in relation to God.

The repetition serves to deepen the contrast between Samuel and his associates. Eli is a priest, but is presented in his first appearance (1:9–17) as policing the holy place and keeping worshipers (Hannah) in line. He has turned into a parody of a priest: religion is his job, his priestly calling reduced to a religious function; he doesn't have to deal with God at all (1:14). Hophni and Phinehas are also parody-priests, only worse; the holy place for them is a place of power and privilege—access to easy women and gourmet food. God is the last thing on their minds. Readers of the Bible are not particularly surprised at modern "sex-and-religion" scandals, which journalists delight in using to shock and titillate the public. They have a long and tiresome history behind them. Holy places provide convenient cover for unholy ambitions—they always have, and they always will.

But Samuel is defined repeatedly (and so far exclusively) as dealing with ("ministering to/before") God. *This* is what interests us. *This* counts as news. This kind of interest in God's word and God-centeredness was no more common then than it is now; the text says it was "rare" and "not widespread." While the sociologists, psychologists, and journalists describe the periphery of our lives and actions, the Samuel storyteller zeroes in at the center. And we are all ears!

God speaks to Samuel; Samuel answers God. The story is a lens through which we see the way language works in the biblical revelation.

God speaks to Samuel. *That* God speaks is the basic reality of biblical faith. The fundamental conviction of our faith is not so much that God *is*, as that God *speaks*. The biblical revelation begins with God creating by word, speaking the cosmos into being (Genesis 1). It concludes with Jesus, the *Word* of God, speaking in invitation, "Come . . . " (Rev. 22:17). All the pages in between are packed with sentences that God speaks—in creation and invitation, in judgment and salvation, in healing and guidance, in oracle and admonition, in rebuke and comfort. The conspicuous feature in all this speaking is that God speaks in personal address. God does not speak grand general truths, huge billboard declarations of truth and morals; the Lord's speaking is *to* persons, *named* persons: Abraham, Moses, Isaiah, Jeremiah, Paul. And Samuel. Personal address, not philosophical discourse or moral commentary or theological reflection, is God's primary form of speech. Whenever we let the language of religious abstraction or moral principles (and we do it often) crowd out the personal address, we betray the word of God.

And Samuel listens. Three times Samuel misidentifies God's words to him as human words. The fourth time, with Eli's help, he listens to them as God's words. Learning to discern the difference between human words and God's word is basic to his prophetic and priestly life: Samuel *listens*. Listening is an act of personal attentiveness that develops into answering. The emphatic "Let anyone with ears listen!" with which Jesus concluded his parables (Matt. 13:9, 43) is repeated in the Spirit's urgent messages to the churches in the Revelation (Rev. 2:7, 11, 17, 29; 3:6, 13, 22). Personal speech, but this time from the human side of things. God's address is not

turned into materials for a Bible study, shaped into a Sunday school cur-
riculum, set as the topic for an academic paper, or trotted into the local bar
as fuel for an evening of boozy gossip. Samuel *answers*, which is to say, he
prays.

Samuel's very existence is a result of prayer, the prayer of his praying
mother, Hannah. The story of his call in the temple, introducing his
prophetic vocation, shows him learning how to pray for himself, that is,
listen to God's personal word to him and then respond.

We are not used to this. Impersonal speech is our métier. Our schools
train us to acquire information. Our culture trains us to get ahead. Parents,
at least for a while, and lovers, at their mature best, give us a taste for a language of personal address and answer. But more often than not the personal is elbowed to the sidelines by the impersonal.

The difficulty in recognizing and responding as persons to God, who
speaks and comes to us as person, is conveyed by the repetitions in the
story: The God-Samuel conversation is repeated three times, and not until the third exchange does it gel. But on the third attempt, Samuel, with
Eli's priestly help, gets it. That is what priests are for—to help us discern
God's personal address to us—and Eli, for all his general ineptitude, comes
through this time.

God's message, while *to* Samuel, is *for* Eli. And for Eli it is not brand-
new; earlier "a man of God" (2:27) had brought the same message, a message of judgment against Eli and his family. But there is this difference:
The first message came from an outsider, the unnamed "man of God."
This time it is from within the family and from within the sanctuary. While
the judgment continues to be a message of harsh doom, it is now conveyed
under conditions of intimacy and trust.

And Eli responds admirably, yes, even courageously. He recognizes the
personal signature of God in the severe message and willingly submits. If
it comes from God, it has to be right, and Eli, when pushed to the wall, is
still enough of a priest to accept what is right.

Here is that word "grow" again (cf. 2:26). This time Samuel's physical
growth is correlated with growth in language, Samuel's words and God's
word coming together. The term "word" is used three times here, the first
and third instances refer to Samuel's words (3:19; 4:1a) held together by
God's word in the middle (3:21). The personal conversational exchanges between God and Samuel have now matured. Samuel has become a
"prophet"—a person whose words are dependably God's word. "The words
the prophet utters are not offered as souvenirs. His speech to the people is
not a reminiscence, a report, hearsay. The prophet not only conveys; he

reveals. He almost does unto others what God does unto him. In speaking, the prophet reveals God. This is the marvel of a prophet's work: in his words *the invisible God becomes audible*" (Heschel, *The Prophets*, 22).

"Dan to Beer-sheba" is the usual Old Testament idiom for "the whole country." Dan was on the northern border of Palestine and Beer-sheba on the southern.

6. The Ark of God
1 Samuel 4:1b–7:2

Samuel's part in this story is now put on hold while a segment in the history of the ark of God is introduced. Samuel is ready to step into the world of God's revelation and play his considerable part. But the world into which he is about to step requires some definition if we are to appreciate Samuel's place in it. Instead of a generalized description of the "times," we are given this highly localized account of the "ark." *This* is the political and religious culture in which Samuel will do his work.

THE ARK OF GOD IS CAPTURED (4:1b–11)

4:1b In those days the Philistines mustered for war against Israel. . . . ² . . . Israel was defeated by the Philistines. . . . ³ . . . the elders of Israel said, "Why has the LORD put us to rout today before the Philistines? Let us bring the ark of the covenant of the LORD here from Shiloh, so that he may come among us and save us from the power of our enemies." ⁴ So the people sent to Shiloh, and brought from there the ark of the covenant of the LORD of hosts, who is enthroned on the cherubim. The two sons of Eli, Hophni and Phinehas, were there with the ark of the covenant of God.

⁵ When the ark of the covenant of the LORD came into the camp, all Israel gave a mighty shout, so that the earth resounded. ⁶ When the Philistines heard the noise of the shouting, they said, "What does this great shouting in the camp of the Hebrews mean?" When they learned that the ark of the LORD had come to the camp, ⁷ the Philistines were afraid; for they said, "Gods have come into the camp. . . . ⁸ . . . Who can deliver us from the power of these mighty gods? . . . ⁹ Take courage, and be men, O Philistines, in order not to become slaves to the Hebrews as they have been to you; be men and fight."

¹⁰ So the Philistines fought; Israel was defeated, and they fled. . . . ¹¹ The ark of God was captured; and the two sons of Eli, Hophni and Phinehas, died.

41

This part of the story revolves around two poles, the cursed Philistines and the blessed ark of the covenant.

The cursed Philistines had been Israel's local enemy par excellence for two hundred years, and would continue as an irritant for another three hundred. During the entire period covered by the Samuel stories, Philistine harassment is continuous. Bracketed by the earlier Egyptian oppression and the later Babylonian exile, the Philistines take their place among the Big Three Enemies in Israel's history. Their five cities on Palestine's coastal plain (Gaza, Ashdod, Ekron, Gath, Ashkelon) were, at least as far as Israel was concerned, used mostly as bases for military operations. The Philistines had a monopoly on iron, which they used primarily to make weapons. Prominent among the artifacts that archaeologists have uncovered in their cities are beer jugs. Fierce fighters, hard drinkers. Our contemporary use of the term "Philistine" to refer to the coarse and unsophisticated seems to be not far off the mark.

The blessed ark of the covenant, on the other hand, was a mere box, not quite four feet in length and a little over two feet in depth and width (see Exod. 25:10). It was built at the outset of Israel's forty years in the wilderness and provided a center to their worship. It was constructed of wood and plated with gold. Its lid of solid gold was called the mercy seat. Two cherubim, angel-like figures at either end, framed the space around the central mercy seat from which God's word was honored. The ark contained three items: the tables of stone that Moses had delivered to the people from Sinai; a jar of manna from the wilderness years of wandering; and Aaron's rod that budded. These objects were the continuing and reminding evidence that God worked among them: commanded them (the tablets), provided for them (the manna), and saved them (the rod). After entrance into the promised land (Palestine), it was placed in the central sanctuary at Shiloh. The ark gave a hard, historical focus to the revealed character of the God that Israel worshiped. The ark did not have magical properties. Superstition was not encouraged in Israel. The people were never taught that the ark was a source of power that they could plug into.

But in the emotional panic caused by the sudden Philistine victory, the Israelite leaders regressed spiritually to gross superstition. The narrative shows what happens when we become superstitious rather than believing; namely, nothing—or worse than nothing.

The national religion over which Hophni and Phinehas presided that day was a far cry from the world of deliverance and salvation and worship into which the people had been led by Moses and Joshua. There is no evidence that anyone prayed that day at Ebenezer and Aphek, where Israel and the Philistines were encamped. The God who was revealed as personal and sovereign at Midian and Sinai had been traded in for a god-in-a-box that the leaders thought could work magic against the Philistines at Aphek.

But the Philistines captured the ark, and the priests Hophni and Phinehas were killed in the battle. That would seem to provide irrefutable evidence against superstitious practices, against the manipulative powers of magic. But the spiritual life of Israel was far gone by this time, and it would be a while before recovery was complete. This kind of stuff dies hard. And it keeps recurring. We humans seem to be religiously addicted to anything that "can be objectified, over against which our ego can be asserted" (Barth, *Church Dogmatics* I/1, 438).

THE ICHABOD EPITAPH (4:12–22)

4:12 **A man of Benjamin ran from the battle line, and came to Shiloh the same day. . . .** [13] **. . . When the man came into the city and told the news, all the city cried out. . . .** [16] **The man said to Eli, "I have just come from the battle. . . ."** **He said, "How did it go, my son?"** [17] **The messenger replied, " . . . there has . . . been a great slaughter among the troops; your two sons also, Hophni and Phinehas, are dead, and the ark of God has been captured."** [18] **When he mentioned the ark of God, Eli fell over backward from his seat by the side of the gate; and his neck was broken and he died, for he was an old man, and heavy. He had judged Israel forty years.**

[19] **Now his daughter-in-law, the wife of Phinehas, was pregnant. . . . When she heard the news that the ark of God was captured, and that her father-in-law and her husband were dead, she bowed and gave birth. . . .** [21] **She named the child Ichabod, meaning, "The glory has departed from Israel," because the ark of God had been captured and because of her father-in-law and her husband. . . .**

She was wrong, of course. The glory of God had by no means left Israel; it was even now in the process of getting ready to reappear. But before the glory could be seen, the shame had to be removed. In naming her son, the widow of Phinehas was only giving voice to the bankrupt legacy of her degenerate priest husband: "Glory" in her vocabulary is equivalent to privilege and power (for Phinehas, it meant gourmandizing and fornicating); if the privilege and power are gone, God is gone. Did she suppose that her husband's connection with the ark of God gave them their higher standard of living? Apparently. But wrongly.

"Glory" has quite another meaning in the biblical story. It is evidence of God's substantial, though invisible, presence—the weight and glow of

God in contrast to the flimsiness of jerry-built structures that we throw together when trying to construct something satisfactory without going to
all the trouble of dealing with God. It conveys a sense of God's foundational solidity as an alternative to a culture built on sand. In a lecture, James
M. Houston, with acerbic wit, once pointed out that we have, for the first
time in history, quite literally constructed a civilization built on sand, for
the silicon chip at the heart of our computers is made of sand.

When the Philistines captured the ark they were carrying out God's
judgment against the rotten religious corruption that was flourishing in
Shiloh. The judgment was neither accidental nor arbitrary—there were
ample forewarnings (the "man of God" in 2:27–36 and Samuel in 3:11–18).
The role of the ark was central in giving content to this judgment, for if
the ark was supposed by the people to give sanction to whoever was in
charge of it, how better to disabuse them of the superstition than to make
a public display of its total ineffectiveness in that regard? If the ark was
worthless as a weapon of war, it was surely also useless as a tool of religion.
The ark was good for *something*, and the Samuel storyteller will get around
to that later, but it is not good for *this*.

The narrative is quick-paced and vivid: the messenger of bad news running the twenty miles from Aphek to Shiloh, most of it uphill; the citywide
dismay; fat Eli falling backward in his chair and breaking his neck; the ill-
naming of a child; and the death of its mother. Anticipation of Samuel's
assumption of leadership, announced in 3:20–4:1a, builds as this much-
needed housecleaning is done.

THE COMEDY OF THE ARK (5:1–12)

> 5:1 When the Philistines captured the ark of God, they brought it . . . to Ash-
> dod [2] . . . into the house of Dagon and placed it beside Dagon. [3] When the
> people of Ashdod rose early the next day, there was Dagon, fallen on his face
> to the ground before the ark of the LORD. So they took Dagon and put him
> back in his place. [4] But when they rose early on the next morning, Dagon had
> fallen on his face to the ground before the ark of the LORD, and the head of
> Dagon and both his hands were lying cut off upon the threshold; only the
> trunk of Dagon was left to him. . . .

When the Philistines carried the ark to their central city, Ashdod, and set
it in the temple of their chief god, Dagon, they thought they were in possession of the God of Israel, that they had captured *him* (much as Israel had
supposed that it had lost him). The sequence is humorous: The citizens get

up early to admire their plunder, only to find their god fallen off his pedestal and in a position of servitude before the ark. The next day is even worse; not only had Dagon fallen, but he was broken, hopelessly incapacitated. Dagon means "grain" in Hebrew (Dagon was the "grain-god"), and was therefore prominent in the vegetation-fertility rites so central to pagan religion.

> 5:6 The hand of the LORD was heavy upon the people of Ashdod, and he terrified and struck them with tumors. . . . [7] And when the inhabitants of Ashdod saw how things were, they said, "The ark of the God of Israel must not remain with us. . . ." [8] [They] . . . said, "What shall we do with the ark of the God of Israel?" The inhabitants of Gath replied, "Let the ark of God be moved on to us." . . . [9] But after they had brought it to Gath, the hand of the LORD was against the city, causing a very great panic; he struck . . . both young and old, so that tumors broke out on them. [10] So they sent the ark of the God of Israel to Ekron. But when the ark of God came to Ekron, the people of Ekron cried out, "Why have they brought around to us the ark of the God of Israel to kill us and our people?" [11] They . . . said, "Send away the ark of the God of Israel. . . . " For there was a deathly panic throughout the whole city. The hand of God was very heavy there; [12] . . . and the cry of the city went up to heaven.

The Philistines, sworn enemies of the Israelites, had at least this in common with them: They both thought that possession of the ark of God would provide them with supernatural advantage. They both thought of it as a spiritual tool, a device for prying power loose from divinity. The Philistines were, perhaps, less culpable in this than the Israelites, for they did it out of ignorance, while the Israelites did it out of forgetfulness stemming from disobedience.

For God had revealed himself to the Israelites, clearly and definitively. Exodus tells that story. God was not at their disposal. God was not a thing. God was not a piece of spiritual technology. The ark of the covenant was one among other material means by which they were trained in obedient and believing worship of their Sovereign. It was a way of nurturing a reverent memory of their origins and God's covenant with them; it was a visibility that kept them focused on the invisible; it kept them mindful that God had entered their history and was shaping God's salvation life among them. But generations of forgetful disobedience, epitomized in the Eli family, had obscured that revelation, so at the time of this story Israel was more like its Palestinian neighbors than different.

The Philistines, on the other hand, knew none of that. They were familiar with hearsay stories of the miraculous and terrifying events involved in the

[margin handwritten note: sacrament = outward sign of inward grace]

Egyptian deliverance, but garbled in the language of paganism (4:8). It was understandable that if the Israelites thought of the ark as a military weapon emitting divine power, they would think the same. Capturing the ark, for them, was capturing the famous God of the exodus—a weapon that would give them dominating power over the entire region (emotionally equivalent in our experience to the nuclear bomb).

But it doesn't turn out that way. The ark does them no more good than it did the Israelites. In fact, it backfires on them.

It is hard to resist the notion that the narrator is having a bit of fun here at the Philistines' expense. Twice their god Dagon falls on his face before the ark, the second time losing his head and hands in the fall. Then an epidemic breaks out among them, something on the order of the bubonic plague, with people dying left and right and the whole population in a panic. With their god Dagon in ruins, they quite naturally jump to the conclusion that the ark is causing the epidemic—obviously they don't know how to operate this weapon, and it is backfiring on them. Overnight the ark, instead of being a prize of war, becomes a hot potato; they pass it from city to city—from Ashdod to Gath to Ekron—each, perhaps, hoping to gain some advantage from it but getting only a deadly infection from the spreading epidemic, disappointing all their persistent superstitious hopes. Between the lines, we detect something on the order of slapstick farce: the powerful and bullying Philistines with their vaunted weaponry are now hysterical over a box no larger than a child's coffin. "He who sits in the heavens laughs" (Ps. 2:4). Finally they have had enough, and determine to get rid of it by dumping it back on Israel.

So much for religion as superstition. First the Israelites and then the Philistines are taught their lesson: The living God cannot be used, manipulated, or managed. Spiritual power is not a matter of getting our hands on the right method or technology. The personal God cannot be reduced to an impersonal power. And further, those who attempt such are judged by this living God; God will not tolerate such blasphemous behavior— sooner or later, death is the consequence. The people so recently used by God to bring judgment against corrupt Canaan are themselves judged. God will not be mocked.

GETTING RID OF THE "HOT-POTATO" ARK (6:1–12)

6:1 **The ark of the LORD was in the country of the Philistines seven months.** ² **Then the Philistines called for the priests and the diviners and said, "What** shall we do with the ark of the LORD? . . . [3] They said, "If you send away the ark of the God of Israel, do not send it empty, but by all means return him a guilt offering. Then you will be healed and will be ransomed. . . . " [4] And they said, "What is the guilt offering that we shall return to him?" They answered, "Five gold tumors and five gold mice, according to the number of the lords of the Philistines. . . . [5] . . . make images of your tumors and images of your mice that ravage the land. . . . [6] Why should you harden your hearts as the Egyptians and Pharaoh hardened their hearts? After he had made fools of them, did they not let the people go, and they departed? [7] Now then, get ready a new cart and two milch cows that have never borne a yoke, and yoke the cows to the cart, but take their calves home, away from them. [8] Take the ark of the LORD and place it on the cart, and put in a box at its side the figures of gold, which you are returning to him as a guilt offering. Then send it off, and let it go its way. [9] And watch; if it goes up on the way to its own land, to Beth-shemesh, then it is he who has done us this great harm; but if not, then we shall know that it is not his hand that struck us; it happened to us by chance."

[10] The men did so. . . . [12] The cows went straight in the direction of Beth-shemesh . . . , and the lords of the Philistines went after them as far as the border of Beth-shemesh.

Getting rid of the ark turns out to be harder than getting it in the first place. A consultation of religious experts produces a plan: Craft five mice and five tumors of gold, place them with the ark, and send the works back to Israel. The plan is based on a religious understanding of the trouble they are in, namely, guilt. They have done something wrong—Who knows exactly what? It probably involved some mishandling of the magic-charged ark.

But why mice and tumors? Early Greek translations of this text expand the story by inserting the detail that the plague was carried by a swarm of mice (or rats)—and we do know that bubonic plague which erupts in tumors is carried by rodents. So the story as we have it assumes that mice caused the epidemic and deadly tumors were the result. The gold mice and tumors are set forth as the homeopathic remedy for healing. (Homeopathy operates on the principle that healing comes from the same source as the illness, but administered in a smaller dose, or in a different form. Vaccination is one application of the principle; "a hair of the dog that bit you" is the equivalent in contemporary folklore.)

They carry out the plan by placing the ark and a container holding the gold replicas on a new cart pulled by two cows who have never yet been yoked. (They were trying to do everything right—neither cart nor cows contaminated with guilt.) Then they put it all on the road to Beth-shemesh, the nearest Israelite town.

They have also built a test into the plan. The yoked cows had calves that

were still nursing. They will test their solution by first penning the calves
in a barn and then sending the cart off. If the full-uddered cows leave their
hungry calves behind, "against nature" so to speak, that will be a clear sign
that the whole business (ark, Dagon, epidemic) is supernatural and not
merely circumstantial, and that they are doing this right—properly ap-
peasing an angry god. The cows head straight for Beth-shemesh, leaving
their hungry calves behind, unfed. The ark is on its way home.

This part of the story is dominated by the superstitious thinking and
practices of the Philistines. But God uses what is at hand to accomplish
the divine will, which is the return of the ark. God does not seem to be
fussy about the character or condition of the culture or people in whom
and with whom the Lord works. What is clear is that out of the mess of
Philistine (and Israelite!) superstition, God's presence in both judgment
and mercy is discernible. The one line in the narration that links this incident of the ark's return to the large background story of Egyptian deliverance is spoken by Philistines (6:6). If Israel has forgotten its past,
Philistia has not! At least an echo of the witness is maintained, if not by
friend, then by foe.

THE FIELD OF JOSHUA (6:13–18)

Meanwhile, tucked away in the obscure village of Beth-shemesh, far from
the worship center at Shiloh (fifty or so miles away) and neighboring on
pagan Philistine territory, there are Israelites who know what the ark is for
and what to do in response to it, namely, *worship God.* One of them, Joshua,
is named. Joshua of Beth-shemesh. His name ought to be more remembered than it is, for he is evidence that faith in the living God can be maintained in remote circumstances and in alien conditions. Bordered on one
side by the degenerate superstitions of his fellow Israelites and on the other
by the ignorant superstitions of the Philistines, somehow he and his friends
have kept God's word alive among them. When the ark arrives by oxcart
they are jubilant, welcome it, and set about at once worshiping God. And
about time! This ark, which has been subjected to the wheeling and dealing of Israel and Philistia respectively, is now being treated properly, with
joyous reverence. (A touch of irony is provided in the detail that the pagan
Philistines supplied both the fuel [the wood of the cart] and the animals for
the sacrificial worship of the true God.) The boulder in Joshua's field
where the worship took place became a landmark in Israel—a witness to
intelligent and obedient worship.

KIRIATH-JEARIM (6:19–7:2)

6:19 The descendants of Jeconiah did not rejoice with the people of Beth-shemesh when they greeted the ark of the LORD; and he killed seventy men of them. The people mourned because the LORD had made a great slaughter among the people. 20 Then the people of Beth-shemesh said, "Who is able to stand before the LORD, this holy God? To whom shall he go so that we may be rid of him?" 21 So they sent messengers to the inhabitants of Kiriath-jearim, saying, "The Philistines have returned the ark of the LORD. Come down and take it up to you." 7:1 And the people of Kiriath-jearim came and took up the ark of the LORD, and brought it to the house of Abinadab on the hill. They consecrated his son, Eleazar, to have charge of the ark of the LORD. . . .

This is a difficult passage to fit into the story as it is being told. The texts that have come down to us in Hebrew and in Greek do not match; scholars exercise considerable ingenuity in figuring out what actually went on. What seems clear, though, is that some kind of disaster associated with impiety or irreverence took place in connection with the ark—even in pious Beth-shemesh. Earlier, the Israelites tried to use God (via the ark) to win their battles; then the Philistines tried to put God on display as a trophy of war; perhaps the disaster at Beth-shemesh was a variation on such sacrilege—this time using God as entertainment. This is all conjecture, of course, but the context permits it. Did some of these people think that the ark was a curiosity to be displayed, a novelty in a religious sideshow? God as entertainment? This "holy God" (v. 20) is a God to be worshiped, not used, a God to be served, not manipulated, a God to be adored, not ordered around. Suddenly uncomfortable with being charged with such a dangerous responsibility, the people of Beth-shemesh asked the people at Kiriath-jearim, about nine miles farther up the road, to take over. And there the ark remained. The story of the ark will be resumed twenty years later, at 2 Samuel 6, when David comes to get it.

Even though the details of this incident remain obscure to us, a basic theme of the ark story is clearly underlined: The ark is not to be toyed with; God is sovereign and takes care of himself; materiality is not incidental to God's revelation, but is a *means* of revelation, and so the way we treat things is part and parcel of the way we treat God. We do not cure superstition by getting rid of things, by avoiding or marginalizing the physical—there remains a holiness of place and thing.

7. Samuel Leads Israel
1 Samuel 7:3–8:22

SAMUEL BEGINS HIS PROPHETIC LEADERSHIP (7:3–6)

In contrast to all the "religious" activity that surrounded the ark, in which it was treated as some kind of portable god, Samuel calls the people to a repentance that emphasizes personal response to the living God.

> 7:3 **Then Samuel said to all the house of Israel, "If you are returning to the LORD with all your heart, then put away the foreign gods and the Astartes from among you. Direct your heart to the LORD, and serve him only, and he will deliver you out of the hand of the Philistines." ⁴ So Israel put away the Baals and the Astartes, and they served the LORD only.**
> ⁵ **Then Samuel said, "Gather all Israel at Mizpah, and I will pray to the LORD for you." ⁶ So they gathered at Mizpah, and drew water and poured it out before the LORD. They fasted that day, and said, "We have sinned against the LORD." And Samuel judged the people of Israel at Mizpah.**

We left Samuel back at 4:1 preaching. The intervening story of the ark of the covenant is a vivid evocation of the corrupt, superstitious, and dangerous conditions in which he did his preaching. He has his work cut out for him! But his preaching is producing effects. Unfortunately, we don't know exactly what effects, for the verb phrase "Israel *lamented* after the LORD" (7:2) is obscure and imprecise. But *something* was going on in the hearts of the people, and Samuel seized the moment to shape whatever it was into the precision of repentance. Religious feeling, as such, never amounts to much. It needs nailing down to a life of commitment to God. Repentance provides the hammer and nails.

"Repent!" summarizes Samuel's actual words, "put away" (a negative action) and "serve" (a positive action). The negative and positive add up to the powerful, biblical "repent." This first item on Samuel's prophetic agenda becomes, a thousand years later, the opening word in the preach-

50

ing of both John the Baptizer and Jesus. An entire culture has been stampeding headlong in the wrong direction; a halt has to be called and a turnaround accomplished before the reformation of worship and manners can take place.   *pivot point*

Samuel's call to "put away" the foreign gods and goddesses (Baals and Astartes) is a call to come clean from the surrounding culture. Baal (male) and Astarte (female) were the dominant deities of the culture. They were the local Canaanite fertility deities, which meant that their worshipers may have been involved in both male and female cultic prostitution. But we would be mistaken to see in these activities simply religiously sanctioned sexual indulgence. Baal/Astarte worship was a way of thinking and living that believed that *human* actions provide the critical element in what happens in life, that the gods can be bribed to throw their weight in our direction. Viewed this way, North American culture is hardly distinguishable from Canaanite—a great deal of contemporary religion is little more than technology designed to get something from God. Fornication at the Baal/Astarte shrines was a kind of "priming of the pump" to get agricultural fertility going, which then had consequences in a more general prosperity.

We cannot, then, understand Samuel's preaching as a mere campaign for moral decency. This is much deeper, a theological/spiritual repentance that involves abandoning the culture's way of doing things, a way in which I determine the outcome with my initiative and action, and instead setting myself unreservedly ("with all your heart," v. 3) under the initiative and action of God. Samuel's preaching rescues the people from their culture. Israel listens and acts: "They served the LORD only" (v. 4).

Mizpah is set as the site for the act of worship that will give expression to this national repentance. Mizpah was both symbolically and strategically an ideal place for the service. Mizpah means "watchtower." (This Mizpah is not to be confused with the Mizpah where Jacob and Laban made their covenant [Gen. 31:43–50]; that one is another fifty miles to the northeast.) Samuel's Mizpah sits astride the high central ridge of Palestine, about eight miles north of Jerusalem, central to the area in which Samuel spent his life (and in which Saul later would spend his). As the people gather, they engage in rituals of repentance, fasting, and confessing their sins. They give every indication of being serious about serving "the LORD only" (v. 4).

The pouring out of water (v. 6) is a ritual otherwise unmentioned in the Bible, but it clearly has something to do with the confession of sin, perhaps a dramatization of what was later described in Lamentations 2:19: "Pour out your hearts like water before the presence of the LORD!"

THE MIZPAH VICTORY (7:7–14)

> 7:7 When the Philistines heard that the people of Israel had gathered at Mizpah, the lords of the Philistines went up against Israel. And when the people of Israel heard of it they were afraid of the Philistines. 8 The people of Israel said to Samuel, "Do not cease to cry out to the LORD our God for us, and pray that he may save us from the hand of the Philistines." 9 So Samuel took a sucking lamb and offered it as a whole burnt offering to the LORD; Samuel cried out to the LORD for Israel, and the LORD answered him. 10 As Samuel was offering up the burnt offering, the Philistines drew near to attack Israel; but the LORD thundered with a mighty voice that day against the Philistines and threw them into confusion; and they were routed before Israel. . . .

Marked by Samuel's preaching and the people's repentance, the domestic life of Israel shows signs of coming together. The polluting degeneracy that had accumulated in the Hophni and Phinehas era is cleansed. But foreign affairs are still anything but comfortable; the Philistines are as aggressive and brutal as ever. When they get word that all Israel has gathered at Mizpah, their knee-jerk reaction is "War!" And they come on the run to do what they do best—fight.

Israel is frightened. Their recent double defeat by the Philistines is still a raw wound in their national psyche. It is natural they would be frightened. But they do not panic. The Philistine attack becomes a test of Israel's spiritual repentance. Is their repentance only cosmetic—a surface piety that will dissipate under Philistine pressure and send them scurrying after the tangible and reassuring gods and goddesses that they have trafficked with for so long? It is not. They call on Samuel to pray for them, a most uncharacteristic action on their part. Samuel prays and leads them in worship. God answers the prayers, and the Philistines are defeated (also most uncharacteristic!).

The story goes on to make it clear that though the Israelites are given a part to play in the action ("pursued the Philistines and struck them down," v. 11), *God* accomplishes the victory, and by his own means (v. 10). The narrator of this story, detail by detail, is shifting the ground of our understanding of life: we *begin* with God, and everything follows from that; the invisible is more real than the visible; we must never permit the secular (or superstitious) outsider to dictate the terms on which we will conduct our lives.

> 7:12 Then Samuel took a stone and set it up between Mizpah and Jeshanah, and named it Ebenezer; for he said, "Thus far the LORD has helped us." 13 So

the Philistines were subdued and did not again enter the territory of Israel;
the hand of the LORD was against the Philistines all the days of Samuel.
¹⁴ . . . There was peace also between Israel and the Amorites.

The promised land that had been slowly eroded through generations of
willfulness and forgetfulness was recovered as Samuel preached God's
word and administered God's law. Enemies to the west (Philistines) and to
the east (Amorites) were put in their place. The life of faith is never only
a matter of the soul; nor is it ever merely circumstantial. The interior and
exterior are always impinging on and affecting each other. Every once in
a while there is a remarkable confluence of the two elements that calls for
recognition. "Ebenezer" is one of those moments of recognition.

"Ebenezer" means "stone of help." It marks the place and time in
Samuel's leadership of Israel when the "insides" and "outsides" of Israel
were in harmony. These moments are not constant in the life of God's
people, but when they arrive they deserve to be memorialized, for they are
evidence of what can happen and what finally will happen as we pray, "Thy
kingdom come."

The Ebenezer story, set in the context of Christian experience by
Robert Robinson's 1758 hymn, "Come, Thou Fount of Every Blessing,"
continues to be sung by God's people:

> Here I raise my Ebenezer,
>   Hither by Thy help I'm come;
> And I hope, by Thy good pleasure,
>   Safely to arrive at home.
> Jesus sought me when a stranger,
>   Wandering from the fold of God;
> He, to rescue me from danger,
>   Interposed His precious blood.

SAMUEL, CHAMPION OF JUSTICE (7:15–17)

¹⁵ Samuel judged Israel all the days of his life. ¹⁶ He went on a circuit year
by year to Bethel, Gilgal, and Mizpah; and he judged Israel in all these places.
¹⁷ Then he would come back to Ramah, for his home was there; he adminis-
tered justice there to Israel, and built there an altar to the LORD.

Samuel *judged* Israel. The verb is used three times, dominating each of
these verses and accumulating in force. The word has far more in it than

the handing down of judicial decisions—it involved a comprehensive leadership that fused prayer and worship, justice and mercy, guidance and wise counsel. Samuel *led* Israel in the ways of God. But while it was a diligent and attentive leadership, Samuel faithful in his annual circuit of visitation, it was not imposed—neither dictatorial nor militaristic. This is not common, but neither is it impossible. Every so often someone comes along and does it right. Samuel did it right.

Three place names in chapter 7 summarize, in turn, stages in the "upward" movement from corruption to reformation: Kiriath-jearim (v. 1), where the ark was returned with reverence and treated with respect; Mizpah (v. 5), where Samuel prayed and the people repented; Ebenezer (v. 12), where the LORD showed saving strength in the midst of the renewed people.

THE PEOPLE DEMAND A KING (8:1–22)

Israel was unique: the people had no government in a conventional sense, for God was their king. From time to time God provided prophets and judges to carry out special tasks of leadership, but the central focus for the common life of the people was not in a political office, but in an act of worship where God was acknowledged as Ruler and Savior. The sanctuary where God was worshiped, not a palace where a king was enthroned, was the visible symbol of government in Israel.

And then suddenly there was a change. Israel, almost overnight as such things go, got a political system along the lines current among its neighbors in the ancient Near East.

> 8:1 **When Samuel became old, he made his sons judges over Israel. . . . ³ Yet his sons did not follow in his ways, but turned aside after gain; they took bribes and perverted justice.**

Samuel is the third leader (Gideon and Eli precede Samuel in this misfortune) whose sons refuse to follow in their father's righteous footsteps.

> 8:4 **Then all the elders of Israel gathered together and came to Samuel at Ramah, ⁵ and said to him, "You are old and your sons do not follow in your ways; appoint for us, then, a king to govern us, like other nations." ⁶ But the thing displeased Samuel. . . . Samuel prayed to the LORD, ⁷ and the LORD said to Samuel, "Listen to the voice of the people in all that they say to you; for they have not rejected you, but they have rejected me from being king over them. ⁸ Just as they have done to me, from the day I brought them up out of**

Egypt to this day, forsaking me and serving other gods, so also they are doing to you. [9] Now then, listen to their voice; only—you shall solemnly warn
them, and show them the ways of the king who shall reign over them."

[10]So Samuel reported all the words of the LORD to the people who were
asking him for a king. [11] He said, "These will be the ways of the king who will
reign over you: he will take your sons and appoint them to his chariots and
to be his horsemen, and to run before his chariots; [12] and he will appoint for
himself commanders of thousands and commanders of fifties, and some to
plow his ground and to reap his harvest, and to make his implements of war
and the equipment of his chariots. [13] He will take your daughters to be per-
fumers and cooks and bakers. [14] He will take the best of your fields and vineyards and olive orchards and give them to his courtiers. [15] He will take
one-tenth of your grain and of your vineyards and give it to his officers and
his courtiers. [16] He will take your male and female slaves, and the best of
your cattle and donkeys, and put them to his work. [17] He will take one-tenth
of your flocks, and you shall be his slaves. [18] And in that day you will cry out
because of your king, whom you have chosen for yourselves; but the LORD
will not answer you in that day."

Here is a curious thing: We are more apt to leave God's ways during times
of well-being than in time of need. Prosperity seems to be a more fertile
breeding ground for discontent and sin than does poverty. Samuel's ex-
cellent leadership as God's prophet in Israel achieved a high level of justice among the people and peace with historic enemies. But in his old age,
the people became restless and dissatisfied. The elders of Israel came to
Samuel and petitioned for a change of government: "Give us a king."

But they already had a king: *God* ruled Israel. Their demand for a king,
in the deepest sense, was an attempt to get out from under the rule of God.
A line in Jesus' parable expresses the hidden motive in the demand, "We
do not want this man [King Jesus!] to rule over us" (Luke 19:14).

The reason the elders gave for their request was that Samuel was old (and
so presumably would not be around much longer), and his sons whom he
was grooming to succeed him were not fit for the work. Samuel didn't take
kindly to the proposal—"displeased" is putting it mildly; he thought it was
a terrible idea, an affront to God's revealed ways among them. Samuel *was*
old, and his sons, with a reputation for taking bribes and corrupting justice,
were obviously not fit to take over his work (he seems to have done no better than Eli at rearing sons). So why did he react so strongly?

Samuel took his displeasure to God in prayer, and in the praying his gut
reaction was clarified. The elders' request was, in effect, a rejection of
Samuel's prophetic leadership, which is to say, his God-oriented leadership.

He had led Israel diligently and well for a long time (we do not know how many years), and now, rather than trusting their lives to the continuing providence of God, which had been featured in Samuel's leadership, they were taking matters into their own hands, *not* living by faith but living defensively, cautiously, planning for their own future. "King" to them meant managed security, living in conformity with the ways of the world ("like other nations").

"Retirement Planning"

When the people demanded a king, what they had in mind was the impressive display of grandeur that would show that they were as important as the neighboring nations and give them a strong central authority that would be able to get rid of the corruption that was so scandalously evident in Samuel's sons quickly and efficiently. They wanted a government that had style and clout. What they never considered was that all the style and clout would be for the king's benefit, not theirs.

All this becomes clear to Samuel as he prays. God reassures him that it is not Samuel's but God's leadership that is being rejected. The sovereign and almighty God is already their king, but now they want a king cut to the size of their sin-defined hopes and fears. This kind of thing, looking for alternatives to a life of faith-freedom, had been going on among these people ever since they were delivered from Egyptian slavery. They were a free people, free to live in faith before a merciful, saving God. But a free life of faith, lived in the vast and gracious mysteries of God, is a large, demanding life—it is far easier to live small, reduced to the visible and tangible requirements of petty gods and tyrant kings. Their leaders, from Moses to Samuel, kept trying to get them to live large; they preferred to live small.

The phrase "ways of the king" is a translation of the Hebrew word *mishpat*, a word that describes the way that the king would operate in God's moral universe. This word recurs throughout this chapter and constitutes its basic theme. The root occurs eight times (vv. 1, 2, 4, 5, 6, 9, 11, 20).

When people transfer their expectations for righteousness and salvation from God to government, they are sure to be disappointed. There are many things that human government is good for, but there are some things that it cannot do. And one of those things is to function as a God substitute. The issue that day at Ramah, when the elders confronted Samuel, was one not of political science, but of spiritual faith.

Hitler!

8:19 **But the people refused to listen to the voice of Samuel; they said, "No! but we are determined to have a king over us, ²⁰ so that we also may be like other nations, and that our king may govern us and go out before us and fight our battles."**

The refusal of the people to pay attention to Samuel's warnings was, in some ways, incredible. What people would deliberately get themselves in for what Samuel had outlined as their future fate? Yet the refusal is true to both personal and historical experience. Ever since Eve succumbed to the tempter's seductions in the garden there has been a certain inevitability to sin: if it is possible to do wrong, there will be someone around to do it.

Eve responded to the tempter out of the hope that she would "be like God" (Gen. 3:5); the Israelites have no higher ambition than to "be like other nations." It is not a very lofty goal, particularly when we ponder the rather dreary repetitions of old and banal sins that constitute the histories of the nations. The ambition doesn't die out; today we call it "peer group" pressure. Paul could very well have been thinking of this story when he wrote, "Do not be conformed to this world, but be transformed by the renewing of your minds, so that you may discern what is the will of God—what is good and acceptable and perfect" (Rom. 12:2); or as Phillips translated it, "Don't let the world around you squeeze you into its own mold."

> **8:21 When Samuel had heard all the words of the people, he repeated them in the ears of the LORD. 22 The LORD said to Samuel, "Listen to their voice and set a king over them." Samuel then said to the people of Israel, "Each of you return home."**

Then this surprising turn in God's word to Samuel: "Go ahead, let them have their king. Warn them of what they're in for; but let them have their way—give them a king."

We read these words and rub our eyes in disbelief: Is God really giving in to their smallness, their unbelief, their world-conforming ways? If having a king is so bad, why is God giving them one? If demanding a king is, in effect, rejecting God as king, why does God assent to being rejected?

But God ever does this. We don't have to come up to God's standards before we are listened to or cared for. God descends to our condition, accommodates to our dulled imaginations and little faith, works with us where we are, and changes us from the inside. Jesus, born in a place of rejection and killed in an act of rejection, is the supreme instance of this, but it is characteristic of God's way with us.

In giving in to their request, though, God doesn't give up on them. The kings they get are going to be a primary means of realizing who the king is that they already have, namely, God. First Saul (a mostly negative lesson), and then David (mostly positive), followed by a succession of kings who in one way or another will be presented by Israel's storytellers in terms of how well or ill they represent God's kingship. And Israel will finally learn who their king is, for when the Babylonian exile takes place some four or five hundred years later, putting a definitive end to kings in Israel, they will spend those years of captivity singing and praying the marvelous psalms that proclaim and praise God as King. Those approximately five hundred years of mostly negative "king" experience, quite unlike what they anticipated along the lines of "the other nations," will play their part in the revelation and recognition and reception of Jesus as King. The result in the Christian church is that the term "king" takes on a coloration all its own, quite distinct from that of "the nations." George Herbert's hymn is typical:

> Let all the world in every corner sing,
> My God and King!
> The heavens are not too high,
> God's praise may thither fly;
> The earth is not too low,
> God's praises there may grow.
> Let all the world in every corner sing,
> My God and King!

Samuel, of course, doesn't see all of this, but he is obedient to God's word and agrees to give them their king, even though it makes no sense at the time and he cannot possibly see the implications of it. But he does warn them about what they are getting themselves in for: high taxes, military conscription, slave labor, and arbitrary exploitation—loss of freedom in every area of their lives. And they must not expect God to rescue them from the consequences of their decision. But even though well warned, they persist in their demands. Samuel, after another session of prayer in which God seconds God's earlier assent, agrees.

We leave this chapter with a sense of nostalgia for a lost opportunity. How would Israel's history have developed if they had followed Samuel's counsel, entered the narrow gate and followed the hard way (Matt. 7:13–14), refused to be "like other nations," and stubbornly lived by faith, with the LORD as their King? What we get instead is about a five-hundred-year history of monarchy in which every detail of Samuel's forecast came true.

8. Samuel Establishes Saul as King
1 Samuel 9–12

Saul, famously described by Milton as "He who seeking asses, found a kingdom," was Israel's first king.

SAUL (9:1–2)

9:1 **There was a man of Benjamin whose name was Kish . . . a Benjaminite, a man of wealth. ² He had a son whose name was Saul, a handsome young man. There was not a man among the people of Israel more handsome than he; he stood head and shoulders above everyone else.**

Compared to Samuel's introduction into the story, Saul's is most auspicious. Samuel entered the story as a "nonperson"—Hannah, childless, despised by Peninnah and condescended to by Eli, is totally dependent on God. The child she conceived, Samuel, is a sheer gift from God, and she then gives him to God. Saul, in contrast, appears fully formed, the impressive son of an impressive father. Whereas Samuel arrives out of nothingness and weakness, Saul appears brimming with "presence" and virility. Is the storyteller signaling us to be on the watch for coming contrasts between appearance and reality?

The genealogy shows that Saul came from a respected and responsible family. The fact that he was from the tribe of Benjamin, the smallest of the twelve tribes, was probably important strategically. A leader chosen from Benjamin would not threaten the relative prestige of the two strongest tribes, Judah (in the south) and Ephraim (in the north). A king selected from either one of those tribes would have had difficulty enlisting the allegiance of the other.

THE KING IS FOUND (9:3–26)

> 9:3 Now the donkeys of Kish, Saul's father, had strayed. So Kish said to his son Saul, "Take one of the boys with you; go and look for the donkeys." ⁴ He passed through the hill country of Ephraim and . . . the land of Shalishah, . . . of Shaalim, . . . of Benjamin, but they did not find them.

Saul is introduced, significantly, as a man who knows how to be obedient to authority. It is an important qualification in a king who will not *be* the authority, but be *under* the authority of God.

The places Shalishah and Shaalim have not been located by geographers, but the general vicinity is central Palestine.

> 9:5 When they came to the land of Zuph, Saul said to the boy who was with him, "Let us turn back, or my father will stop worrying about the donkeys and worry about us." ⁶ But he said to him, "There is a man of God in this town. . . . Whatever he says always comes true. . . . Perhaps he will tell us about the journey on which we have set out." ⁷ Then Saul replied to the boy, "But if we go, what can we bring the man?" . . . ⁸ The boy answered Saul again, "Here, I have with me a quarter shekel of silver; I will give it to the man of God, to tell us our way." . . . ¹⁰ Saul said to the boy, "Good; come, let us go." . . .
> ¹¹ As they went up the hill to the town, they met some girls coming out to draw water, and said to them, "Is the seer here?" ¹² They answered, "Yes, there he is just ahead of you. Hurry; he has come just now to the town, because the people have a sacrifice today at the shrine. . . . " ¹⁴ So they went up to the town. As they were entering the town, they saw Samuel coming out toward them on his way up to the shrine.

The words paint a picture: The city is on the side of a hill, with the place of worship at the apex and the well for water at the foot, both outside the city gates. From an earlier description (1 Sam. 7:15–17) we know that Samuel went on a circuit through the country, making regular rounds as judge. It sounds as if Samuel has just returned to his home town of Ramah after completing his annual circuit.

> 9:15 Now the day before Saul came, the LORD had revealed to Samuel: ¹⁶ "Tomorrow about this time I will send to you a man from the land of Benjamin, and you shall anoint him to be ruler over my people Israel. He shall save my people from the hand of the Philistines; for I have seen the suffering of my people, because their outcry has come to me."

The word "king" is conspicuous by its absence here. "Ruler" (*nagid*) is used instead, a "prince" or "captain." The Hebrew text carefully surrounds the employment of this term with its verbal forms (*nagad*) in verses 6, 8, 18, and 19, and in 10:15. This is no accident; it emphasizes that Saul is being brought to the position of leadership in God's way. The term "king" will be used later, but by putting it off as long as possible the narrative emphasis falls on the behind-the-scenes action in which God is selecting the proper leader and preparing the way for his presentation.

> 9:17 **When Samuel saw Saul, the LORD told him, "Here is the man of whom I spoke to you. He it is who shall rule over my people." ¹⁸ Then Saul approached Samuel inside the gate, and said, "Tell me, please, where is the house of the seer?" ¹⁹ Samuel answered Saul, "I am the seer. . . . ²⁰ As for your donkeys that were lost three days ago, give no further thought to them, for they have been found." . . . ²¹ Saul answered, "I am only a Benjaminite, from the least of the tribes of Israel, and my family is the humblest of all the families of the tribe of Benjamin. Why then have you spoken to me in this way?"**

Saul's evident surprise and self-deprecating words in the face of Samuel's greeting show that being king over Israel is the farthest thing from his mind. The one thing, more than anything else, that would have disqualified him from the position would have been a burning desire for it. God, through Samuel, is looking for him; Saul is only looking for some lost donkeys. But the two searches connect, and God's will is done.

> 9:22 **Then Samuel took Saul and his servant-boy and brought them into the hall, and gave them a place at the head of those who had been invited. . . . ²³ And Samuel said to the cook, "Bring the portion I gave you, the one I asked you to put aside." ²⁴ The cook took up the thigh and what went with it and set them before Saul. Samuel said, "See, what was kept is set before you. Eat; for it is set before you at the appointed time. . . . "**

Despite the ambiguity and reluctance associated with the request for a king in chapter 8, chapter 9 begins as well as such a story can. Saul enters his new place in history indirectly, artlessly, unself-consciously. As he looks for his father's lost donkeys, it turns out that he himself is the one being looked for. After three days of aimless, unguided, and unsuccessful hunting for the lost donkeys, he is himself found by someone who is not out searching but simply waiting for him to show up. Saul, frustrated in his search for dumb animals, looks for spiritual guidance in his quest, and when he finds it (him) discovers that he himself is the wanderer (through Ephraim, Shalishah, Shaalim, Benjamin) who is found.

In contrast to Saul's blind roaming through the countryside, looking, looking, looking, Samuel waits. And prepares. For by the time Saul in his hunt enters the town, hunting now for help rather than for the donkeys as such, a sacrificial feast is prepared and ready to be eaten, with thirty invited guests in place. Samuel puts the stranger who has just shown up unannounced and uninvited in a place of honor. After the meal, Saul is shown to a guest room and spends the night in hospitable comfort. In the morning Samuel personally wakes him and sends him on his way home, having earlier reassured him that the straying donkeys have been recovered.

The story makes it quite clear that even though a "king" was the last thing God (and Samuel) wanted for Israel, when it became clear that Israel would settle for nothing less, God entered into the process of selection in minute detail. There is nothing haphazard or meandering in Samuel's God-directed finding of Saul.

And is there also a hint at the edges of the story that while Israel, like Saul looking for the donkeys in all the wrong places, is trying to get itself a king, God, behind the scenes, is using Samuel to do the actual work?

SAMUEL ANOINTS SAUL AS KING (9:27–10:16)

9:27 As they were going down to the outskirts of the town, Samuel said to Saul, "Tell the boy to go on before us . . . that I may make known to you the word of God." 10:1 Samuel took a vial of oil and poured it on his head, and kissed him; he said, "The LORD has anointed you ruler over his people Israel. You shall reign over the people of the LORD and you will save them from the hand of their enemies all around. Now this shall be the sign to you that the LORD has anointed you ruler over his heritage: 2 When you depart from me today you will meet two men by Rachel's tomb . . . ; they will say to you, 'The donkeys that you went to seek are found, and now your father has stopped worrying about them and is worrying about you. . . . 3 Then you shall go on from there further and come to the oak of Tabor; three men going up to God at Bethel will meet you there, one carrying three kids, another carrying three loaves of bread, and another carrying a skin of wine. 4 They will greet you and give you two loaves of bread, which you shall accept from them. 5 After that you shall come to Gibeath-elohim . . . you will meet a band of prophets coming down from the shrine with harp, tambourine, flute, and lyre playing in front of them; they will be in a prophetic frenzy. 6 Then the spirit of the LORD will possess you, and you will be in a prophetic frenzy along with them and be turned into a different person. 7 Now when these signs meet you, do whatever you see fit to do, for God is with you. . . ."

⁹ As he turned away to leave Samuel, God gave him another heart; and all these signs were fulfilled that day. ¹⁰ When they were going from there to Gibeah, a band of prophets met him; and the spirit of God possessed him, and he fell into a prophetic frenzy along with them. ¹¹ When all who knew him before saw how he prophesied with the prophets, the people said to one another, "What has come over the son of Kish? Is Saul also among the prophets?" ¹² . . . it became a proverb, "Is Saul also among the prophets?" ¹³ When his prophetic frenzy had ended, he went home.

¹⁴ Saul's uncle said to him and to the boy, "Where did you go?" And he replied, "To seek the donkeys; and when we saw they were not to be found, we went to Samuel." ¹⁵ Saul's uncle said, "Tell me what Samuel said to you." ¹⁶ Saul said to his uncle, "He told us that the donkeys had been found." But about the matter of the kingship, of which Samuel had spoken, he did not tell him anything.

The sanctuary feast, presided over by Samuel and with Saul as guest of honor, was a public affair. Saul was picked out, as it were, from nowhere, and set down at the head table, surrounded by thirty guests. But while Saul was for this moment in the spotlight, no one would have known why. Only Samuel knew what was really going on—that this was, in fact, a preinauguration banquet. It is sheer speculation, but one wonders if any of the elders who had petitioned Samuel for a king were among those thirty guests. At any rate, the storyteller is letting us readers in on the real action of the day—God already at work without calling attention to it, using the seemingly intractable material of the people's hankering after something less than God to fashion the kingdom of God.

The actual king-making took place in private between Samuel and Saul the next day, marked by oil, symbol of God's Spirit, poured on Saul's head, and the prophetic kiss, sign of God's blessing. Saul is king.

In the Bible, anointing with oil designates a person as set apart to a special position of leadership. Both priests (Exod. 29:7) and prophets (1 Kings 19:16) were thus anointed. But the ritual was especially associated with the kings, who were often called "the LORD's anointed." In Isaiah 61:1 the word is used to describe the future messiah (literally, "anointed one"). The Hebrew word "messiah" translates into Greek as "Christ."

This is a radical moment in Israel's history: they have their first king! But Samuel is the only person in the country who knows it. Trained by journalists to notice significance only in a blaze of flashbulbs, we miss most of what makes history. But the God-revealing moments—moments of obedient faith and faithful prayer—characteristically take place in obscurity, inaccessible to curious spectators.

Meanwhile, before Saul is presented to the people as their king, *he* has to be prepared—provided an internal identity as the one in whom God is exercising rule. If kingship is going to be more than a role, hung on him like a suit of ill-fitting clothes, he needs confirmation that there is more to this than Samuel's action, more in it than Samuel's bright idea. If Saul is, in fact, God's king, he needs more than Samuel's word for it before it becomes public. And that is what he gets: circumstantial signs that will validate Samuel's action, and a deep change within him that makes it possible to understand himself in God's terms, not his own.

Samuel tells him to expect three signs. The first two, meeting the two men at Rachel's tomb and the three men at the oak of Tabor, are circumstantial and seemingly random, arbitrary even. But they will convey to Saul that Samuel's anointing and blessing was not an isolated act—there's a lot more going on here than "Saul." God works comprehensively, interconnectedly. The third sign will take place at Gibeah and begin circumstantially—a troop of prophets will come down the road singing, dancing, and prophesying ecstatically—but it will turn into something inward and personal; Saul will become one with them and "be turned into a different person" (v. 6).

As Saul left Samuel, God made him on the inside what Samuel had just made him from the outside: "God gave him another heart" (v. 9). The three signs then took place just as Samuel had described them, in the local and familiar settings of a tomb and a tree and a town. Saul was not sent off to prestigious Egypt or Babylon for an orientation in his new position as king, but kept firmly on home ground. Whatever else being king meant for Saul, that day's events would mean that it had primarily to do with God in *this* place, at *this* time—the ways in which God would work around and within him.

The elders had said that they wanted a king "like other nations" (8:5); but the king that they now had (although they didn't know it yet) was not at all "like [the] other nations." Saul was one detail among others in which God's presence could be detected—at Rachel's tomb, at the oak of Tabor, at Gibeah. And Saul's authority was not to be imposed from without, but would issue from within, of a kind with the worshipful singing and dancing of the prophets. It is significant for the way the story is being told that Saul first comes to public notice in association with prophets, that is, with the people whose primary identity was with God in worship and utterance. The identification stuck and became proverbial: "Is Saul also among the prophets?" (10:11; see also 19:24). It looks as if the people are going to get a king who is far more like one of their prophets than like a king after the pattern of the "other nations." "King" in Israel, if God has anything to

say about it (and God most certainly does!), is going to have far more to
do with dealing with God than with competing with the "other nations."
When God answers our prayers, it is rarely on our terms—we get more,
and better (but not always more to our liking), than we bargained for.

SAUL PROCLAIMED KING (10:17–27a)

10:17 Samuel summoned the people to the LORD at Mizpah 18 and said to
them, "Thus says the LORD, the God of Israel, 'I brought up Israel out of
Egypt, and I rescued you from the hand of the Egyptians and from the hand
of all the kingdoms that were oppressing you.' 19 But today you have rejected
your God, who saves you from all your calamities and your distresses; and
you have said, 'No! but set a king over us.' Now therefore present yourselves
before the LORD by your tribes and by your clans."

At Mizpah, the site of Samuel's earlier call to repentance (7:5–6), he again
preaches. With impressive succinctness he summarizes Israel's history in
two propositions: God has done everything possible to save them; and Israel has stubbornly rejected God's ways.

10:20 Then Samuel brought all the tribes of Israel near, and the tribe of Benjamin was taken by lot. 21 . . . and Saul the son of Kish was taken by lot. But
when they sought him, he could not be found. 22 So they inquired again of
the LORD, "Did the man come here?" and the LORD said, "See, he has hidden himself among the baggage." 23 Then they ran and brought him from
there. When he took his stand among the people, he was head and shoulders
taller than any of them. 24 Samuel said to all the people, "Do you see the one
whom the LORD has chosen? There is no one like him among all the people."
And all the people shouted, "Long live the king!"
. . . 27 But some worthless fellows said, "How can this man save us?" They
despised him and brought him no present. But he held his peace.

Saul was secretly selected and anointed as Israel's first king. In tension with
the fact that *asking* for a king was a faithless, God-rejecting act on Israel's
part, the storyteller intends that we understand that actually *getting* the
king was God's work from start to finish.

Now as Saul is about to be brought out into the open and publicly proclaimed king, God's shaping providence is still more or less hidden, this
time through an apparent election. ("Casting lots" was their equivalent to
our "casting votes." We do not know exactly how it was carried out—

presumably objects such as pebbles or dice or arrows were used to select between two possibilities. Slightly more detail is given in 14:40–42, the second instance of casting lots that involved Saul.) An orderly process of selection was followed, and Saul was chosen.

But before Saul is presented as the first king, Samuel goes over the old ground again (groundwork laid in 8:4–22) in a brief but pungent "Thus-says-the-LORD" sermon: "In asking for a king you are rejecting the God who saved and continues to save you! But if you insist, we'll do it."

Repetitively Again in this story we are struck with the remarkable gospel fact that though the people reject God, God doesn't reject them. He stays with them through the entire process, using his prophet Samuel both to interpret and to carry out the action. Even though their agenda excludes God, God is silently, hiddenly there, sovereign *in* their agenda. It is not that easy to get rid of God.

But, once chosen, Saul is nowhere to be found! He has gone into hiding. Did that last sermon by Samuel put the fear of God in him? Did he have a premonition that despite all the signs of God's Spirit in his choosing, the kingship was flawed from the start by the people's God-rejecting ambitions, and it was going to be a rocky road ahead? The story does not provide us with Saul's motives for hiding. What it makes quite clear, though, is that this whole king business was going to be a mixed bag, involving both God's mercy and God's judgment.

And here is a telling detail: They are now forced to pray to God to help them find the king they have just chosen with God's help, but against God's will (v. 22). God graciously condescends to do for them what they cannot do for themselves.

But for the moment these shadows recede as Samuel presents Saul to the people as God's choice for their first king. Finally, the people have gotten their way, and they shout in acclamation, "Long live the king!" (v. 24). The minimal dissent registered that day (v. 27) had nothing to do with the fear of God. It was a landslide victory for the "king" party—Israel was embarked on a roughly five-hundred-year experience of living under kings, a half-millennium that will end ignominiously by living under a foreign king in Babylon.

SAUL DEFEATS THE AMMONITES (10:27b–11:14)

Outwardly, the story of Saul's life is dominated by wars against enemies. But that is mere scaffolding. The real drama is inward—the relationships he develops with the God of Israel. There is sharp irony as this narrative unfolds, for while he is mostly successful against the enemies, a grave weakness appears in his relationship with God. The storytelling skillfully sets these two truths off one against the other, in a kind of counterpoint. Saul leads the people in stirring military victories, but in the process he repeatedly falters in matters of faith. In the long run, it is the loss of spiritual poise and the failure to develop a mature faith, and not his Ammonite/Philistine/Amalekite successes, that set their mark on his reign like a clef on a music staff.

> **10:27b Now Nahash, king of the Ammonites, had been grievously oppressing the Gadites and the Reubenites. He would gouge out the right eye of each of them and would not grant Israel a deliverer. No one was left of the Israelites across the Jordan whose right eye Nahash, king of the Ammonites, had not gouged out. But there were seven thousand men who had escaped from the Ammonites and had entered Jabesh-gilead.**

This first paragraph in this section of the story, the unnumbered verses at the end of chapter 10, was lost accidentally early on in the process of transmission. But in the astonishing finds of Hebrew scrolls at Qumran near the Dead Sea in 1947, and continuing for the next several years, scrolls predating all existing Old Testament manuscripts, the Samuel scroll includes this paragraph. Most scholars today agree that it belongs with the original text, and so it is included here.

> **11:1 About a month later, Nahash the Ammonite went up and besieged Jabesh-gilead; and all the men of Jabesh said to Nahash, "Make a treaty with us, and we will serve you." ² But Nahash the Ammonite said to them, "On this condition I will make a treaty with you, namely that I gouge out everyone's right eye, and thus put disgrace upon all Israel." ³ The elders of Jabesh said to him, "Give us seven days' respite." . . . ⁴ [The messengers] reported the matter in the hearing of the people; and all the people wept aloud.**
> **⁵ Now Saul was coming from the field behind the oxen; and Saul said, "What is the matter with the people, that they are weeping?" So they told him. . . . ⁶ And the spirit of God came upon Saul in power when he heard these words, and his anger was greatly kindled. ⁷ . . . Then the dread of the LORD fell upon the people, and they came out as one. ⁸ . . . from Israel were three hundred thousand, . . . from Judah seventy thousand. ⁹ They said . . . "say to the inhabitants of Jabesh-gilead: 'Tomorrow . . . you shall have deliverance.'" When the messengers came and told the inhabitants of Jabesh, they rejoiced. . . . ¹¹ The next day Saul . . . cut down the Ammonites until the heat of the day; and those who survived were scattered, so that no two of them were left together.**

> [12] The people said to Samuel, "Who is it that said, 'Shall Saul reign over us?' Give them to us so that we may put them to death." [13] But Saul said, "No one shall be put to death this day, for today the LORD has brought deliverance to Israel."
>
> [14] Samuel said to the people, "Come, let us go to Gilgal and there renew the kingship." [15] So all the people went to Gilgal, and there they made Saul king before the LORD in Gilgal. There they sacrificed offerings of well-being before the LORD, and there Saul and all the Israelites rejoiced greatly.

Saul is king over Israel. But what does a king in Israel do? There is no precedent or tradition in Israel for kings. Since being delivered from Egypt under the leadership of Moses they have, to be sure, been a kingdom (Exod. 19:6), but *God* has been their king. Now Saul has been chosen king—Israel's first experience with a *human* king. Saul has no court, no palace, no throne. He has a job, but no job description. So what does he do? After the exhilarating acclamation, "Long live the king!" (10:24), the next mention of Saul has him back on the farm, plowing the ground (11:5). The new king, finding no kingly work to do, went back to his old occupation of dirt farming.

That is the setting for the scene in which Saul puts his hand to his first kingly work, which turns out to be rescuing an oppressed minority people from the most brutal sort of tyranny. After he has been back on the farm for a month or so, Saul hears of the outrageous abuse being visited on these people, goes into action, and saves them.

It is difficult to imagine a provocation more extreme: Nahash (the "Snake"), king of Ammon, the country to the east of the Jordan River, made a practice of gouging out the right eye of the Israelites whom he conquered. The tribes of Gad and Reuben, who had settled in this area (Gilead), were the primary victims. The cruel blinding combined torture and humiliation. Imagine a population of one-eyed men walking the streets, daily reminders of the sadistic monster Nahash. But seven thousand Israelites escaped and took refuge in the walled fortress village of Jabesh-gilead. Nahash came after them, and laid siege to the village. When the men of Jabesh offered themselves up as slaves in return for peace, Nahash made the outrageous counteroffer: "Only on the condition that I gouge out everyone's right eye." At that moment Nahash stepped into the front ranks of the world's most brutal oppressors, where he rubs shoulders with Herod the Great and Nero, Tamerlane and Genghis Khan, Hitler and Stalin, and Pol Pot. Inflicting gratuitous pain and humiliation on the hapless is by no means rare in this fallen world, but it never fails to shock us.

When Saul heard of it he was not only shocked, he was moved to action—*kingly* action, for the same spirit of God that marked him for a holy vocation at the time of his anointing (10:10) was in evidence again (11:6) as he plunged into the holy work of delivering the oppressed. Saul pulled an army together, made a forced march through the night across the Jordan to Jabesh (the distance was only about nine miles, but the terrain was difficult), and that was the end of the sadistic Nahash brutalities. Nahash at Jabesh launched Saul into his kingly work. Until Nahash, Saul was a king plowing a field with a single yoke of oxen; with the appearance of Nahash, Saul, galvanized by the spirit of God, became a king commanding a large army and working justice among the most wretched of victims.

But even though Saul now moves to center stage, Samuel continues to play a major role in the life of both Saul and the people. Before the battle, when Saul called for people to come fight with him against Nahash, he did it in the name of "Saul and Samuel" (11:7). And now, after the battle, Samuel continues to be prominent. Two significant items follow the victory, and both involve Samuel. First, the people come to Samuel to ask him to turn over the "worthless fellows" (10:27) for execution, the men who had earlier opposed Saul's becoming king. Samuel, in other words, was still seen as the person with primary authority among them. But Saul intervened and said there was to be no more killing that day; Saul wanted this to be remembered as a day of God's deliverance, not of Saul's revenge (11:13). Saul, in the presence of Samuel and under the authority of Samuel, acted in the spirit of Samuel—he experienced and interpreted his kingly work as God's work of salvation. He understood his leadership as being part of the long history of God's deliverance of the people from Egyptian and Canaanite oppression and in strong distinction to the prevalent brutalities of Nahash and his ilk.

The second item is initiated by Samuel: He calls the people to Gilgal to "renew the kingship."

SAMUEL'S VALEDICTORY ADDRESS (12:1–25)

Samuel is about to step off the stage. He will make a few marginal, although still critical, appearances in the subsequent chapters, but the "kings" now move into the front and center. It is time to sum up leadership among the people.

12:1 **Samuel said to all Israel, "I have listened to you in all that you have said to me, and have set a king over you. ² See, it is the king who leads you** now; I am old and gray. . . . [3] Here I am; testify against me before the LORD and before his anointed. Whose ox have I taken? Or whose donkey have I taken? Or whom have I defrauded? Whom have I oppressed? . . . Testify against me and I will restore it to you." [4] They said, "You have not defrauded us or oppressed us or taken anything from the hand of anyone." [5] He said to them, "The LORD is witness against you, . . . that you have not found anything in my hand." And they said, "He is witness."

[6] Samuel said to the people, . . . [7] "Now therefore take your stand . . . and I will declare to you all the saving deeds of the LORD that he performed for you and for your ancestors. [8] . . . The LORD sent Moses and Aaron, who brought forth your ancestors out of Egypt. . . . [11] And the LORD sent Jerubbaal and Barak, and Jephthah, and Samson, and rescued you out of the hand of your enemies on every side; and you lived in safety. [12] But when you saw that King Nahash of the Ammonites came against you, you said to me, 'No, but a king shall reign over us,' though the LORD your God was your king. [13] See, here is the king whom you have chosen. . . . [14] If you will fear the LORD . . . , and if both you and the king who reigns over you will follow the LORD your God, it will be well; [15] but if you will not heed the voice of the LORD, . . . then the hand of the LORD will be against you and your king. [16] Now therefore take your stand and see this great thing that the LORD will do before your eyes. [17] . . . I will call upon the LORD, that he may send thunder and rain; and you shall know and see that the wickedness that you have done in the sight of the LORD is great in demanding a king for yourselves." [18] So Samuel called upon the LORD, and the LORD sent thunder and rain that day; and all the people greatly feared the LORD and Samuel.

[19] All the people said to Samuel, "Pray to the LORD your God for your servants, so that we may not die. . . . " [20] And Samuel said to the people, "Do not be afraid; you have done all this evil, yet do not turn aside from following the LORD, but serve the LORD with all your heart. . . . [22] For the LORD will not cast away his people. . . . [23] Moreover as for me, far be it from me that I should sin against the LORD by ceasing to pray for you. . . . [24] Only fear the LORD, and serve him faithfully. . . . [25] But if you still do wickedly, you shall be swept away, both you and your king."

Samuel's address to the people completes a major and radical transition in Israel's life, from leadership by men and women whose primary orientation was to God, to a leadership by kings, leaders whose primary orientation was to the people: God *raised up* judges; the people *demanded* a king. The prophetic judges were God-appointed; the political kings were people-acclaimed. The contrast is not absolute, for God continued to be involved in the setting up of kings, but as Samuel steps aside and Saul steps forward there is a distinct sense of decline setting in. Samuel announces the era of the "second best." For a long time now, leadership has come from God's saving initiative; now it takes shape from the people's fears and wishes.

The kind of leadership that began so magnificently with Moses ends graciously with Samuel. In this succession of God-appointed prophetic leaders, God's action held center stage, actions of deliverance and judgment. Six of these leaders are named: Moses, Aaron, Jerubbaal (Gideon), Barak, Jephthah, and Samson. They were effective against Egyptians, Canaanites, Philistines, and Moabites. And Samuel himself—what an impeccable and honorable leader he was! What more could you ask?

And what did the people have to complain of? Samuel reviews his own leadership record: He asks five rhetorical questions (12:3) that contrast with the warnings he had previously issued regarding what they could expect from a rule by kings (8:11–17). The people admit that they have had it pretty good under Samuel (12:4).

But it is not more justice or prosperity that the people are after—they want to rule themselves, or be ruled by one like themselves. It is God's sovereignty that they are rejecting. The root of their demand for a king is not political aspiration, but a spiritual dodge. They suppose that getting rid of God as their king will give them more "say-so" over their own lives. Every political system before and since, whether monarchy or democracy, socialism or communism, has encouraged that supposition.

There is no suggestion in Samuel's address that the change of government is going to precipitate them into a decline in standard of living, military security, or cultural advantages. The difference is not in "benefits." Iron Age culture set the conditions in which they lived, with or without a king. Samuel forces them to face the enormous shift that they have just made in their willful ignorance. They have thrown out one government and embraced another, and the governments could hardly be more different. They have just elected to live under human sovereignty instead of divine sovereignty. Their participation in government until now has been dominated by listening to, crying out to, and obeying God. But no longer.

Samuel minces no words as he tells the people that they have made a grave mistake (a great "wickedness," 12:17) in demanding a king. And the people, to their credit, recognize through Samuel's prophetic speech their sin in "demanding a king for ourselves" (12:19). But it is too late now. They have a king. Saul is their king.

Now here is the surprise, the "gospel," if you will, in this story: Neither Samuel nor (more importantly) God walks off and leaves the people to suffer the consequences of their bad decision. God promises to stay with them. If they, in the aftermath of their faithless demand, reverence and obey God, "it will be well" (12:14). God continues to be their God. It is not a carte-blanche promise of blessing, for their disobedience will also surely be pun-ished. But *God* will be there, whether in salvation or in judgment.

Samuel articulates here one of the fundamental features of the biblical message: No evil, no sin in itself, can separate us from God's gracious mercy toward us. Nothing we do puts us outside the power of God's grace to forgive and reconcile. A thousand years later Jesus embodied what Samuel preached: Do not be afraid. . . . Yes, you have sinned, but don't let your sin paralyze you with guilt; don't let your sin dupe you into thinking you are irredeemable; don't for a minute suppose that God has called it quits on you. It is God's business to save you, and God is not giving up (12:20–22).

Further, Samuel himself intends to continue living what he preaches. Even though he has been displaced as leader, he has no plans for slipping off into retirement. He will stay on, praying for these people and teaching them to live rightly before God (12:23). His prophetic presence will con-tinue to play an important role in the early years of the monarchy.

But we must not misunderstand. This is no easygoing religion being proclaimed, which divinely subsidizes self-centered willfulness and spiri-tual sloth. Twice in this address Samuel says, "Now therefore take your stand . . ." (12:7, 16). "Stand" precludes indolence or slouching—they are in God's courtroom, after all: "God the LORD, speaks and summons the earth" (Psalm 50:1). It is as if Samuel is saying, "Attention! Look me in the eye! You are in crisis, the *nation* is in crisis. Just because you are not being damned on the spot for your sins doesn't mean you are off the hook. Judg-ment, yes, but salvation also. And the two together require everything you have in you—'all your heart' " (12:24). God's grace is not slipshod indul-gence, but a rigorous enlistment in God's ways with us.

Samuel's address takes its place with two other key transitional ad-dresses, one before and one after: Joshua's (Joshua 23–24) and Solomon's (1 Kings 8:12–61). The three farewell addresses are similar in that at high historical moments of change, they look both backward and forward, re-peating God's unchanging covenantal provisions and faithfulness, keeping the story line intact and clear.

Part 3. The Story of Saul as King

1 Samuel 13–15

Introduction

Saul looms out of the past as a tragic figure, a dark, spectral, craggy eminence—a doomsday warning to all men and women who would hear and take seriously God's word in their lives. "Oh, the grievous shipwrecks of some great ships! We see some boards and planks lying in the mud at low water, but that is all!" (Thomas Shepherd quoted in Alexander Whyte, *Bible Characters*, vol. I, page 234). A thousand years separate Saul and Judas Iscariot, but the two men share the dubious honor of being persons called into positions of leadership, betraying that calling, and ending their lives by suicide.

Saul's position in history is marked by two items: iron and politics. The discovery of iron marked a new era in civilization, designated by our archaeologists as the Iron Age. The Philistines were the first people in Palestine to learn to use iron, and they used it primarily for military purposes. This made them immediately superior to the Israelites in armed combat. Excavations have shown that they kept a ruthless control of the manufacture of iron tools and weapons, a virtual iron monopoly. Iron, and the Philistine monopoly of it, account for the desperate conditions against which Saul's life is a response. Saul takes his place on the stage of history at a crisis moment. Every move he makes is fraught with significance. The sheer survival of Israel as a distinct people is at stake. No matter what Saul does, it will count one way or another.

And politics: Human kingship is introduced into Israel in the person of Saul. But what exactly would "king" in Israel look like? Saul is the person in whom the word "king" begins to be defined, in contrast to the way the surrounding cultures understood it. As it turns out, Saul will primarily serve as a negative example. One of our greatest Old Testament scholars, Martin Noth, wrote that Saul's term as king was "as hopeless as it could possibly be" (Noth, *The History of Israel*, 178). If it is true that we learn more from our failures than from our successes, we can expect to learn

75

much from Saul. The initial working out of this radical innovation in politics took place in the person of Saul. Herbert Butterfield, former professor of modern history at Cambridge University, would never permit a separation between politics and person: " Certainly for my part, I do not see why in politics even the virtues which I associate with the Christian religion should be suspended for a moment. I mean humility, charity, self-criticism, and acceptance of the problem that Providence sets before one; also a disposition not to seek to direct affairs as though one had a right to assert a sovereign will in the world—a disposition rather to see that one's action takes the form of a cooperation with Providence" (Butterfield, *International Conflict in the Twentieth Century*, 16). Saul's life compresses into a brief span a great deal of what is involved for all of us as we refuse to reduce spirituality to something purely private and inward, and determine to live well and wisely in the political conditions of our own time.

Saul is the first of Israel's twenty-three kings. The last one, Jehoiachin (Jeconiah), will round out approximately five hundred years of monarchy (2 Kings 25). Some kings were good, others bad; none made it big on the world's wide screen. But between Saul and Jehoiachin, we are immersed in a culture and politics that counter the world's prevailing ideas on what it means to live realistically in the midst of powers and principalities. Saul is the opening chapter in this extensive biblical text that teaches us to pray intelligently and devoutly, "Thy kingdom come." And learning to pray that way does have consequences. Citizens in the Roman colony of Thessalonica complained to their civil authorities that the Christians, converted by Paul to this way of praying and living, "have been turning the world upside down . . . saying that there is another king named Jesus" (Acts 17:6–7).

9. King Saul Fights the Philistines
1 Samuel 13–14

THE PHILISTINE HORNETS STIRRED UP (13:1–7)

> 13:1 **Saul was . . . years old when he began to reign; and he reigned . . . and two years over Israel.**

The exact number of years is missing in two places in our text. Was there a large lapse of time between Saul's anointing and this first battle about to be narrated? We don't know how old Saul was when Samuel anointed him, but he *sounds* young. Still, at this point he has a grown son, Jonathan— there is so much that we don't know about this man!

> 13:2 **Saul chose three thousand out of Israel; two thousand were with Saul in Michmash . . . and a thousand were with Jonathan in Gibeah. . . .** [3] **Jonathan defeated the garrison of the Philistines that was at Geba; and the Philistines heard of it. . . .** [4] **. . . the people were called out to join Saul at Gilgal.**
> [5] **The Philistines mustered to fight with Israel . . . and encamped at Michmash, to the east of Beth-aven.** [6] **When the Israelites saw that they were in distress (for the troops were hard pressed), the people hid themselves in caves and in holes and in rocks and in tombs and in cisterns.** [7] **Some Hebrews crossed the Jordan to the land of Gad and Gilead. Saul was still at Gilgal, and all the people followed him trembling.**

Saul's first act of leadership in Israel, which precipitated his public coronation at Gilgal, was a military victory over Nahash and the Ammonites, enemies to the east (chapter 11). The second is a military victory over the Philistines, enemies to the west. It began as a minor skirmish against an outpost of Philistine soldiers at Geba with Saul's son Jonathan leading the attack, but it ignited an all-out war between Israel and Philistia.

The Philistines, Israel's archetypal enemies, had been subdued under Samuel (7:13), and the country had enjoyed a season of security on the western front. But the Geba adventure, like a stone thrown into a hornets' nest, stirred up the old hostilities. The Philistines were *buzzing*.

Saul prepared for a major battle, assembling his troops at Gilgal, the site of his recent coronation (11:14–15), while the Philistines gathered their forces at Michmash, three or so miles from Geba. When Israel saw the Philistine army, it was obvious that they were greatly outnumbered; they were, quite understandably, terrified. They took "bomb shelter" cover wherever they could find it, and many escaped across the Jordan River to the east.

We get a picture of King Saul, acclaimed as king on the strength of his military prowess against the Ammonites, his leadership of Israel now circumstantially defined in wholly military terms, suddenly threatened from an aroused Philistine army and faced with almost certain defeat. He is desperate.

Implicit in what follows is that there had been some sort of agreement or understanding between Saul and Samuel that Saul was to lead in matters of warfare, while Samuel retained the priestly and prophetic responsibility for dealing with God. Saul was in charge of fighting; Samuel in charge of praying.

And then this:

SAMUEL CALLS SAUL ON THE CARPET (13:8–15)

13:8 He waited seven days . . . , but Samuel did not come to Gilgal, and the people began to slip away from Saul. 9 So Saul said, " Bring the burnt offering here to me, and the offerings of well-being." And he offered the burnt offering. 10 As soon as he finished offering the burnt offering, Samuel arrived; and Saul went out to meet him and salute him. 11 Samuel said, " What have you done?" Saul relied, " When I saw that the people were slipping away from me, and that you did not come within the days appointed, and that the Philistines were mustering at Michmash, 12 I said, 'Now the Philistines will come down upon me at Gilgal, and I have not entreated the favor of the LORD'; so I forced myself, and offered the burnt offering." 13 Samuel said to Saul, " You have done foolishly; you have not kept the commandment of the LORD your God, which he commanded you. The LORD would have established your kingdom over Israel forever, 14 but now your kingdom will not continue; the LORD has sought out a man after his own heart; and the LORD has appointed him to be ruler over his people. . . .

Saul did not keep his part of the bargain. When Samuel did not show up on time, Saul took over. Saul intruded in matters in which he had no business. But his offering of the sacrifices was not a mere technical violation of an agreement; it is interpreted as a lack of trust in God, motivated by fear of losing his position and power. He has reduced his concept of king to military terms; he thinks that the authority of his kingship depends (as to all appearances it began) on his success in battle. In the story, it is clear that he is king because God chose him to be king, prior to any military achievement; his primary relation is with God, not Philistines or Israelites.

It is hard to resist the temptation, especially when we suppose that we are doing something special for God, to expect special favors from God, and on occasion to use forms that are virtually equivalent to theological blackmail. Such attempts, ancient and modern, are of dubious morality; they present us with a God who may be forced by pressure groups. A God who can be so coerced is not much of a God, but a merely capricious and fickle ruler who is never sure of his own mind and can be flattered into granting favors to favorites.

The concern of the storyteller is not with military operations as such, even though the passage is packed with fascinating detail on terrain and troop movements. The way the story is told guarantees that we will recognize that acts of faith take place in the so-called "real world"—a world of named towns, of strategic troop deployments, of military statistics, of probabilities and "odds." *This* is the setting for understanding faith and obedience. Saul believes or disbelieves, is obedient or disobedient to God, trusts or mistrusts God *in* his daily work as a military leader, not abstracted from it. As it turns out, he is unbelievingly disobedient.

Samuel, when he eventually does show up, is sharp and direct in his rebuke: Saul has, in effect, just abdicated his throne. In a seemingly inoffensive act of disobedience (but disguised as an act of worship), Saul has forfeited his kingdom. Instead of living in the fear of God, he has lived in fear of Philistines, and the consequence is that he will no longer be king— someone else has been chosen and appointed (13:14). Three chapters later we will get that story. Preoccupied with Philistines, Saul forgot God, forgot what he had been anointed to be and do; at that moment Samuel announced that he was bankrupt. It will take a while for the collapse to become apparent, but we, the readers, know that from now on we will be reading the story of the dismantling of Saul as king—and that it will have nothing to do with Philistines; it will have been caused from within, by his defection from God. The inner world of obedience to God is far more "real" than the outer world of war.

BUSINESS AS USUAL (13:15–18)

Saul goes on, oblivious to Samuel's prophetic rebuke, and continues with business as usual. Did he hear a single word of these words of Samuel, which we have just read? Listening does not seem to have been one of Saul's strong points.

AN ASIDE: THE PHILISTINE MONOPOLY OF IRON (13:19–22)

13:19 Now there was no smith to be found throughout all the land of Israel; for the Philistines said, " The Hebrews must not make swords or spears for themselves"; 20 so all the Israelites went down to the Philistines to sharpen their plowshare, mattocks, axes, or sickles. . . . 22 So on the day of the battle neither sword nor spear was to be found . . .; but Saul and his son Jonathan had them.

The narrative now shifts abruptly from Samuel's searing prophetic indictment of the king back to everyday matters of battle strategies and cultural conditions. But it doesn't strike us as abrupt; it is one world. The prosaic note regarding the Philistine monopoly on iron keeps the story rooted in the everyday world of tools and economics.

THE BATTLE AT MICHMASH PASS (13:23–14:23)

13:23 Now a garrison of the Philistines had gone out to the pass of Michmash. . . .
14:6 Jonathan said to the young man who carried his armor, " Come, let us go over to the garrison of these uncircumcised; it may be that the LORD will act for us. . . . " 7 His armor-bearer said to him, " . . . I am with you; as your mind is, so is mine." 8 Then Jonathan said, " Now we will cross over to those men and will show ourselves to them. 9 If they say to us, 'Wait until we come to you,' then we will stand still in our place. . . . 10 But if they say, 'Come up to us,' then we will go up; for the LORD has given them into our hand. That will be the sign for us." 11 So both of them showed themselves to the garrison of the Philistines; and the Philistines said, "Look, Hebrews are coming out of the holes where they have hidden themselves." 12 The men of the garrison hailed Jonathan and his armor-bearer, saying, " Come up to us, and we will show you something." Jonathan said to his armor-bearer, " Come up after me; for the LORD has given them into the hand of Israel." 13 Then Jonathan climbed up on his hands and feet, with

his armor-bearer following after him. The Philistines fell before Jonathan, and his armor-bearer, coming after him, killed them. [14] In that first slaughter Jonathan and his armor-bearer killed about twenty men within an area about half a furrow long in an acre of land. [15] There was a panic in the camp. . . .

[16] Saul's lookouts in Gibeah of Benjamin were watching as the multitude was surging back and forth. [17] Then Saul said . . . , "Call the roll and see who has gone from us." When they had called the roll, Jonathan and his armor-bearer were not there. [18] Saul said to Ahijah, " Bring the ark of God here." . . . [20] Then Saul and all the people who were with him rallied and went into the battle; and every sword was against the other, so that there was very great confusion. . . . [23] So the LORD gave Israel the victory that day. . . .

Jonathan started this fight (13:3), which resulted in a massive mobilization of Philistine troops and a retaliation that spelled, it seemed, certain doom for Israel. And it is Jonathan who now ends it, with his daring, single-handed (accompanied by his armor-bearer) assault on the Philistines, which quickly turned into a full-scale battle, all the Israelites pouring into the field of battle and the Philistines routed totally.

The account of the battle at Michmash Pass is extraordinarily vivid, etched in fine detail, the plot's movement fueled with energetic dialogue. The story stands on its own; little commentary is needed. But some notes may be helpful in clarifying certain words:

1. "Ark" in verse 18 in the Greek translation is "ephod," a priestly garment used for, among other things, divination, and ephod is almost certainly the right word here. We last heard of the ark being left at Kiriath-jearim (7:1–2); it will not enter the story again until David retrieves it after the death of Saul (2 Samuel 6).
2. "Hebrews" (13:3, 7, 19; 14:11, 21) most probably refers here to a fickle, riffraff fringe of Israelites who defect and return depending on the fortunes of war. All Hebrews were Israelites, but not all Israelites were Hebrews.
3. "Bozez" and "Seneh" (14:4) in Hebrew were something like " thorn" and " tooth"—dramatic, craggy outcroppings.
4. Geba (14:5) and Gibeah (14:2) are most probably alternate spellings for the same place, a village on the summit of a hill about three miles north of Jerusalem. Gibeah was Saul's home base; archaeologists excavated on this site the oldest Iron Age fortification in Palestine; it is plausible that it was Saul's citadel, a simple, unpretentious structure.

THE CURSING OF JONATHAN (14:24–46)

14:24 Now Saul committed a very rash act on that day . . . saying, "Cursed be anyone who eats food before it is evening and I have been avenged on my enemies." So none of the troops tasted food. 25 All the troops came upon a honeycomb. . . . 26 . . . but they did not put their hands to their mouths, for they feared the oath. 27 But Jonathan had not heard his father charge the troops with the oath; so he extended the staff that was in his hand, and dipped the tip of it in the honeycomb, and put his hand to his mouth; and his eyes brightened. 28 Then one of the soldiers said, "Your father strictly charged the troops . . . , 'Cursed be anyone who eats food this day.'" . . . 29 Then Jonathan said, "My father has troubled the land. . . . 30 How much better if today the troops had eaten freely of the spoil." . . .

36 Then Saul said, "Let us go down after the Philistines by night and despoil them until the morning light; let us not leave one of them." They said, "Do whatever seems good to you." But the priest said, "Let us draw near to God here." 37 So Saul inquired of God, "Shall I go down after the Philistines?" . . . But he did not answer him that day. . . . 41 Then Saul said, "O LORD God of Israel, why have you not answered your servant today? If this guilt is in me or in my son Jonathan, O LORD God of Israel, give Urim; but if this guilt is in your people Israel, give Thummim." And Jonathan and Saul were indicated by the lot, but the people were cleared. 42 Then Saul said, " Cast the lot between me and my son Jonathan." And Jonathan was taken.

43 Then Saul said to Jonathan, "Tell me what you have done." Jonathan told him, " I tasted a little honey with the tip of the staff that was in my hand; here I am, I will die." 44 Saul said, " God do so to me and more also; you shall surely die, Jonathan!" 45 Then the people said to Saul, "Shall Jonathan die, who has accomplished this great victory in Israel? Far from it! As the LORD lives, not one hair of his head shall fall to the ground; for he has worked with God today." So the people ransomed Jonathan, and he did not die. 46 Then Saul withdrew from pursuing the Philistines; and the Philistines went to their own place.

In this segment of the story, Jonathan is used as a foil to expose the failing kingship of Saul: Saul panics as the Philistines gather their vastly superior forces and, failing to trust God, usurps Samuel's place by offering the sacrifice; meanwhile Jonathan courageously attacks the Philistines with intrepid trust, saying, "Nothing can hinder the LORD from saving by many or by few" (14:6). Saul ignorantly (and probably superstitiously) orders a fast on the troops in order to gain a military advantage; Jonathan, unaware of this, breaks the fast, and when informed of his father's oath counters it with plain common sense; Saul with kingly authority orders Jonathan executed; the people royally ignore the order, and Jonathan is saved.

In detail after detail we see Saul's kingship coming up empty. Ostensibly, Saul is king, but Jonathan is doing all the work.

In all of this, we see Saul acting as a very religious king: consulting the priest Ahijah (14:18), commanding the troops to keep a religious fast (14:24), providing for "kosher" butchering (14:34), building an altar to God (14:35), praying to God by using the Urim and Thummim in the venerable ephod (14:36–42). But we can only conclude that it was all for either manipulation or show. As God's Spirit recedes from Saul, he becomes more and more "religious." But all his religion is on the outside.

SAUL THE VALIANT (14:47–52)

14:47 When Saul had taken the kingship over Israel, he fought against all his enemies on every side—against Moab, against the Ammonites, against Edom, against the kings of Zobah, and against the Philistines; wherever he turned he routed them. [48] He did valiantly, and struck down the Amalekites, and rescued Israel out of the hands of those who plundered them. . . .

Following on the heels of high drama, this matter-of-fact summary gives the narrative breathing room. It also provides perspective: God's word and command are as effectively at work when God is not mentioned as when God is featured. But note these names: Many of them will play significant roles as the story develops.

Surprisingly, or maybe not, Saul's military prowess continues unimpaired. Outwardly, King Saul is valiantly successful against enemies on every side. The listing of his victories, along with the listing of his family and associates, gives an appearance that everything is just fine. But by now we know that the reality is quite different. The world is full of appearances like this.

10. Saul Fights the Amalekites
1 Samuel 15

Saul was never an out-and-out rebel against God. He always did most of what God commanded. Only on a few, seemingly minor occasions, did he substitute his own will for God's. And even then he had plausible, even pious, reasons for them. Most disobedience is like that—not absolute defiance, but a nibbling away at the edges of God's authority.

"HOLY WAR" (15:1–9)

15:1 **Samuel said to Saul, . . .** [2] **"Thus says the LORD of hosts, 'I will punish the Amalekites for what they did in opposing the Israelites when they came up out of Egypt.** [3] **Now go and attack Amalek, and utterly destroy all that they have; do not spare them, but kill both man and woman, child and infant, ox and sheep, camel and donkey.'"**
. . . [7] **Saul defeated the Amalekites. . . .** [8] **He took King Agag of the Amalekites alive, but utterly destroyed all the people. . . .** [9] **Saul and the people spared Agag . . . and all that was valuable . . . ; all that was despised and worthless they utterly destroyed.**

The Amalekites were a bedouin tribe from the steppes of the deep south. They had been Israel's chief enemy during the wilderness wanderings under Moses. It was decreed then that "the LORD will have war with Amalek from generation to generation" (Exod. 17:16). They were the enemy who first and most obviously sought to deny Israel entry into the promised land. In Deuteronomy they are denounced for having picked off the stragglers from the Israelite column of march (Deut. 25:17–19). They had come to be regarded as *the* opponents of God's guidance and providence. So in the memory of Israel they were far more than one more military enemy; they were the archetypal opponents of the LORD's ways.

Samuel maintains his prophetic presence in the midst of Saul's doomed rule. He continues to speak God's word of command on the basis of the previous anointing. And Saul continues to avoid simple and devout obedience.

The command to "utterly destroy" (15:3) is difficult for us to hear. It is not difficult to understand historically, for the "holy war" that involved the total destruction of an enemy was an accepted feature in the military landscape of the age—all the surrounding countries practiced it also; the command would not have jarred the ethical sensibilities of anyone in the story. But it jars ours (and we are, after all, also in this story). This is neither the first nor the last time that we are faced with ethical difficulties in our understanding of the biblical story. One way to account for this is that God does not stand aloof from our moral conditions, but *enters* them and works with us where we are, working out salvation among us with the cultural materials at hand. There are no ethical and cultural prerequisites to the work of salvation; God's sovereign purposes are worked out in the most depraved and brutal of conditions by God's descending into them, not criticizing them from above.

Haman, in Esther 3:1, is named as an Agagite, an indication that in Israel's memory Agag had become a representative figure of enmity against God and God's people. (Was Agag the archetypal anti-Semite?)

UNHOLY KING (15:10–35)

15:10 **The word of the LORD came to Samuel:** [11] **"I regret that I made Saul king, for he has turned back from following me, and has not carried out my commands."** . . . [12] **Samuel rose early in the morning to meet Saul.** . . . [13] **When Samuel came to Saul, Saul said to him,** . . . **"I have carried out the command of the LORD."** [14] **But Samuel said, "What then is this bleating of sheep in my ears, and the lowing of cattle that I hear?"** [15] **Saul said, " They have brought them from the Amalekites; for the people spared the best of the sheep and the cattle, to sacrifice to the LORD your God; but the rest we have utterly destroyed."** [16] **Then Samuel said to Saul,** . . .

[18] **" . . . [T]he LORD sent you on a mission, and said, 'Go, utterly destroy the sinners, the Amalekites'** . . . [19] **Why then did you not obey the voice of the LORD?** . . . **"** [20] **Saul said to Samuel, "I have obeyed the voice of the LORD.** . . .
[21] **But from the spoil the people took sheep and cattle** . . . **to sacrifice to the LORD your God in Gilgal."** [22] **And Samuel said,**
    "Has the LORD as great delight in burnt offerings and sacrifices,
        as in obeying the voice of the LORD?

Surely, to obey is better than sacrifice,
    and to heed than the fat of rams.
23 . . .
    Because you have rejected the word of the LORD,
        he has also rejected you from being king."
    . . . 30 Then Saul said, "I have sinned; yet honor me now before the elders
of my people and before Israel, and return with me, so that I may worship
the LORD your God." 31 So Samuel turned back after Saul; and Saul worshiped the LORD.
    32 Then Samuel said, " Bring Agag king of the Amalekites here to me." And
Agag came to him haltingly. . . . 33 . . . And Samuel hewed Agag in pieces
before the LORD in Gilgal.
    . . . 35 . . . Samuel grieved over Saul. And the LORD was sorry that he had
made Saul king over Israel.

If the first part of this chapter (vv. 1–9) confronts us with ethical difficulties, this second part throws up theological roadblocks: How do we account
for the fact that the God who does "not recant or change his mind" (v. 29)
now changes it? God clearly anointed Saul as king (10:1); now, just as
clearly, God regrets that choice and rejects Saul as king (15:11, 23, 26, 35).

But rather than trying to sort out a theological puzzle, we do better to
submit ourselves to the story as it is: What kind of story is being told here,
and what is the storyteller intending to convey? When we ask the question
that way, we realize that what we have before us is a story of Saul's hard-
hearted and somewhat calculated refusal of God (he won't *listen*), set
alongside God's heartbroken disappointment in Saul. Saul is presented as
a man to whom God speaks in promise and command (15:1), but who then
modifies God's words to suit his own convenience; God is presented as the
one rejected and avoided (15:23, 26). Samuel, who speaks for God in all
this, is terribly upset, spends an entire night in prayer over Saul (15:11),
and later grieves over him (15:35); God is "sorry" (15:35). The picture we
get is one of Saul coldly and deviously trimming his obedience to terms
that serve his own interests (he never rejects God as such; he continues to
be *very* religious), and of God (and Samuel) experiencing the effects of his
sin in regret and grief and sorrow. While Saul calculates, God *cares*. This
is not an abstract "theology" of God, but a story of God's sensitivity to human sin. As Saul becomes less human, God becomes more human, anticipating the incarnation: " For we do not have a high priest who is unable to
sympathize with our weaknesses, but we have one who in every respect has
been tested [or tempted] as we are" (Heb. 4:15).

It is common (and tempting) to treat Saul as a tragic figure and fill in psychological and political details that give him romantic stature. But the biblical narrator does not do that: Saul is treated with considerable respect, and even dignity, but also as a man who makes deliberate choices calculated to put himself at the center and God on the sidelines. Saul turned the famous aphorism of John the Baptizer (John 3:30) on its head: "*I* must increase; *He* must decrease."

The reign of Israel's first king is virtually finished, although it will be years before the journalists find out. Politically, Saul gets high marks, but it is not the politics of the kingdom of God.

Part 4. The Story of Saul and David's Rivalry

1 Samuel 16–31

Introduction

Saul's successor has been alluded to twice, although not by name: first, as a "man after his [God's] own heart" (13:14); and second, as the "neighbor" (15:28). Now we are told his name, David.

But the succession is not immediate. It is a dozen or so years (the storyteller does not provide an exact chronology) before Saul leaves the stage and David takes over. Meanwhile the two lives become fascinatingly and inextricably intertwined and treated with parallel dignities. G. K. Chesterton once pilloried "two despicable modern doctrines, one that geniuses should be worshiped like idols and the other that criminals should be merely wiped out like germs. That both clever men and bad men ought to be treated like men does not seem to occur to them" (Chesterton, *George Bernard Shaw*, 164). Our narrative treats both Saul and David first of all like men.

But there is far more than these two lives involved; there is *God's* life— God's promises and judgments, God's word and will, God's sovereignty worked out in the lives of these two men chosen to represent and give witness to that sovereignty on a few hundred square miles of Palestinian soil in the culture of the Iron Age. This is a history permeated with theology. The interest of the narrator is not merely in telling us what happened, but in helping us to realize and recognize *God* in the happenings.

Such recognitions are not easily achieved, for God works, for the most part, behind the scenes. It takes a skillful storyteller (and this one is most skillful) to train us in an awareness of God's quiet but decisive presence when human beings are making all the noise.

In the process of attending to this story, we realize that good and bad are not as easily distinguishable as we wish they were. Saul the "bad" king is not all bad, and David the "good" king is not all good. There is tension and ambiguity, testing and temptation, all through the narrative. The story of salvation is never a cut-and-dried, black-and-white scheme; it takes place in the colorful mess and pageantry of history. Black and white are not, after all, the only two colors in the world. The divine sovereignty of God is not arbitrarily *imposed* on the parallel sovereigns Saul and David, but painstakingly worked out from within their very human lives.

And, in the process of reading this story, we realize that however surely God's purposes are enacted, they are not accomplished quickly. God's rejection of Saul was decisive; God's choice of David to replace him was decisive; but it took years to effect the transition from the one to the other, during which time it was not at all clear to those within the story how things would turn out. God does not run roughshod over any of us just to get things done in a hurry. The Saul/David story supplies a much needed living context, not merely an abstract admonition, for appreciating the urgency of the repeated calls throughout scripture for patience and endurance.

Scholars have discerned that at this point in the story, and continuing to 2 Samuel 5, there is also a strong political theme: David's rise to power is narrated in such a way that it justifies his succession to Saul, not as usurpation, but as God-willed. Politics is woven into the story: God's ways with us can never be only a matter of our personal or private dealings with God, but include the entire spectrum of social, cultural, and governmental aspects of life. In reading this story, we are getting a feel for "kingdom," the kingdom of God that Jesus preached and taught.

11. David Anointed King
1 Samuel 16:1–13

SAMUEL GOES TO BETHLEHEM (16:1–5)

16:1 **The LORD said to Samuel, "How long will you grieve over Saul? I have rejected him from being king over Israel. Fill your horn with oil and set out; I will send you to Jesse the Bethlehemite, for I have provided for myself a king among his sons." 2 Samuel said, "How can I go? If Saul hears of it, he will kill me." And the LORD said, "Take a heifer with you, and say, 'I have come to sacrifice to the LORD.' 3 Invite Jesse to the sacrifice, and I will show you what you shall do; and you shall anoint for me the one whom I name to you." 4 Samuel did what the LORD commanded. . . .**

The same Samuel who anointed the first king is now to anoint the second. Samuel's prophetic authority continues intact, defining "king" as a God-appointed position. Politics is never "just politics" in Israel.

The first move in this God-initiated replacement of Saul is framed by the human emotion of fear: Samuel is afraid of Saul, and Bethlehem is afraid of Samuel (16:4). This is dangerous business! That Samuel is in danger from Saul is obvious; from Saul's perspective, he is acting traitorously. But what danger would Samuel pose to Bethlehem? Probably the simple assumption that a visit by God's prophet could very well mean that serious wrong was about to be addressed—they were in for it! People in general carry enough residual guilt around with them that the very mention of the word "God" provokes uneasiness, if not downright terror. Until we know, we have as much, maybe more, to fear from the good (Samuel) as from the bad (Saul). The double dangers (Saul to Samuel and Samuel to Bethlehem) inject a keen emotional energy into the scene.

Samuel Anoints David King (16:6–13)

16:6 **When they came, he looked on Eliab and thought, "Surely the LORD's anointed is now before the LORD." 7 But the LORD said to Samuel, "Do not look on his appearance or on the height of his stature, because I have rejected him; for the LORD does not see as mortals see; they look on the outward appearance, but the LORD looks on the heart." . . . 10 Jesse made seven of his sons pass before Samuel, and Samuel said to Jesse, "The LORD has not chosen any of these." 11 Samuel said to Jesse, "Are all your sons here?" And he said, "There remains yet the youngest, but he is keeping the sheep." And Samuel said to Jesse, "Send and bring him. . . . " 12 . . . Now he was ruddy, and had beautiful eyes, and was handsome. The LORD said, "Rise and anoint him; for this is the one." 13 Then Samuel . . . anointed him in the presence of his brothers; and the spirit of the LORD came mightily upon David from that day forward. . . .**

The choosing of David is contrasted with that of Saul. Saul was outstandingly impressive (9:1–2); David was a virtual nonentity in the Jesse family, left behind to tend the sheep while his seven brothers were off being presented to Samuel at the festivities being held in Bethlehem. The contrast is further emphasized in the rejection of Eliab who, like Saul, had all the appearance of being first-class leadership material. Narrative tension builds as the seven sons are one by one presented to Samuel, only to be turned down. "Are all your sons here?" It apparently never occurred to father Jesse that David, the "little brother," was good for anything other than menial farmwork.

The choice of David, the most unlikely of the brothers (the family runt?), has entered the Christian imagination as a characteristic mark of God's electing grace. Paul's way of putting it was, "God chose what is low and despised in the world, things that are not, to reduce to nothing things that are, so that no one might boast in the presence of God" (1 Cor. 1:28–29).

The "spirit of the LORD" that came on David on the occasion of his anointing (v. 13) was God working in David's life—God at work in David's muscles and mind. Saul was likewise visited and energized after his anointing (10:6, 10; 11:6). "Spirit" in Hebrew (and Greek) has the basic meaning of "breath" or "wind"—the invisible that moves the visible. But the metaphorical use of the word throughout scripture for God's life present and at work in men and women keeps us continuously alert to the working of the God whom we cannot see in the people and events that we do see.

12. David Joins Saul's Court
1 Samuel 16:14–18:5

DAVID SERVES SAUL AS COURT MUSICIAN (16:14–23)

16:14 Now the spirit of the LORD departed from Saul, and an evil spirit from the LORD tormented him. [15] And Saul's servants said to him . . . [16] " . . . command the servants who attend you to look for someone who is skillful in playing the lyre; and when the evil spirit from God is upon you, he will play it, and you will feel better." . . . [18] One of the young men [said], "I have seen a son of Jesse the Bethlehemite who is skillful in playing, . . . and the LORD is with him." . . . [21] And David came to Saul, and entered his service. Saul loved him greatly, and he became his armor-bearer. . . . [23] And whenever the evil spirit from God came upon Saul, David took the lyre and played it with his hand, and Saul would be relieved and feel better, and the evil spirit would depart from him.

The phrase "an evil spirit from the LORD" grates on our ears, but it cannot be avoided—it opens and closes this part of the story (vv. 14, 23). It contrasts with Saul's earlier visitations by God's spirit (10:6, 10; 11:6), and David's anointing by God's spirit, "mightily" (v. 13), in the preceding verses. We cannot reduce this story to politics or psychology—*God* provides the central presence and energy. Our biblical writers have a comprehensive understanding of God—everything comes through God's hand, blessings and curses, good and evil. The "evil" in this instance is not arbitrary, but clearly an aspect of judgment, the result of Saul's bullheaded disobedience. It is not the only word, however, for David is graciously provided by God for Saul's comfort and healing.

David, who has just been chosen to succeed Saul as king, begins by serving him. David gets his first training in ruling by serving. His service involves healing the distress brought on by divine judgment (playing the lyre), and acting as a personal aide to the king (armor-bearer). He does it so well, so personally, that Saul loves him. Human emotions play a prominent part in this story.

Ironically, the person who will eventually supplant Saul as king begins by helping him survive what kingship he has left to him. Saul *invites* (unknowingly, of course) his replacement into his most intimate service.

DAVID SERVES SAUL AGAINST THE PHILISTINES (17:1–58)

The story of David and Goliath is, deservedly, one of the best known and most often told stories of the Bible. Too often, however, it is identified merely as a children's story. That is understandable, for the drama of the youth against the giant catalyzes a whole array of childhood emotions. But it is an unfortunate identification, for it effectively removes it from the consideration of adults, the very adults for whose sake it was first told.

> 17:1 **Now the Philistines gathered their armies for battle . . . and encamped . . . in Ephes-dammim. ² Saul and the Israelites gathered and encamped in the valley of Elah. . . . ³ The Philistines stood on the mountain on the one side, and Israel stood on the mountain on the other side, with a valley between them. ⁴ And there came out from the camp of the Philistines a champion named Goliath, of Gath, whose height was six cubits and a span. . . . ⁸ He stood and shouted to the ranks of Israel, "Why have you come out to draw up for battle? Am I not a Philistine, and are you not servants of Saul? Choose a man for yourselves, and let him come down to me. ⁹ If he is able to fight with me and kill me, then we will be your servants; but if I prevail against him and kill him, then you shall be our servants and serve us." . . . ¹¹ When Saul and all Israel heard these words of the Philistine, they were dismayed and greatly afraid.**
> **. . . ¹³ The three eldest sons of Jesse had followed Saul to the battle. . . . ¹⁴ David was the youngest, . . . ¹⁵ . . . David went back and forth from Saul to feed his father's sheep at Bethlehem. ¹⁶ For forty days the Philistine came forward and took his stand, morning and evening.**
> **¹⁷ Jesse said to his son David, "Take . . . this parched grain and these ten loaves . . . to your brothers; ¹⁸ also take these ten cheeses to the commander of their thousand. . . . "**

Goliath enters the story immense and defiant and arrogant. His stature (over nine feet tall) and outsized weaponry set him apart as larger than life.

David enters the story as a menial shepherd and unimportant errand boy. His three eldest brothers are in on important actions of the day, while David works two servant jobs, running back and forth between Saul's court and his father's sheep. The comparison between David and his brothers here is similar to what we read in David's first appearance, in Bethlehem before Samuel (16:6–11). There are also echoes from the story of Joseph and his brothers in what David now encounters (see Genesis 37).

> . . . 17:20 **David rose early in the morning, left the sheep with a keeper, took the provisions, and went as Jesse had commanded him. . . .** [21] **Israel and the Philistines drew up for battle, army against army.** [22] **David . . . ran to the ranks, and went and greeted his brothers.** [23] **. . . the champion, the Philistine of Gath, Goliath by name, came up out of the ranks of the Philistines, and spoke the same words as before. And David heard him.**
> [24] **All the Israelites, when they saw the man, fled from him and were very much afraid. . . .** [26] **David said to the men who stood by him, " . . . who is this uncircumcised Philistine that he should defy the armies of the living God?" . . .**
> [28] **His eldest brother Eliab heard him talking to the men; and Eliab's anger was kindled against David. He said, "Why have you come down? . . . you have come down just to see the battle."** [29] **David said, "What have I done now? It was only a question." . . .**

David arrives at the camp as a naive outsider, able to see and hear with fresh eyes and ears what is going on. The battle-weary, fear-paralyzed troops are stuck; they can see no way out of the impasse posed by Goliath. After forty days of insult from the strutting giant, they are beaten down. As David takes in the situation, he is clearly intrigued by the possibilities of reward; he also expresses shock that God's people are intimidated by an "uncircumcised Philistine." Eliab's rebuke of his little brother accurately expresses "Philistine realism." But a totally other reality is being formed in our imaginations as the story develops.

The oldest brother, Eliab, and the youngest brother, David are at odds at this point; they see the same "facts" in the Valley of Elah, but they interpret them differently. The "Eliab mind" is impressed with size and power; the "David mind" is attentive to God and the right. When David showed up at the camp that day, Goliath dominated the scene. The huge giant twirling his twenty-five-pound spear with the careless ease of a cheerleader twirling her baton was completely intimidating. His taunts across the valley, teasing and provoking the Israelites, each day made each man a little more of a coward. Goliath—his size, his brutality, his cruelty— centered the world. Goliath was the polestar around which everyone else took bearings.

The same debased imagination that treated Goliath as important treated David as insignificant. Eliab, who was in awe of Goliath, was contemptuous of David; he treated David with withering scorn. His imagination was so ruined by Goliath watching that he was incapable of seeing and accepting a simple act of friendship from his little brother, let alone the possible presence of God.

But David entered the Valley of Elah with a God-dominated imagination. He was incredulous that everyone was cowering before the infidel giant. Weren't these men enlisted in the army of the living God? God was the reality with which David had to deal; giants didn't figure largely in David's understanding of the way the world worked.

> ... 17:32 **David said to Saul, "Let no one's heart fail because of him; your servant will go and fight with this Philistine." 33 Saul said to David, "You are not able ... you are just a boy. . . . " 34 But David said to Saul, "Your servant used to keep sheep for his father; and whenever a lion or a bear came, and took a lamb from the flock, 35 I went after it and struck it down. . . . 36 Your servant has killed both lions and bears; and this uncircumcised Philistine shall be like one of them, since he has defied the armies of the living God." 37 . . . So Saul said to David, "Go, and may the LORD be with you!"**
>
> 38 **Saul clothed David with his armor; he put a bronze helmet on his head and clothed him with a coat of mail. 39 David strapped Saul's sword over the armor, and he tried in vain to walk, for he was not used to them. Then David said to Saul, "I cannot walk with these; for I am not used to them." So David removed them. 40 Then he took his staff in his hand, and chose five smooth stones from the wadi, and put them in his shepherd's bag, in the pouch; his sling was in his hand, and he drew near to the Philistine.**

David comes to Saul's attention as a possible contender against Goliath, and presents his credentials. Saul is persuaded to let David face Goliath, but because he doesn't see the actual qualities that fit David for the task, he proceeds to equip him in conventional terms, piling armor on him. It doesn't seem to occur to him that if this royal armor didn't qualify him, Saul, for fighting Goliath, it could hardly benefit David. Saul's imagination is restricted by the conventions of the day, and stunted with fear. David, innocent of the conventions, is large with hope. An innocent in all matters Philistine, he is not innocent in the ways of God. He knows that he cannot fight Saul's battle in Saul's way.

The phrase "Saul's armor" has entered Christian discourse as a metaphor for tools or methods of doing God's work that are inauthentic or inappropriate to our identity as servants and disciples of Jesus. These "means" are often professionally validated and carry connotations of "expertise." But "means," the way we do something, must be authentic, true, appropriate to our prayers and proclamations. The Quaker Isaac Pennington used to exclaim, "There is that near you which will guide you; O! wait for it, and be sure ye keep to it."

> ... 17:42 When the Philistine looked and saw David, he disdained him. ...
> 43 ... "Am I a dog, that you come to me with sticks?" ... 45 But David said to the Philistine, "You come to me with sword ... but I come to you in the name of the LORD of hosts, the God of the armies of Israel, whom you have defied. ... 47 ... for the battle is the LORD's and he will give you into our hand."
> 48 ... David ran quickly. ... 49 David put his hand in his bag, took out a stone, slung it, and struck the Philistine on his forehead ..., and he fell face down on the ground.
> 50 So David prevailed over the Philistine with a sling and a stone. ...
> 51 Then David ran and stood over the Philistine; he grasped his sword, drew it out of its sheath, and killed him; then he cut off his head with it.
> When the Philistines saw that their champion was dead, they fled. ...

The confrontation, for which the storyteller has so carefully prepared us, now takes place: Goliath and David face each other in the Valley of Elah. The brutal giant is disdainful of David. He belches Philistine curses across the valley. Like mortars, they batter the ears of David and the Israelite army with the invective of the coarse pantheon of Canaanite gods. Then David, oblivious to what impresses everyone else, picks five stones from the brook, preaches a sermon of judgment to Goliath that proclaims God's sovereignty over meanness and might, and kills the giant.

This final scene is framed by the image of David running (vv. 48 and 51), running toward the living embodiment of evil, running to the stunned body collapsed on the ground, and turning it into a corpse. The paralyzing standoff is over: "I run the way of your commandments, for you enlarge my understanding" (Psalm 119:32).

The only person fully in touch with reality that day in the Valley of Elah was David. Reality is mostly made up of what we cannot see. This human life is mostly a matter of what never gets reported in the newspapers. Only a God-saturated, as opposed to a Goliath-saturated, mind can account for what made holy history that day in the Valley of Elah.

> 17:55 When Saul saw David go out against the Philistine, he said ..., "Abner, whose son is this young man? ... 56 ... Inquire whose son the stripling is." 57 On David's return from killing the Philistine, Abner took him and brought him before Saul. ... 58 Saul said to him, "Whose son are you,

young man?" And David answered, "I am the son of your servant Jesse the Bethlehemite."

Earlier we read the account of David in Saul's court, which conveys a considerable degree of acquaintance and even intimacy between the two (16:14–23). Now we read of Saul asking questions about David as if he had never heard of him. This is best accounted for by remembering that there were undoubtedly many David stories in circulation, and the storyteller of 1 and 2 Samuel kept as many as served his purpose. His task was not to provide a meticulous journal of day-by-day events, but to tell and retell the stories that best showed God working through the people and events of the day to accomplish the purposes of God's rule and salvation. Side-by-side stories that bring different perspectives on a truth are not unusual in the Bible. Alert readers will notice other details in the overall narrative that don't comfortably fit into what we can piece together of the history. The narrator was not writing a government report.

If we knew enough—all the facts as they occurred and all the details involved in arriving at the final text as we have it—we might see how all these seemingly disparate and sometimes out of place items fit together. But since we do not, it is better to take the story as given to us and let God reveal what God wills in it as is. It is, when all is said and done, a God story.

DAVID SERVES SAUL'S FAMILY (18:1–5)

The David and Goliath story is followed up by the contrasting David and Jonathan story. The first is a war story, the second a love story. War and love map most of the territory both of human experience in general and of David's experience in particular.

> 18:1 . . . [T]he soul of Jonathan was bound to the soul of David. . . . ³ Then Jonathan made a covenant with David, because he loved him as his own soul. ⁴ Jonathan stripped himself of the robe that he was wearing, and gave it to David, and his armor, and even his sword and his bow and his belt. . . .

This is the first notice of the justly celebrated friendship between Jonathan and David. Jonathan came to our notice earlier in his daring assault on the Philistines at the Pass of Michmash, after which he bravely faced his father's death sentence for an inadvertent transgression (chapter 14). Now he comes into the story as David's soul friend.

Friendship of this depth and quality (we will get details on that in chapter 20) is remarkable in itself; it is all the more remarkable here because the most natural way for Jonathan to treat David would be as a rival—both as a warrior and as a favorite son. David is at the point of replacing Jonathan both functionally, as leader against Philistines, and in his father's affection.

Friendship, much esteemed by our ancestors, has fallen on hard times among us moderns. We have acquaintances that we pick up from time to time to augment our pleasures or needs, but the kind of spiritual kinship energized by affection and sealed by covenant between David and Jonathan is rare. It is the least demanding and least needy of human relationships. But it is also the most necessary for realizing who we are, for becoming ourselves (and letting others become themselves) with no strings attached. C. S. Lewis prized this kind of friendship as the form of love by which God reveals to each the beauties of all the other forms of love (Lewis, *The Four Loves*, chapter 4). This David-Jonathan sort of friendship is a love that sets the other free to be himself or herself—a commitment with no demands. In a culture like ours in which there is widespread avoidance of commitments because they are confining, this story of a love commitment that is freeing is a breath of fresh air. Healthy relationships do not restrict our lives; they expand our lives.

13. Saul Turns against David
1 Samuel 18:6–20:42

David, the future king, is now firmly established in Saul's court as loyal and trusted on all fronts, personally and publicly a member of the family and a defender of the kingdom. The story makes it clear that there is not a hint of underhanded scheming in David. David's life is God's gift to Saul, who needs all the help he can get; and Saul embraces David as such. But not for long.

SAUL BECOMES JEALOUS (18:6–16)

18:6 . . . [W]hen David returned from killing the Philistine, the women came out . . . singing and dancing. . . . [7] And the women sang to one another as they made merry,

> "Saul has killed his thousands,
>   and David his ten thousands."

[8] Saul was very angry, for this saying displeased him. He said, " . . . what more can he have but the kingdom?" [9] So Saul eyed David from that day on.
[10] The next day an evil spirit from God rushed upon Saul . . . while David was playing the lyre. . . . Saul had his spear in his hand; [11] and Saul threw the spear, for he thought, "I will pin David to the wall." But David eluded him twice.
[12] Saul was afraid of David, because the LORD was with him but had departed from Saul. [13] So Saul removed him from his presence, and made him a commander. . . . [14] David had success in all his undertakings; for the LORD was with him. [15] . . . Saul . . . stood in awe of him. [16] But all Israel and Judah loved David. . . .

In contrast to Jonathan's covenantal friendship with David and the people's extravagant and celebratory love, King Saul became jealous. A succession of verbs develops the enmity that will dominate his soul until his death: he was "very angry" (v. 8); "raved" (v. 10); "threw the spear" (v. 11); "was afraid" (v. 12); "removed him" (v. 13); and, finally, "stood in awe of him" (v.15), sensing, for the first time, perhaps, that more than mere popularity was involved—that God's purposes were being worked out in this young man. When we read that "Saul eyed David" (v. 9), we know that it was a very evil eye indeed.

SAUL SCHEMES AGAINST DAVID (18:17–30)

18:20 Now Saul's daughter Michal loved David. Saul was told, and the thing pleased him. [21] Saul thought, "Let me give her to him that she may be a snare for him and that the hand of the Philistines may be against him." Therefore Saul said to David . . . , "You shall now be my son-in-law." . . . [25] Then Saul said [to his servants], "Thus shall you say to David, 'The king desires no marriage present except a hundred foreskins of the Philistines, that he may be avenged on the king's enemies.'" Now Saul planned to make David fall by the hand of the Philistines. . . . [27] David . . . killed one hundred of the Philistines; and David brought their foreskins . . . that he might become the king's son-in-law. Saul gave him his daughter Michal as a wife. [28] But when Saul realized that the LORD was with David, and that . . . Michal loved him, [29] Saul was still more afraid of David. So Saul was David's enemy from that time forward. . . .

Saul's generalized enmity now settles into hate, with a blueprint. Using his daughters as bait, he schemes to trick David into Philistine dangers in which he will most certainly be killed—a cold-blooded connivance of murder by marriage.

The first attempt, an offer of marriage to his older daughter, Merab, on condition that he prove himself in battle, is withdrawn at the last minute. When David shows up after the Philistine battles alive and ready for the wedding, Saul hastily marries Merab off to another (18:17–19). He never had any intention of conferring son-in-law status on David.

When he learns that his daughter Michal is in love with David, he tries again. This time he sets the bride-price at an outrageous hundred Philistine foreskins. Did he intend it as a coarse joke? "Go out and circumcise a hundred Philistines and bring me the evidence." David gives no sign that he thinks the demand either dangerous or demeaning. He simply does it, comes back alive carrying a gunnysack of Philistine foreskins, and marries Michal.

Despite Saul's calculated scheming, everything turns up in David's favor: Saul's son Jonathan loves him, his daughter Michal loves him, the people love him. And, to top if off, "the LORD was with him." Only the Philistines hate him. And Saul.

As part of the subtheme in the story, demonstrating that David's rise to power was not unlawful usurpation, it is noteworthy that in both marriage offers David disclaims any worthiness to be the king's son-in-law (18:18, 23). Becoming the king's son-in-law, and therefore a member of the royal family, is not *his* idea. David's steady rise to the kingship is not a matter of ambition. God is behind it, using Saul as his instrument.

SAUL ORDERS DAVID'S MURDER (19:1–17)

19:1 **Saul spoke with his son Jonathan and with all his servants about killing David. But Saul's son Jonathan took great delight in David. ² Jonathan told David, "My father Saul is trying to kill you; therefore be on guard tomorrow morning; stay in a secret place and hide yourself." . . . ⁶ Saul heeded the voice of Jonathan; Saul swore, "As the LORD lives, he shall not be put to death."** **⁷ . . . Jonathan then brought David to Saul, and he was in his presence as before.**

⁸ Again there was war, and David went out to fight the Philistines. . . . ⁹ Then an evil spirit from the LORD came upon Saul, as he sat in his house with his spear in his hand, while David was playing music. ¹⁰ Saul sought to pin David to the wall with the spear. . . . David fled and escaped that night.

¹¹ Saul sent messengers to David's house to keep watch over him, planning to kill him in the morning. David's wife Michal told him, "If you do not save your life tonight, tomorrow you will be killed." ¹² So Michal let David down through the window; he fled away and escaped. . . .

When Saul's scheme of murder-by-marriage doesn't work, he abandons the more subtle strategies and announces plans for killing David openly. The first time he is talked out of it by Jonathan, who talks reason to him; Saul is still capable of listening to reason, and rescinds the assassination order.

The second time he stakes out David's house with his henchmen by night, with plans to murder David first thing in the morning. Michal helps David escape that night through a window, and puts a dummy with a goat's-hair wig in his bed. When the assassins come to get David, Michal tells them that her husband is sick and cannot see them. The killers must have been operating under some ancient code of honor by which they felt constrained not to murder a defenseless sick man; instead of barging in to make short work of him, they report back to King Saul that David is ill in bed and cannot come to get murdered. Saul orders David brought to him, bed and all, and he himself will kill him. But when the men arrive back, they find that all they have done is deliver a bed with a dummy in it.

Sandwiched between these two plans, the first set aside through his son's arguments, the second foiled by his daughter's trick, is another irrational outburst of murderous jealousy, in which Saul throws his javelin at David while David plays music for him—the second such episode (the first is in 18:10–11).

David is doing everything right when Saul tries to kill him. He has brought healing to Saul's tortured spirit and has killed the Philistine giant—ending the impasse with Israel's enemy and quieting the turbulence in the troubled king. He is just what the nation needs; he is just what the king needs. He seems to have done both kinds of work modestly and unassumingly, without showing off. For doing these good works, he nearly gets himself killed.

SAUL HIMSELF GOES AFTER DAVID (19:18–24)

19:18 **Now David fled and escaped; he came to Samuel at Ramah.** . . . **20 Then Saul sent messengers to take David. When they saw the company of the prophets in a frenzy, with Samuel standing in charge of them, the spirit of God came upon the messengers of Saul, and they also fell into a prophetic frenzy. 21 When Saul was told, he sent other messengers, and they also fell into a frenzy. Saul sent messengers again the third time, and they also fell into a frenzy. 22 Then he himself went to Ramah . . . 23 . . . and the spirit of God came upon him. As he was going, he fell into a prophetic frenzy. . . . 24 . . . He lay naked all that day and all that night. Therefore it is said, "Is Saul also among the prophets?"**

What precisely the "prophetic frenzy" was eludes our understanding, but the thrust of the story is clear enough. The same spirit from God that overwhelmed Saul at the outset of his kingship (10:9–13) also marks the end of it. David, after Saul's sixth attempt on his life, runs for protection to the prophet Samuel at Ramah, where Samuel presides over a school of prophets. Saul sends messengers to bring him back, but when the messengers enter the spiritual assembly they are caught up in the prophetic ecstasies, overwhelmed by God's spirit. A second and then a third group of messengers fare identically. Disgusted, Saul takes matters into his own hands and goes to Ramah. He arrives with murder on his mind, but he and his evil intent are no better able to withstand God's spirit than did the messengers. He is soon completely under the influence of God's spirit, stripped of his royal robes and prostrate before Samuel, giving witness to God's power and presence. "This once great man, still tall but no longer great . . . clearly not in control, shamed, now rendered powerless in a posture of submissiveness" (Brueggemann, *First and Second Samuel*, 145). He has fallen under the spell of goodness and is rendered temporarily incapable of evil. In the long run, evil does not stand a chance against goodness.

SAUL HARDENS IN HIS HATE OF DAVID (20:1–42)

Both David and Jonathan want what is best for King Saul. Day after day, though, the signs accumulate: Saul's intermittent rages and sporadic jealousies have settled into something determined and calculated. Still, they seem most reluctant to come to that conclusion, giving Saul every benefit of the doubt. Finally, though, there is no room for doubt: "Jonathan knew that it was the decision of his father to put David to death" (v. 33).

> 20:1 **David fled from Naioth in Ramah. He came before Jonathan and said, " . . . what is my sin against your father that he is trying to take my life?"** [2] **He said to him, "Far from it! You shall not die. My father does nothing either great or small without disclosing it to me." . . .** [3] **But David also swore, ". . . truly as the LORD lives and as you yourself live, there is but a step between me and death." . . .** [5] **David said to Jonathan, "Tomorrow is the new moon and I should not fail to sit with the king at the meal; but let me go, so that I may hide in the field until the third evening.** [6] **If your father misses me at all, then say, 'David earnestly asked leave of me to run to Bethlehem his city; for there is a yearly sacrifice there for all the family.'** [7] **If he says, 'Good!' it will be well with your servant; but if he is angry, then know that evil has been determined by him.** [8] **Therefore deal kindly with your servant, for you have brought your servant into a sacred covenant with you." . . .**
> [12] **Jonathan said to David, . . .** [13] **. . . "if my father intends to do you harm, the LORD do so to Jonathan, and more also, if I do not disclose it to you, and send you away, so that you may go in safety. . . .** [14] **If I am still alive, show me the faithful love of the LORD; but if I die,** [15] **never cut off your faithful love from my house. . . . "** [16] **Thus Jonathan made a covenant with the house of David. . . .** [17] **Jonathan made David swear again by his love for him; for he loved him as he loved his own life. . . .**

As the final break between Saul and David approaches, the pace of the narrative slows down. The accumulation of precise detail and the rendering of most of the action in the form of dialogue gives us room to take in all the implications of what is going on—political and personal. The stakes are enormous for both Jonathan and David.

> 20:24 **So David hid himself in the field. When the new moon came, the king sat at the feast to eat. 25 . . . but David's place was empty. . . .**

At the first of each month a prescribed three-day religious feast takes place, over which the king presides (Num. 28:11–15). As it turns out, it provides a perfect setting for testing out the king's attitudes toward David, and so Jonathan structures his investigation into the king's intentions around this.

> 20:30 **Then Saul's anger was kindled against Jonathan. He said to him, "You son of a perverse, rebellious woman! Do I not know that you have chosen the son of Jesse to your own shame . . . ? 31 . . . Now send and bring him to me, for he shall surely die." 32 Then Jonathan answered his father Saul, "Why should he be put to death? What has he done?" 33 But Saul threw his spear at him to strike him; so Jonathan knew that it was the decision of his father to put David to death. 34 Jonathan rose from the table in fierce anger . . . because his father had disgraced him.**

Jonathan had successfully talked his father out of an earlier decision to kill David (19:1–7), but not so this time. The reprieve was short-lived—after the influence of reason had subsided, Saul, in an evil outburst, threw his spear at David, trying to kill him. Now, as Jonathan attempts to talk reasonably to his father again, Saul throws the same spear at him.

> 20:35 **In the morning Jonathan went out into the field to the appointment with David. . . . 42 Then Jonathan said to David, "Go in peace, since both of us have sworn in the name of the LORD, saying, 'The LORD shall be between me and you, and between my descendants and your descendants, forever.'"**

This is our final David and Jonathan story. The two friends will meet one more time, briefly and furtively, at Horesh (23:15–18). It is significant that the story that settles, once and for all, Saul's determination to kill David is at the same time the most elaborately narrated and emotionally moving of the friendship stories. Jonathan's covenant friendship with David brackets Saul's repeated attempts, ranging from irrational to rational, to kill David. The front bracket of the story is set at 18:2–3; the end bracket is set in 20:42.

Jonathan lives out his covenantal friendship in hard circumstances. The friendship covenant serves God's purposes in David, but Jonathan gets little or no emotional reward; Jonathan never sees David again. Jonathan lives out the covenant in circumstances and conditions that are relentlessly anti-David. For the rest of his life he serves in Saul's court, fighting with his father in the Philistine wars and accompanying his father, presumably, on the David hunts. But the circumstances do not cancel out the covenant; rather, the covenant is used in the purposes of God to overcome the circumstances. Many a covenantal friendship is lived out similarly in "Saul's court," in marital, family, work, and cultural conditions that are hostile to a vowed intimacy. But it is the covenant, not the conditions, that carries the day.

14. David's Wilderness Years
1 Samuel 21–30

The break with Saul is final; David's exile years begin. David does not start out in the wilderness, and he does not end up in the wilderness. But he does spend highly significant years in the wilderness. Everybody—at least everybody who has anything to do with God—spends time in the wilderness, so it is important to know what can take place there.

David does not choose to enter the wilderness; he is chased there. He did not go to the wilderness to take photographs of the wild goats and draw pictures of the exquisite wilderness wildflowers, but to escape from murderous King Saul. He lives a dangerous and precarious existence in the wilderness. During these wilderness years his anointing to the kingship is contradicted detail after detail by daily events. David has had much help and support up until now—Samuel and Michal and Jonathan are the conspicuous names—but now he is on his own. Still, the *plot* continues to center in David. Saul is increasingly isolated from the providence of God, while David is emphatically at its center.

For those of us who live comfortably in civilization, there is something enormously attractive about wilderness, so attractive that we set aside tracts of land preserving them as wilderness so that we know we can enter wilderness when we feel the "call of the wild." When we are in the wilderness, we are not in control, we have no assignment, no appointments to keep. Stay alert, stay alive—that's it. When we are in the wilderness, we commonly feel our lives simplifying and deepening. Many people, after a few days in the wilderness (sometimes after only a few hours) feel more themselves, uncluttered and spontaneous. Very often, even though otherwise unaccustomed to it, they say the name *God*. There is something wonderfully attractive about wilderness.

But there is also something frightening about wilderness. The wild, while it may be breathtakingly beautiful, is also dangerously unpredictable. A storm can turn an angel-caressed sky into a devil's cauldron. An animal can change in an instant from an elegant icon into a fierce killer. The wilderness has a hundred different ways to kill us.

This is the wilderness that David enters: both beautiful and dangerous. He will see, hear, and experience things in the wilderness that can be seen, heard, and experienced nowhere else. When we find ourselves in the wilderness, we do well to be frightened (like David); we also do well to be alert and open-eyed (like David). In the wilderness, we are plunged into an awareness of danger and death; at the very same moment we are plunged, if we let ourselves be, into an awareness of the great mystery of God and the extraordinary preciousness of life. David's wilderness years combine these elements of preciousness and precariousness.

There are fifteen wilderness stories ahead.

DAVID AT NOB (21:1–9)

21:1 **David came to Nob to the priest Ahimelech. Ahimelech came trembling to meet David, and said to him, "Why are you alone, and no one with you?"** [2] **David said to the priest Ahimelech, "The king has charged me with a matter, and said to me, 'No one must know anything of the matter about which I send you. . . .** [3] **Now then, what have you at hand? Give me five loaves of bread, or whatever is here."** [4] **The priest answered David, "I have no ordinary bread at hand, only holy bread—provided that the young men have kept themselves from women."** [5] **David answered the priest, "Indeed women have been kept from us as always when I go on an expedition. . . . "** [6] **So the priest gave him the holy bread. . . .**

[7] **Now a certain man of the servants of Saul was there that day. . . ; his name was Doeg the Edomite, the chief of Saul's shepherds.**

[8] **David said to Ahimelech, "Is there no spear or sword here with you? I did not bring my sword or my weapons with me. . . . "** [9] **The priest said, "The sword of Goliath the Philistine, whom you killed in the valley of Elah, is here . . . ; if you will take that, take it. . . . " David said, "There is none like it; give it to me."**

David's first stop is at Nob, where there was a sanctuary and a large community of priests led by Ahimelech. The location of Nob is uncertain, but certainly within the vicinity of Gibeah—some think only a mile or so away. References in Isaiah 10:32 and Nehemiah 11:32 put it in the neighborhood of Anathoth, and therefore somewhere between Gibeah and Jerusalem.

In his hurried escape from Saul, David is without either food or weapons; he gets both at Nob. The priest Ahimelech is cautious about giving up the holy bread for David to use as field rations, but when he is assured that David is ritually clean and that human need necessitates it, he goes ahead. (David plays fast and loose with the facts at this point, presenting himself as still working *for* Saul instead of running *from* him.) The incident is referred to with approval by Jesus in Matthew 12:3–4. The regulations regarding the holy bread are set down in Leviticus 24:5–9.

The conversation presumes a previous acquaintance. David, as leader of military expeditions, would have been a frequent visitor at the priestly sanctuary in order to consecrate his troops before going into battle.

David's need for a weapon is satisfied by Ahimelech's offer of Goliath's sword. It has been in the sanctuary at Nob ever since David's youthful triumph over the giant, years earlier in the Valley of Elah. The recollection of that event juxtaposes David's earlier favor with his present plight: David, unknown and untested, came before Goliath with nothing but his staff, sling, a stone, and prayers and gained victory in God; now, years later, he is a veteran warrior with many campaigns to his credit, famous and well respected throughout Israel, but again weaponless. The sword of Goliath, then, is charged with symbolic meanings: a trophy of the unconquerable enemy conquered by faith; a token of the first great Davidic victory in the service of Saul, and now used in defense against Saul.

David is provisioned and armed at the holy sanctuary. The God who had anointed David for the kingship now provides for his needs in the long struggle to become king.

The brief notice given to Doeg (v. 7) is important because it provides a connection with a later development of the story in chapter 22. Edomites were a traditionally hostile people (ranging across the entire horizon of biblical history, from Esau to the Idumean King Herod), and so the description of Doeg as an Edomite introduces a note of villainy into the narration. His designation as "chief of Saul's shepherds" probably means that he held a high position as a mercenary bodyguard to Saul.

DAVID AT GATH (21:10–15)

21:10 **David rose and fled that day from Saul; he went to King Achish of Gath. [11] The servants of Achish said to him, "Is this not David the king of the land? Did they not sing to one another of him in dances,**
> **'Saul has killed his thousands,**
>> **and David his ten thousands'?"**
[12] **David took these words to heart and was very much afraid of King**

Achish of Gath. [13] So he changed his behavior before them; he pretended to be mad. . . . He scratched marks on the doors of the gate, and let his spittle run down his beard. [14] Achish said to his servants, "Look, you see the man is mad. . . . [15] . . . Shall this fellow come into my house?"

David's next wilderness stop is Gath, one of the five Philistine cities on the lowland plain. Had he hoped to slip into their city unnoticed? Did he not know how famous he was? At any rate, he is immediately spotted and reported to Achish, king of Gath. The servants' report on David describes him as "king of the land" (v. 11), which is surprising, for they would not have known of his private anointing. But his reputation throughout the countryside as Israel's leader has filtered down among the Philistines: As far as they are concerned, David, not Saul, is king. In the very act of fleeing from Saul, David throws himself into the hands of Israel's longtime enemies.

When David realizes that he has been recognized, he is afraid and knows he has to act quickly. Even if admired at a distance, there could not be a person more hated in the city of Gath than he is. He has been the chief nemesis of the Philistines for years. Goliath was from Gath (17:4), and that alone secured David the position of Public Enemy Number 1. To save himself from mob lynching, he throws himself into the pose of a madman, acting crazy. Insanity was regarded in ancient cultures with some measure of awe; so instead of killing him, Achish simply wants to get rid of him. He does not even want him in his prison. Once again David defeats the Philistines, but this time with his wits instead of weapons.

DAVID AT ADULLAM (22:1–2)

22:1 David left there and escaped to the cave of Adullam; when his brothers and all his father's house heard of it, they went down there to him. [2] Everyone who was in distress, and everyone who was in debt, and everyone who was discontented gathered to him; and he became captain over them. Those who were with him numbered about four hundred.

Geographers have located Adullam about eighteen miles southwest of Jerusalem in the hill country. The hills in this area are riddled with caves. Interestingly, this was not far from the Valley of Elah, the scene of the contest with Goliath. Near the foot of the hill at Adullam there is a fine well of spring water, so the place was ideally suited to David's circumstances. He knew the country well, the hills and valleys providing adequate cover for a guerrilla existence, a good water supply, the morale-boosting memory of the defeated Goliath—a made-to-order wilderness hideout.

The mention of his brothers is a bit of a surprise, for they seem not to have held him in great affection previously. But as family members they were probably in danger of reprisals from Saul, and the inhospitable desert was the safest place for them, and along with them all kinds of other people, most of them disreputable, who had gotten into trouble with the government or were discontented with Saul's leadership. The social and economic life under Saul apparently did not suit everyone; getting a king had not solved all the political problems of Israel.

David's four hundred were not Israel's "brightest and best," but more like the early Christians in Corinth to whom Paul wrote, "Not many of you were wise by human standards. . . . God chose what is low and despised in the world, things that are not, to reduce to nothing things that are, so that no one might boast in the presence of God" (1 Cor.1:26–29).

DAVID AT MIZPEH IN MOAB (22:3–5)

22:3 **David went from there to Mizpeh of Moab. He said to the king of Moab, "Please let my father and mother come to you, until I know what God will do for me." . . .⁵ Then the prophet Gad said to David, "Do not remain in the stronghold; leave, and go into the land of Judah." So David left, and went into the forest of Hereth.**

David's parents would have been quite old at this time. David as the youngest of eight sons and now a mature man decides that the Cave of Adullam is not safe for his parents, nor would they be up to the rigors of a fugitive existence. The trip across the Jordan to Moab to look for sanctuary for his parents had a certain logic to it, for David had old ancestral ties in Moab: his great-grandmother Ruth was a Moabitess (see Ruth 4:17). So Moab, which had provided sanctuary years before at the time of the Bethlehem famine, again provides refuge during a difficult time.

The prophet Gad is mentioned again in 2 Samuel 24 in an episode occurring near the close of David's life, his spiritual counsel spanning David's career as outlaw and king. David did not live entirely by his wits. David is quick to respond to the prophet's counsel and return to dangerous Judah. The location of the "forest of Hereth" is not known; what we know is that David is on the run.

THE MASSACRE AT NOB (22:6–23)

. . . 22:7 Saul said to his servants who stood around him, "Hear now, you Benjaminites; will the son of Jesse give every one of you fields and vineyards . . . ?
[8] Is that why all of you have conspired against me? No one discloses to me when
my son makes a league with the son of Jesse, none of you is sorry for me. . . ."
[9] Doeg the Edomite, who was in charge of Saul's servants, answered, "I saw the
son of Jesse coming to Nob, to Ahimelech son of Ahitub; [10] he inquired of the
LORD for him, gave him provisions, and gave him the sword of Goliath the
Philistine."

[11] The king sent for the priest Ahimelech son of Ahitub and for all his father's house, the priests who were at Nob; and all of them came to the king.
[12] Saul said, "Listen now, son of Ahitub. . . . [13] . . . Why have you conspired
against me, you and the son of Jesse . . . ?"

[14] Then Ahimelech answered the king, "Who among all your servants is
so faithful as David? . . . [15] . . . your servant has known nothing of all this,
much or little." [16] The king said, "You shall surely die, Ahimelech, you and
all your father's house." [17] The king said to the guard who stood around him,
"Turn and kill the priests of the LORD. . . . " But the servants of the king would
not raise their hand to attack the priests of the LORD. [18] Then the king said
to Doeg, "You, Doeg, turn and attack the priests." Doeg the Edomite turned
and attacked the priests; on that day he killed eighty-five who wore the linen
ephod. [19] . . . men and women, children and infants, oxen, donkeys, and
sheep, he put to the sword.

[20] But one of the sons of Ahimelech son of Ahitub, named Abiathar, escaped and fled after David. [21] Abiathar told David that Saul had killed the
priests of the LORD. [22] David said to Abiathar, "I knew on that day, when
Doeg the Edomite was there, that he would surely tell Saul." . . .

Saul is now racked with paranoia. When he learns of David's whereabouts,
he feels the precariousness of his position. David is in a position to raise a
standard against Saul and plunge the country into civil war, and Saul assumes that he will do just that. He bitterly accuses his servants, and especially his son Jonathan, for siding with David. In the midst of this tirade,
Doeg the Edomite realizes that he can use his information from Nob to
his own advantage and tells Saul what he saw that day. The picture we get
of Saul is not a pretty one: sitting on his throne surrounded by frightened
servants, unnerved by the rash of dissidents deserting to David, and listening to the talebearing of the informer Doeg.

On the basis of Doeg's information, Saul summons Ahimelech and his
company of priests and accuses them of assisting David with food, arms, and
spiritual counsel. Ahimelech's denial of the charge doesn't put even a dent

in Saul's full-blown paranoia. When Saul orders the massacre of the priests, the servants refuse to so much as lay a hand on them—a bold piece of courage on their part. But Doeg has no scruples against either sacrilege or violence, and does the job single-handed. Calvin refers to Doeg as the "consummate villain" (Calvin, *Commentary on the Book of Psalms*, vol. 2, 311).

The massacre at Nob, bloody and senseless, enters history as one of the major crimes. The king who began his decline by refusing to destroy the heathen Amalekite king Agag, disobeying the clear command of God (chapter 15), now utterly wipes out the priests and inhabitants at Nob on the evidence of a scoundrel. The comparison of the two events is a graph of Saul's decline.

But the massacre is not quite total—Abiathar, Ahimelech's son, escapes and reports the catastrophe to David. David remembers Doeg's skulking presence back at the sanctuary at Nob and takes the blame for the massacre on himself. Abiathar will continue in David's company.

David now has both a prophet (Gad) and a priest (Abiathar) with him in his wilderness exile, signs of the guidance and protection of God, while Saul, enthroned in Gibeah, is isolated in paranoia and jealousy.

DAVID AT KEILAH (23:1–14)

23:1 Now they told David, "The Philistines are fighting against Keilah, and are robbing the threshing floors." ² David inquired of the LORD, "Shall I go and attack these Philistines?" The LORD said to David, "Go and attack the Philistines and save Keilah." . . . ⁵ So David and his men . . . rescued the inhabitants of Keilah.

⁶ When Abiathar son of Ahimelech fled to David at Keilah, he came down with an ephod in his hand. . . . ⁸ Saul summoned all the people to war, to go down to Keilah, to besiege David and his men. ⁹ When David learned that Saul was plotting evil against him, he said to the priest Abiathar, "Bring the ephod here." ¹⁰ David said, "O LORD, the God of Israel . . . ¹¹ . . . will Saul come down . . . ? ¹¹ . . . I beseech you, tell your servant." The LORD said, "He will come down." . . . ¹³ Then David and his men, who were about six hundred, set out and left Keilah. . . .

The village of Keilah is about three miles south of Adullam. The Philistines have come up after the grain harvest is completed to plunder the harvested crop from the threshing floors. It is an easy way to farm: Let the people of Keilah do the hard work of sowing, cultivating, reaping, and threshing, and then, when all the work is done, arrive in time to plunder the crop.

The point of interest here is that even though David is no longer a part of Saul's army, he keeps on doing Saul's work, protecting and helping Israelites against Philistine banditry. His leadership skills and commitments come into focus here. For David's men, intervention in the affairs of Keilah seems ill-advised—they already have their hands full staying out of Saul's clutches; they do not need to cultivate yet another enemy. David listens to the counsel of his soldiers, but does not take it. He listens to God's counsel and gains the victory.

Saul, thinking that he has David cornered, comes after him at Keilah. The irony of the Keilah episode is that while David was willing to risk his life in saving Keilah from the Philistines, Keilah was not willing to protect David from Saul, and so David was forced back into the precarious, chancy wilderness once again. Good deeds are not always reciprocated.

DAVID AT HORESH (23:15–29)

> 23:15 David was in the Wilderness of Ziph at Horesh when he learned that Saul had come out to seek his life. ¹⁶ Saul's son Jonathan set out and came to David at Horesh; there he strengthened his hand through the LORD. ¹⁷ He said to him, "Do not be afraid; for the hand of my father Saul shall not find you. . . . " ¹⁸ Then the two of them made a covenant before the LORD. . . .

This is the last meeting between Jonathan and David, the final scene in their celebrated friendship. The brief visit, certainly dangerous for Jonathan to undertake, gives much-needed encouragement to David during the years when he is being hunted down relentlessly by Saul. But there is more than just friendship here—there is God: Two prepositional phrases, "*through* the LORD" and "*before* the LORD," reveal a friendship that is more concerned with God than with each other. These friends do not get in each other's way in their primary and essential dealings with God. That, and *covenant*, that rare commitment that keeps personal relationships from being sucked into and destroyed in the fetid swamps of subjectivism. Covenant keeps us available to one another for affection and help without using the other for personal convenience or social and political gain.

After this final declaration of friendship between David and Jonathan at Horesh, the hunt accelerates—David is chased from pillar to post, relentlessly, from one wilderness refuge to another, and, as the setting for the next story, to En-gedi.

DAVID AT EN-GEDI (24:1–22)

24:1 **When Saul returned from following the Philistines, he was told, "David is in the wilderness of En-gedi." ² Then Saul . . . went to look for David. . . . ³ He came to the sheepfolds beside the road, where there was a cave; and Saul went in to relieve himself. Now David and his men were sitting in the innermost parts of the cave. ⁴ The men of David said to him, "Here is the day of which the LORD said to you, 'I will give your enemy into your hand. . . . '" Then David went and stealthily cut off a corner of Saul's cloak. ⁵ Afterward David was stricken to the heart because he had cut off a corner of Saul's cloak. ⁶ He said to his men, "The LORD forbid that I should do this thing to my lord, the LORD's anointed. . . . " ⁷ . . . Then Saul got up and left the cave, and went on his way.**

⁸ Afterwards David . . . went out of the cave and called after Saul, "My lord the king!" . . . ⁹ David said to Saul, "Why do you listen to the words of those who say, 'David seeks to do you harm'? . . . ¹¹ See, my father, see the corner of your cloak in my hand; for by the fact that I cut off the corner of your cloak, and did not kill you, you may know for certain that there is no wrong or treason in my hands. . . .

¹⁶ . . . Saul said, . . . ¹⁷ . . . "You are more righteous than I; for you have repaid me good, whereas I have repaid you evil." . . .

En-gedi (literally, "spring of the kid") is an oasis on the western side of the Dead Sea, a country of steep ravines and deep caves. A reference in the Song of Solomon (1:14) shows that it was once a vineyard district. The wilderness of En-gedi includes caves where some of the celebrated Dead Sea Scrolls were discovered in the middle of the twentieth century. A few pottery shards from the Iron Age (the time of Saul and David) have been found in them. Some of the caves were large enough to accommodate David and a bodyguard of considerable size without their being seen.

David's position at this juncture is desperate, for even though the wild country is honeycombed with caves and crisscrossed with ravines, offering innumerable hiding places, caves and ravines are also potential traps. If David were ever trapped, there would be no contest, for Saul outnumbers David five to one.

As the narration builds, all the ingredients for a coarse farce are present: Saul moves from sun glare into the dark cave to respond to a call of nature. His eyes are not yet used to the darkness and so do not pick out the figures in the shadows. There he is, the king on his "throne" viewed from the backside, outlined against the deep blue of the Dead Sea and the red mountains of Moab in the distance. Saul has thrown his garments and weapons aside, and so is defenseless and vulnerable.

When David and his men see what is going on, they know that Saul, oblivious to their presence, ungirded, unarmed, is as good as dead. The obvious thing to do is to kill the king. But David forbids it; instead he slips through the shadows, cuts a piece off the king's garment that has been thrown aside, and returns to his men. In a short while, Saul leaves. David lets him walk a healthy distance away, then goes to the mouth of the cave and calls to him, "My lord the king!" Saul looks back, astonished. The two men exchange speeches with each other, David protesting his loyalty and Saul conceding David's moral superiority. The two speeches are artfully presented, and put on display God's work in both men.

The detail that holds the narrative dynamics together is David's statement, "I will not raise my hand against my lord; for he is the LORD's anointed" (v. 10). David's actions and words are shaped by his conviction that God is present and active in everything. Saul, in contrast, has little God awareness in who he is and what he does. Political and military considerations from which God has been eliminated dominate his life.

Saul's speech in response to David (vv.17–21) is a classic instance of a sentimentalized spirituality. Saul concedes that David is right and attests that he knows David is the rightful king who will eventually take over. He acknowledges all that the circumstance in the cave reveals as the truth of their respective kingships. There is nothing in the account that suggests that Saul does not feel and believe what he is saying while he is saying it. But there is no character to back it up, no covenant (as there is between his son and David) on which to build a life of repentance and prayer, relationship and obedience. Saul displays exquisite religious emotions, but his life does not change in the slightest degree.

SAMUEL'S FUNERAL (25:1)

The prophet Samuel has not been mentioned in the story since the time that David, escaping from Saul's death squad, went to him in Ramah for counsel and refuge (19:18). But while not contributing to the action, his presence must have still been large, for his funeral brought everyone together in mourning. Outwardly, prospects are not bright for David—his patron is dead and he is still stuck in the wilderness. But quietly and behind the scenes we readers of the story, page after page, are acquiring a strong sense of providential inevitability. David is on the rise.

DAVID AT CARMEL: NABAL AND ABIGAIL (25:2–42)

25:2 There was a man in Maon, whose property was in Carmel. The man was very rich. . . . He was shearing his sheep in Carmel. [3] Now the name of the man was Nabal, and the name of his wife Abigail. The woman was clever and beautiful, but the man was surly and mean. . . . [5] . . . David sent ten young men . . . "Go up to Carmel, and go to Nabal, and greet him in my name. [6] . . . 'Peace be to you. . . . [7] I hear that you have shearers; now your shepherds have been with us . . . and they missed nothing, all the time they were in Carmel. [8] . . . let my young men find favor in your sight; for we have come on a feast day. Please give whatever you have at hand to your servants and to your son David."

[9] When David's young men came, they said all this to Nabal. . . . [10] But Nabal answered . . . , "Who is David? . . . There are many servants today who are breaking away from their masters. [11] Shall I take my bread and my water and the meat . . . and give it to men who come from I do not know where?" [12] So David's young men . . . told him all this. [13] David said . . . , "Every man strap on his sword!" . . . and about four hundred men went up after David. . . .

[14] But one of the young men told Abigail, Nabal's wife, "David sent messengers out of the wilderness to salute our master; and he shouted insults at them. [15] Yet the men were very good to us . . . ; [16] they were a wall to us both by night and by day, all the while we were with them keeping the sheep. [17] Now therefore . . . consider what you should do; for evil has been decided against our master and against all his house; he is so ill-natured that no one can speak to him."

[18] Then Abigail hurried and took . . . loaves . . . wine . . . sheep . . . grain . . . raisins, and . . . figs. She loaded them on donkeys [19] and said to her young men, "Go on ahead of me; I am coming after you." But she did not tell her husband Nabal. . . .

[23] When Abigail saw David . . . [24] [s]he fell at his feet and said, . . . [25] "My lord, do not take seriously this ill-natured fellow, Nabal; for as his name is, so is he; Nabal is his name. . . .

. . . [28] "Please forgive the trespass of your servant. . . . [29] . . . the life of my lord shall be bound in the bundle of the living under the care of the LORD your God. . . . [31] . . . And when the LORD has dealt well with my lord, then remember your servant."

[32] David said to Abigail, "Blessed be the LORD, the God of Israel, who sent you to meet me today! [33] Blessed be your good sense, and blessed be you, who have kept me today from bloodguilt and from avenging myself by my own hand! . . . [35] Then David . . . said to her, "Go up to your house in peace; . . . I have granted your petition."

[36] Abigail came to Nabal; he was holding a feast in his house . . . he was very drunk; so she told him nothing at all until the morning light. [37] . . . when the

wine had gone out of Nabal, his wife told him these things, and his heart died within him. . . . [38] About ten days later the LORD struck Nabal, and he died.

[39] When David heard that Nabal was dead, he . . . sent and wooed Abigail, to make her his wife.

The dramatic center of this story is Abigail on her knees in the wilderness, on her knees before David. David is rampaging, murder in his eyes, and Abigail blocks his path, kneeling before him. David has been grossly insulted, and he is out to avenge the insult with four hundred men on the warpath. Abigail, solitary and beautiful, kneels in the path before David and stops him in his tracks (vv. 23–31). The David that we are used to seeing as full of God is, at this moment, full of himself. David has been described earlier as beautiful (16:12 and 17:42), but there is no sign of that beauty here. Now "beautiful" Abigail (v. 3) becomes the person who calls David back to himself, his real self, and helps David recover his true identity.

The background to this story is David's wilderness work. During the wilderness years he has formed his company of men into a disciplined band of "good Samaritans." In addition to the natural dangers of wilderness living, the wilderness was also a high-crime district. Bandits frequented the wilderness, preying on travelers, plundering the defenseless. One of Jesus' most famous stories is about a traveler in the Judean wilderness getting robbed, beaten, and then rescued by a Samaritan. This is the kind of work David and his men have been doing. We can imagine David's men as a kind of unofficial neighborhood watch and emergency ambulance service. Among those whom they have helped are the herdsmen of the rich stockman, Nabal. One of the herdsmen confirms David's help through the vulnerable days of sheepherding (v. 16). Nabal's name means "fool." Psalm 14 provides a good description of the man.

Fool is the Bible's most contemptuous term. The fool is the person who doesn't know what is going on in God's cosmos. Fools are not ignorant and searching, not lost and looking; Nabal knows it all, has it figured out, knows the ropes. The fool lacks all the material for maintaining the self. Fools cannot devise plans that are worth anything, and they finally collapse. The Hebrew verb from which "fool" is derived means "to collapse." Closely connected with this is the word for "corpse." When the hot air has left the gaudy balloon, all that is visible is a limp bladder.

When sheepshearing time arrives, in that culture traditionally a season of festivity and generosity, David asks to be included—a not unreasonable request in the circumstances. But when Nabal hears the request, he acts as if he has never so much as heard of David, lumps him with the riffraff of wilderness outlaws, and refuses him with insults.

David, who has just displayed the greatest restraint and tenderness with King Saul, now loses his temper and determines to kill Nabal. David, who has been able to see murderous Saul as God's anointed, can see nothing in Nabal's coarse curses but an ugly piece of garbage that is stinking up his life.

And then Abigail intervenes. In her intervention, she gives witness to David's vocation as God's leader, his position as witness to God's royalty. In her poetic plea, she faces David with his primary involvement with *life*, not death, and recalls the Goliath event in her allusion to his "sling" (v. 29). Abigail says, in effect, "Your task, David, is not to exact vengeance; vengeance is God's business, and you are not God. You are out here in the wilderness to find out what God is doing and who you are before God. The wilderness is not an experimental station in which you test yourself to find out how strong and resilient you are; it is where you discover the strength of God and God's faithful ways of working in and through your life. Nabal is a fool, but don't you also become a fool. One fool is enough in this story."

David is a good listener. He listened to Samuel, to God, to Abiathar, to Jonathan—and now to Abigail.

The story began with a love-and-death triangle made up of Nabal, David, and Abigail. It ends with a similar but totally different triangle composed of God, David, and Abigail. If Nabal had been permitted to push God out of the lead role in the plot and take it over himself, both David and Abigail would have been diminished. As it turns out, David and Abigail are both blessed extravagantly (note the triple blessing in vv. 32–33).

There is a long tradition in the Christian life, which is most developed in Eastern Orthodoxy, of honoring beauty as a witness to God and a call to prayer. Beauty is never only what our senses report to us, but always also a sign of what is just beyond our senses—an innerness and depth. There is more to beauty than we can account for empirically. In that *more* and *beyond* we discern God. Artists who wake up our jaded senses and help us attend to these matters are gospel evangelists. In the presence of the beautiful, we have access to the "beauty of the Lord."

It was Abigail's beauty that put David in touch again with the beauty of the Lord that was nearly obliterated in his proposed vengeance-obsessed, honor-defending, out-for-blood rampage against Nabal.

DAVID IN THE WILDERNESS OF ZIPH (26:1–25)

> 26:1 **Then the Ziphites came to Saul at Gibeah, saying, "David is in hiding on the hill of Hachilah, which is opposite Jeshimon."** [2] **So Saul rose and went down to the Wilderness of Ziph, with three thousand chosen men of Israel, to seek David in the Wilderness of Ziph. . . .**
>
> **. . .** [7] **So David and Abishai went to the army by night; there Saul lay sleeping within the encampment, with his spear stuck in the ground at his head. . . .** [8] **Abishai said to David, "God has given your enemy into your hand today; now therefore let me pin him to the ground with one stroke of the spear. . . ."** [9] **But David said to Abishai, "Do not destroy him; for who can raise his hand against the LORD's anointed, and be guiltless? . . .** [11] **. . . but now take the spear that is at his head, and the water jar, and let us go." . . .**
>
> [13] **Then David went . . . and stood on top of a hill far away. . . .** [14] **David called . . . to Abner . . . , "Abner! Will you not answer? . . .** [15] **. . . Why . . . have you not kept watch over your lord the king? . . .** [16] **. . . See now, where is the king's spear, or the water jar that was at his head?"**
>
> [17] **Saul recognized David's voice, and said, "Is this your voice, my son David?" David said, "It is my voice, my lord, O king."** [18] **And he added, "Why does my lord pursue his servant? . . .** [20] **. . . for the king of Israel has come out to seek a single flea. . . ."**
>
> [21] **Then Saul said, "I have done wrong; . . . I have been a fool, and have made a great mistake."** [22] **David replied, " . . .** [24] **As your life was precious today in my sight, so may my life be precious in the sight of the LORD, and may he rescue me from all tribulation."** [25] **Then Saul said to David, "Blessed be you, my son David!" . . .**

David is done with the "fool" Nabal (chap. 25), but not with fools, for he now comes face to face with Saul again in an episode in which Saul calls himself a fool (26:21).

This story of David and Saul in the wilderness of Ziph is very similar to the one of David and Saul in the wilderness at En-gedi (chap. 24). The content is essentially the same, but the details are different. The thematic repetition emphasizes a primary concern of the storyteller as these wilderness years wind to a conclusion: the true king, David, is recognized as such by the very king he will soon displace, namely Saul; and David continues to refuse to lift so much as a finger to get rid of Saul and put himself on the throne. If David is God's choice for king, God will do whatever needs to be done to make it happen; David will not make a grab for power; he will not take matters into his own hands. The reticence that David displays in these incidents of disciplined waiting is something of the quality that Jesus blessed in the "meek" who will "inherit the earth" (Matt. 5:5).

"Meekness" designates the controlled strength that turns its back on self-aggrandizing opportunism and stands patiently firm while waiting for God's "day," God's timing. In honoring Saul as God's anointed, David honors God, who works his will in history when and where and how he wills.

In addition to the pattern repeated from the recent event at En-gedi (chap. 24), there are some verbal echoes from much earlier in the story. In the early days of David's service in the royal court, Saul at two different times threw his spear at David. Each time the action was accompanied by the phrase "pin David to the wall" (18:11 and 19:10). He also tried to kill his son Jonathan with that same spear (20:33). After David fled, Saul is pictured seated at Gibeah "with his spear in his hand" (22:6). Was Saul ever without his spear? And now, years later, when David and Abishai come upon Saul asleep in the encampment at Ziph, Saul's spear is prominently there (26:7). Abishai offers to kill Saul with Saul's spear, using the same verb "pin him" (26:8). It would have been a fine stroke of poetic justice, the same spear and spear language that Saul had used against David boomeranging back on himself. But David does not permit it. He is not operating out of the old "eye for an eye, tooth for a tooth" book of ethics.

This is the last meeting between Saul and David. After Saul's many and persistent attempts to eliminate David from his life, it is a surprise, but also surprisingly fitting, that Saul's last words to David are a blessing (26:25).

Within the larger story of the wilderness years, there is a symmetry in the central chapters 24, 25, and 26. All three chapters show David favorably as Israel's true king, soon to supplant Saul. The first and third are made up of conversations between David and Saul, in which David refuses to kill Saul and take over the kingship, and in which Saul acknowledges David as his superior and God-blessed successor. The middle chapter (25) shows David refraining from killing the fool Nabal (even though mightily provoked), and shows the woman Abigail, an outsider to the story, giving independent witness to David's royal status and coming rule.

DAVID AT GATH (AGAIN) (27:1–28:2)

27:1 **David said in his heart, "I shall now perish one day by the hand of Saul; there is nothing better for me than to escape to the land of the Philistines. . . . " ² So David . . . went over, he and the six hundred men . . . , to King Achish son of Maoch of Gath. ³ David stayed with Achish at Gath, he** and his troops. . . . [4] When Saul was told that David had fled to Gath, he no longer sought for him.

[5] Then David said to Achish, "If I have found favor in your sight, let a place be given me in one of the country towns. . . . " [6] So that day Achish gave him Ziklag. . . .

[8] Now David and his men went up and made raids on . . . the landed settlements from Telam . . . to the land of Egypt. . . . [10] When Achish asked, "Against whom have you made a raid today?" David would say, "Against the Negeb of Judah," or "Against the Negeb of the Jerahmeelites," or, "Against the Negeb of the Kenites." [11] David left neither man nor woman alive to be brought back to Gath, thinking, "They might tell about us, and say, "David has done so and so.'" . . . [12] Achish trusted David. . . .

28:1 In those days the Philistines gathered their forces for war, to fight against Israel. Achish said to David, " . . . you and your men are to go out with me in the army. [2] . . . I will make you my bodyguard for life."

Gath again. And Achish. Achish figured prominently at the outset of David's wilderness exile (21:10–15); now Achish reappears at the end of the period. But in a reversed role. When David entered the wilderness, Achish was David's enemy; now Achish is his patron. David escaped from Achish in the first place by acting like a madman; David now enters the service of Achish and enjoys his patronage.

 The irony of the role of Achish does not escape us: A king from Israel's archenemy provides the context for preserving Israel's fugitive and coming king. Achish of *Gath* no less, Goliath's town. Pagan and hostile Philistia is host to God's anointed; Philistia has become an instrument for accomplishing God's sovereign purpose. An aphorism out of medieval times is apt here: "God rides the lame horse and writes straight with a crooked stick."

This part of the story is filled with tension. David despairs of ever getting free from Saul's pursuit, and so defects to the enemy, the Philistine Achish. The strategy works, for Saul gives up on David, and Achish welcomes him as a valuable ally in the perpetual Philistine work of ravage and plunder. David requests and is given a town of his own, away from the immediate surveillance of Achish. Things are settling down very nicely: David and his men no longer have to live on the desert economy, but are in a position to set up housekeeping with their wives and families in the town of Ziklag.

But the defection to the Philistines is only apparent; David is playing a dangerous double game. He pretends to be raiding and looting the towns of southern Judah (v. 10), carrying out the Philistine policy of harassing

God's people, but in fact he is out making hash of Israel's historic enemies farther south along the route from Judah to Egypt, the exact route that Israel had traveled from Egyptian slavery to their promised land. He protects himself from detection by killing everyone in the camps he raids, leaving no witnesses to bring a report back to Achish. So David, under the patronage of the Philistine Achish, is secretly working for his fellow Israelites. For sixteen months, David's final stint in the wilderness, this goes on. Achish suspects nothing. Achish is proud of having the famous David as an ally, diligently employed in the Philistine cause.

But it works almost too well, for as war breaks out again between the Philistines and Israel, Achish assigns David a place in the battle plan. What will David do now? Will he have to fight against the very people God has chosen him to shepherd? David is on the spot: David cannot refuse, since Achish believes that this is what he has been doing all along; but neither can he do it—it would go against every fiber of covenant and anointing that defines him. Twice recently David has refused to kill Saul; now he is about to enter a battle in which he is part of the Philistine strategy to kill Saul. If he refuses to kill Saul in service of the Philistines, he will be exposed as a traitor to the people who have become his protectors. If he takes up arms against Saul, he will become a traitor to his own people. We readers feel the mounting tension (which will be resolved in chapter 29).

SAUL AND THE WITCH OF ENDOR (28:3–25)

The fresh outbreak of Philistine fighting, which has just put David in a murkily compromising position, puts Saul in clearly defined, dangerous straits. His back is against the wall; he is in a desperate way.

> 28:3 **Now Samuel had died, and all Israel had mourned for him. . . . Saul had expelled the mediums and the wizards from the land. ⁴ The Philistines assembled and came and encamped at Shunem. . . . ⁵ When Saul saw the army of the Philistines, he was afraid. . . . ⁶ When Saul inquired of the LORD, the LORD did not answer him, not by dreams, or by Urim, or by prophets. ⁷ Then Saul said to his servants, "Seek out for me a woman who is a medium. . . . " His servants said to him, "There is a medium at Endor."**
>
> ⁸ **So Saul disguised himself . . . and went there, he and two men. . . . They came to the woman by night. And he said, "Consult a spirit for me, and bring up for me the one whom I name to you." ⁹ The woman said to him, "Surely you know what Saul has done, how he has cut off the mediums and the wizards from the land. Why then are you laying a snare for my life . . . ?" ¹⁰ But**

Saul swore to her . . . , "As the LORD lives, no punishment shall come upon you for this thing." [11] Then the woman said, "Whom shall I bring up for you?" He answered, "Bring up Samuel for me." . . . [13] . . . The woman said to Saul, "I see a divine being coming up out of the ground. [14] . . . An old man is coming up; he is wrapped in a robe." . . .

[15] Then Samuel said to Saul, "Why have you disturbed me by bringing me up?" Saul answered, "I am in great distress, for the Philistines are warring against me, and God has turned away from me and answers me no more, either by prophets or by dreams; so I have summoned you to tell me what I should do." [16] Samuel said, " . . . [17] . . . the LORD has torn the kingdom out of your hand, and given it to your neighbor, David. . . . [19] . . . and tomorrow you and your sons shall be with me. . . . "

[20] Immediately Saul fell full length on the ground, filled with fear. . . . [21] The woman came to Saul, " . . . I have taken my life in my hand, and have listened to what you have said to me. [22] Now therefore, you also listen to your servant; let me set a morsel of bread before you. Eat, that you may have strength."

Trafficking with the dead by calling up their spirits from the underworld was forbidden in Israel. Necromancy (consulting the dead through a medium) continues, though, to attract, even fascinate, many people. The usual term for it today is "channeling." It seems to offer supernatural experience without any of the inconveniences of relationship and commitment, without, in fact, dealing with God. It is a kind of spiritualist technology that offers supernatural thrills to bored or desperate people. In Deuteronomy such practices are lumped among "the abhorrent practices of those nations" (Deut. 18:9–11). Saul himself in his earlier years had led a reform against such occult seances conducted by spiritualists.

It is a mark of just how desperate Saul is that he goes to the spiritualist underworld looking for a medium. Samuel, the wisest person he has ever known, is dead—but maybe, just maybe, he can find someone to bring Samuel's ghost back for consultation.

The narration is artful, colorful—and theological. For this same Saul, reduced to sneaking around the back alleys of Israel looking for a witch to replace God, had been the beneficiary of the best of revelation and anointing. The last (and perhaps greatest) of the prophetic judges was his personal adviser for years. He has been placed in a position of being Israel's first king, with all that involves in making a transition from a loose tribal confederation, with more or less informal charismatic leaders, to a central government that would give witness to God's sovereignty. But the cumulative effects of a long disobedience, along with the steady rise of David, have taken their toll: Saul is at the end of his rope. Out of touch with God, out of touch with his true self, he grasps at anything, a straw as it turns out—a woman at Endor who has a reputation as a medium.

The woman is able to do what Saul asks from her—bring up the ghost of Samuel from the world of the dead. But there is nothing new to be learned from the seance: The ghost of Samuel tells Saul only what the fully embodied Samuel had already told him many times over—Saul's rule is finished; David's is about to begin. Whatever reality there may be in the disreputable business of spiritualism, one thing seems evident: God does not reveal saving truth through such methods. What Samuel said before he says again; what Saul heard before he hears again.

Saul hears nothing to his advantage, but even here, in this unsavory and shadowy underworld, Saul experiences compassion. The woman, a most reluctant medium, is zealous in mercy. She insists on providing Saul with the hospitality of a nourishing meal. Saul has hit bottom, and at the bottom there is someone who cares for him just as he is, in his fatigue and despair. This is his last meal; he will die the next day.

DAVID EXCUSED FROM THE PHILISTINE ARMY (29:1–11)

The story of Saul and the seance at Endor was an aside; the main story now resumes: David in the company of Achish, off to fight with the Philistines against Saul and Israel.

29:2 **As the lords of the Philistines were passing on . . . and David and his men were passing on in the rear with Achish, ³ the commanders of the Philistines said, "What are these Hebrews doing here?" Achish said . . . , "Is this not David . . . ? Since he deserted to me I have found no fault in him to this day." ⁴ But the commanders of the Philistines . . . said to him, "Send the man back . . . ; he shall not go down with us to battle. . . . ⁵ Is this not David, of whom they sing to one another in dances,**

> **'Saul has killed his thousands,**
> **and David his ten thousands'?"**

⁶ Then Achish called David and said to him, " . . . ⁷ . . . go back now. . . . "
⁸ David said to Achish, "But what have I done? . . . " ⁹ Achish replied . . . , "I know that you are blameless in my sight as an angel of God; nevertheless, the commanders of the Philistines have said, 'He shall not go up with us to the battle.'" . . . ¹¹ So David set out with his men . . . to return to the land of the Philistines. But the Philistines went up to Jezreel.

Achish thinks David is wonderful. He trusts him completely. For sixteen months now he has been the beneficiary (he thinks) of David's plundering raids, certainly a long enough time to test both his competence and his loyalty. But the other Philistine leaders are not so sure—can anyone who has made his reputation killing Philistines so easily change sides and begin killing his fellow Israelites? They are not convinced. They tell Achish that they will not have David fighting in their ranks. Achish defends David to them, insisting on his usefulness and trustworthiness. But in the end he must give in to his military leaders and dismiss David from his ranks. He does it reluctantly and apologetically, hoping David will not take offense at being rejected. But the other Philistine leaders are right about David, and Achish is wrong. Everything Achish believes about David is based on David's deception; David, duplicitous David, has been pulling the wool over Achish's eyes ever since he moved into Ziklag. Unknowingly, Achish has been harboring the enemy. David continues his pose of loyal friendship to the end.

That is the surface story, conveyed by means of lively dialogue in the voices of the Philistine lords, Achish, and David. But just under the surface we are aware of the workings of a divine providence. When our narrative attention was temporarily redirected from David to Saul in the previous chapter (at 28:3), David was in a dilemma: the Philistines were preparing for a major assault against the Israelites, and Achish quite naturally wanted to bring David along on the Philistine side. But though Achish does not know it, David is *Israel's* king. If Achish knows David's true identity, he will kill him; if David fights for Achish, he repudiates his true identity.

And then the dilemma is resolved without David's having to do anything: The Philistines (the ungodly, *enemy* Philistines) angrily reject David and unwittingly do God's work of saving both his life and his integrity. This is another of the many instances commonly experienced by God's people that are so well expressed in the Psalm line, "Human wrath serves only to praise you" (Psalm 76:10).

DAVID AT THE WADI (BROOK) BESOR (30:1–31)

While preparation for the much publicized "main event," the major war between the Philistines and Israel, proceeds in Jezreel, the narrator once again shifts our attention south to something going on behind the scenes.

This is one of the most endearing of David stories. David has been pulled out of the main action, where history is being made, and sent home to his out-of-the-way village. But what happens in the obscurity of Ziklag, far from the headline-making battle of Jezreel, turns out to be fraught with "gospel." An incident at the Brook Besor captures our attention and holds it fast. The word *besor* means "good news" or, as we often render it, "gospel." Many, perhaps most, of the actions that critically influence humankind take place far from where the journalists assemble and post their stories. This is the final entry in the cycle of stories from David's wilderness years.

30:1 . . . [T]he Amalekites had made a raid on . . . Ziklag . . . burned it down, [2] and taken captive the women . . . and went their way. [3] When David and his men came to the city, they found it burned down, and their wives and sons and daughters taken captive. [4] Then David and the people who were with him raised their voices and wept. . . . [5] David's two wives also had been taken captive, Ahinoam . . . and Abigail. . . . [6] David was in great danger; for the people spoke of stoning him, because all the people were bitter in spirit for their sons and daughters. But David strengthened himself in the LORD his God.

[7] David said . . . , "Bring me the ephod." . . . [8] David inquired of the LORD, "Shall I pursue this band . . . ?" . . . He answered him, "Pursue. . . . " [9] So David set out, he and the six hundred men who were with him. They came to the Wadi Besor. . . . [10] . . . David went on with the pursuit, he and four hundred men; two hundred stayed behind, too exhausted to cross the Wadi Besor.

[11] In the open country they found an Egyptian. . . . They gave him bread and . . . water to drink; [12] . . . for he had not eaten bread or drunk water for three days and three nights. [13] Then David said to him, " . . . Where are you from?" He said, "I am . . . servant to an Amalekite. My master left me behind because I fell sick three days ago. [14] We had made a raid on the Negeb . . . and we burned Ziklag down." [15] David said to him, "Will you take me down to this raiding party?" He said, " . . . I will take you down to them."

[16] When he had taken him down, they were spread out all over the ground, eating and drinking and dancing. . . . [17] David attacked them. . . . [18] David recovered all that the Amalekites had taken; and David rescued his two wives. [19] . . . David brought back everything. . . .

[21] Then David came to the two hundred men who had been too exhausted to follow David. . . . [22] Then all the corrupt and worthless fellows among the men who had gone with David said, "Because they did not go with us, we will not give them any of the spoil. . . . " [23] But David said, "You shall not do so, my brothers. . . . [24] . . . For the share of the one who goes down into the battle shall be the same as the share of the one who stays by the baggage. . . . "

While the dismissal from the Philistine ranks is clearly providential, the sense of grateful relief turns immediately to bitter anger when David and his men return and see their village Ziklag plundered and burned out, and all their wives and children gone.

The anguished anger finds an easy target in David—after all, he *is* their leader and therefore to be held accountable for this holocaust. The cry goes up, "Stone David!" David's life has been under threat from King Saul and from the Philistines; this is the first time that his own company has turned against him. David has had his share of enemies to deal with. The frequent "enemy" citations in the Psalms have an extensive base in David's life experience: "Let God rise up, let his enemies be scattered" (Psalm 68:1).

Desperate, David turns to God and God's priest, Abiathar (vv. 6–7). David prays. At roughly the same time that Saul is superstitiously setting up a seance with the medium at Endor (ch. 28), David is consulting the biblically sanctioned ephod with his priest. Both of them know that their very lives are on the line, but David prays to the God who reveals himself, while Saul consults an insubstantial ghost.

Given the go-ahead, David is able to rally his angry and exhausted men and set out in pursuit of the marauders. They have just come off a three-day march (of about sixty miles) from Aphek, where they have been with the Philistines getting ready for the big battle; by the time they arrive at the Brook Besor later that day, another fifteen miles, they are thoroughly fatigued, and two hundred of the men, a third of the company, drop out. Those two hundred dropouts are going to figure prominently in the story.

The pursuers, though, know neither who they are looking for nor where to find them. And then they come upon a sick Egyptian, half dead. They treat him tenderly and compassionately (the "good Samaritan" theme again), and when he revives he becomes their guide, for it turns out that he is a servant to an Amalekite and has been on the raid that destroyed Ziklag. When he fell ill in the desert his master discarded him as useless, leaving him to die. After David's men restore him to life, they find they have the one person in that trackless desert who can lead them to their quarry.

When they do come on the Amalekites, they find them carousing wildly. The Amalekites are sitting ducks; soon they are dead ducks. All the women and children are recovered, as well as all the Amalekite booty.

On returning, they stop at the Brook Besor to pick up the two hundred left behind, rejoining them with their wives and children. But some of the mean-spirited in the company refuse to share the extensive plunder—the dropouts do not deserve it, sitting at the brook soaking their feet while the others did all the work. David intervenes: It is to be share and share alike. The entire campaign was a gift from God: the sick Egyptian to guide them, the unwary and undefended Amalekites, all the women and children alive.

Two acts of generosity occur in this story, one to the left-behind Egyptian, the other to the left-behind two hundred. David's gracious generosity sets the standard for Israel ever after. The story has since embedded itself in the Christian imagination as the narrative counterpart to Paul's teaching, "For by grace you have been saved through faith, and this is not your own doing; it is the gift of God—not the result of works, so that no one may boast" (Eph. 2:8–9).

Because this Brook Besor incident is taking place at the same time that Saul is fighting for his life in the Valley of Jezreel, we cannot help noticing certain Amalekite echoes. Saul was confirmed in his downward slide when he disobeyed orders in an Amalekite campaign (chap. 15). And now at the very moment that Saul's kingship is coming to an end, David is being prepared to step into it on the heels of a victory over Amalekites. Narrative connections are thus made between Saul's rejection and David's rise as both are marked, but in contrasting ways, with an Amalekite presence.

> 30:26 **When David came to Ziklag, he sent part of the spoil to his friends, the elders of Judah, saying, "Here is a present for you from the spoil of the enemies of the LORD"; 27 it was for those in . . . 31 all the places where David and his men had roamed.**

Twelve towns or regions are named, the final one, Hebron. This is the territory in which David has been double-crossing Achish, pretending to be plundering his fellow Israelites, but in fact protecting them by raiding and harassing their enemies. For years now, David has been proving himself loyal to his own people, cultivating their respect, caring for their needs. It is just a short time from now that David takes up residence in Hebron and begins his uncontested rule as Judah's king (2 Sam. 2:1–4). This is country David knows well and a people who know him well. Everything that has happened through the fugitive wilderness years is coming together as David is about to emerge as king.

The wilderness stories that began at Nob (chap. 21) are now complete. The significance of these wilderness years increases when we see them bracketed by two other wilderness stories: On one side the forty years that Moses led the Israelites through the Sinai wilderness; on the other, the forty days that Jesus fasted in the Judean wilderness. Three great wilderness stories—Moses, David, and Jesus.

Wilderness stories are temptation and testing stories. Wilderness is a place of testing, a place of tempting. Wilderness is wildness. Nothing is tamed or domesticated. The accustomed supports of civilization are not there, and life is sheer survival.

In the Moses wilderness story, the people of Israel are trained to discern the difference between idols and the living God, taught to worship; through their wilderness experience they are prepared to live totally before God. In the Jesus wilderness story, our Lord learns to distinguish between religion that uses God and spirituality that enters into what God does. He is thereby prepared to be our Savior, not merely our helper or adviser or entertainer. In the David wilderness story, we see a person hated and hunted like an animal, his very humanity profaned, forced to decide between a life of blasphemy and a life of reverence and prayer—and choosing prayer.

15. The End of Saul
1 Samuel 31

Again the scene shifts back to the Philistines, where we had left them marching to battle (29:11). While David has been creating a community of compassion in the south in the vicinity of the Brook Besor, the Philistine-Israel battle has gotten under way in the north.

> 31:1 **Now the Philistines fought against Israel; and the men of Israel fled . . . and many fell on Mount Gilboa.** [2] **The Philistines . . . killed Jonathan and Abinadab and Malchishua, the sons of Saul.** [3] **The battle pressed hard upon Saul . . . and he was badly wounded. . . .** [4] **Then Saul said to his armor-bearer, "Draw your sword and thrust me through. . . . " But his armor-bearer was unwilling. . . . So Saul took his own sword and fell upon it.** [5] **. . . his armor-bearer . . . also fell upon his sword and died with him. . . .**

The armor-bearer's refusal to obey Saul's command to finish him off is remarkable for the contrast it provides to our present culture's glib appeals to and apologies for mercy-killing. One can hardly fault King Saul for ordering his servant to end his misery. He was already dying and in agony—"Kill me and get it over with," under the circumstances, makes perfect sense to us. It was a royal command backed by reasons of compassion. But the armor-bearer refused. His respect for royalty itself, this God-anointed vocation, weighed stronger in his scale of values than any particular royal command. Yet, there may be something more: The dignity of life itself, even those final pain-racked minutes of it, at that moment outweighed not-life. It would be precarious to bring in the armor-bearer as a contemporary witness against euthanasia—after all, he did kill himself moments later. But his instinctive negative response to what much of today's medical and moral culture would legitimate does challenge our frequent preference on so many fronts for convenient deaths.

31:8 The next day, when the Philistines came to strip the dead, they found Saul and his three sons fallen on Mount Gilboa. 9 They cut off his head . . . 10 . . . and they fastened his body to the wall of Beth-shan. 11 But when the inhabitants of Jabesh-gilead heard what the Philistines had done to Saul, 12 . . . [they] took the body of Saul and the bodies of his sons from the wall of Beth-shan . . . 13 . . . and buried them under the tamarisk tree in Jabesh.

Saul's end has been a long time in coming, and now it is complete. Saul dies, the first and failed king. But even though we have long known, in the telling of this story, that Saul is fatally flawed and divinely rejected, the account of his death is given reverently. He dies magnificently in the company of his three sons and his loyal armor-bearer. There is no hint of disparagement or denigration in the telling of the story. Saul, despite everything, dies as God's anointed.

The Philistines, of course, do not see it that way—for them the royal bodies are an object of sport. They violate them horribly and hang them on the city walls of Beth-shan to be mocked and further violated.

But that barbaric desecration is not the final scene in Saul's life. The Philistines do not get the last word. The people of Jabesh-gilead are told of the desecration of the corpses and come running. They remember Saul with gratitude; they were the beneficiaries of Saul's first kingly act: deliverance from the cruel oppression of Nahash ("Snake") the Ammonite (see chapter 11). They seize the opportunity to honor him when he falls to the Philistines. Saul stood by them; they will stand by Saul, even if all that's left of him is his mutilated corpse. No matter what Saul has done wrong since, nothing is able to obliterate their gratitude for that tremendous deliverance. So on hearing of the Philistine outrage, they risk their lives to rescue the violated bodies of Saul and his sons, take them back home, and give them a decent burial.

Part 5. The Story of David as King

2 Samuel 1–24

Introduction

As we look over the record, it is clear that Hebrew kings did not amount to much, either politically or spiritually. Politically, they were dwarfed by the giant powers of Assyria and Babylon to the northeast and Egypt to the southwest. Spiritually, they lived in the shadows of Moses and the judges who preceded them, and Elijah and the prophets who appeared during their reigns, taking up the leadership that the kings themselves seemed incapable of exercising. In the long history of Israel, "king" is not a term that excites admiration.

Except for David. David's life is narrated as pivotal in the history of salvation. David's name occurs nearly eight hundred times in the Old Testament, and another sixty times in the New. David's name is taken up a thousand years later as a title for Jesus, "son of David." And David's name is honored and revered still—Christians and Jews commonly name their children "David." No other name from the extensive list of Hebrew kings has anywhere near the prominence of "David." In fact, no other life in the biblical record, with the exception of Jesus, is given such extensive and detailed attention. The effect of this sustained narrative treatment is to immerse us in the *human* condition—*this* is what is involved in being a human being, created and called, judged and saved by God—all the complexity of glory and difficulty involved in our human condition.

It is useful to pause at this midpoint in the David narrative and call to notice the way the story keeps us immersed in and attentive to our human condition. For it is not easy to attend to ourselves; it is more attractive to try to rise above our human condition (like the angels?); it is easier to sink below our human condition and live like animals. But "human" is unique, and we require a long growing up to realize *who* we are and the *way* we are before God. It comes as something of a surprise to find that religion, as often as not, is used as a means to avoid or escape our actual humanity. Moral engineering is the strategy of choice for avoidance, devising ways to remake our lives (and the lives of family and friends) into ways more to our own liking. Miracle is set forth as the standard means of escape, calling on or expecting God to intervene in conditions we find uncongenial. The David narrative is reticent on both counts: there is virtually no imposed morality or intervening miracle in the story. The morality is there, to be sure, but it is worked out within the conditions of the story; and the miracle is there most emphatically, but it is behind the scenes and hidden in the circumstances of the story.

The David story is told in such a way as to accustom us to the human condition as it is, not as it might be glamorized in the glossy brochures, and to develop the spiritual character commensurate with our humanity—character consisting of humility and adoration, sacrifice and courage, repentance and obedience, loyalty in the community, and love of God. David's life is intensely moral, but there is no moral bullying. David's life is pervasively supernatural, but there are no miraculous interventions.

It is not uncommon for Christian readers to embellish the David story with moralizing "lessons" and to glamorize the story with supposed "miracles." But we would do well not to tamper with the text as the storyteller gives it to us. The narrative provides us a sustained immersion in the human condition as it is, not as we wish it were: no imposed moralism, no miracle escapism. We get no encouragement from the David story for using the spiritual life as an alternative to being authentically human, by cramming ourselves and others, for instance, into moral cages, or fantasizing God as an escape from the limits and conditions of our humanity. As we men and women honor and submit to the story as it comes to us, our lives are shaped in this telling and listening into obedient and believing participation in God's ways with us.

16. David Made King over Judah
2 Samuel 1:1–2:11

DAVID'S LAMENT OVER SAUL (1:1–27)

This final scene in the extensive back-and-forth narration of Saul and David is the opening scene in the story of David as king. The story of David's ascent to the throne and Saul's decline from it, which began in 1 Samuel 16, is now nearly complete.

It would be easy to read the Saul and David conflict as a classic drama of the kind that Sophocles and Shakespeare have given us: volatile issues of right and wrong, family intrigue and betrayal, divided loyalties, developing intensities of madness and hate, political scheming, hidden moral undercurrents that surface in unexpected places. It is all of that, to be sure, but not *only* that.

Emotionally, we are set up to cheer the demise of Saul and celebrate the ascendancy of David. But the story does not permit it.

> 1:1 **After the death of Saul, when David had returned from defeating the Amalekites, David remained two days in Ziklag.** 2 **On the third day, a man came from Saul's camp, with his clothes torn and dirt on his head. . . . he fell to the ground and did obeisance.** 3 **David said to him, "Where have you come from?" He said to him, "I have escaped from the camp of Israel."** 4 **David said to him, "How did things go? . . . " He answered, " . . . many of the army fell and died; and Saul and his son Jonathan also died. . . .** 6 **. . . I happened to be on Mount Gilboa; and there was Saul leaning on his spear. . . .** 9 **He said to me, 'Come, stand over me and kill me. . . . '** 10 **So I stood over him, and killed him. . . . I took the crown that was on his head and the armlet that was on his arm, and I have brought them here to my lord."**

The Amalekite is a liar. We have just been told that Saul, seriously wounded, commanded his armor-bearer to kill him. When his armor-bearer refused, Saul killed himself, his armor-bearer joining him as a suicide (1 Sam. 31:3–5).

David, listening to the story, didn't know that. But we the story *readers* know it. While David was down south doing battle with Amalekites and then returning to Ziklag, the battle of Gilboa raged in the north at Jezreel. David would have known nothing yet of the outcome of that battle. This Amalekite was the first to bring a report.

We know that the Amalekite is an opportunistic schemer. He has ostentatiously outfitted himself as a tragic figure—torn clothes, dirt on his head, a survivor of terrible catastrophe. He has a plan, but he needs to test David's response. He cautiously measures out his report. First, the bare facts of his escape from the battlefield with so many dead—and Saul and Jonathan dead! David presses for details.

Emboldened by David's interest, he claims responsibility for Saul's death. What Saul's armor-bearer refused to do, he now says that he himself did. Whereas the actual death is reported sparely (1 Sam. 31:4–5), the Amalekite elaborates his story with details—where he was standing at the time, Saul's position, the conversation between them, Saul's condition, how he assessed the situation. Every good liar knows the importance of providing details. The Amalekite is a good liar. Sure of himself now—David has been listening so attentively!—he finishes his concocted report with a flourish: He presents David with the insignia of royalty, Saul's crown and armband. He just happened to grab them up as he ran for his life from the battlefield! In presenting Saul's crown and armband, he supposes that he is making David king. The reward will certainly be substantial.

The story is working at two levels here: There is the story that we know to be true, which David does not know (1 Samuel 31); and there is the story that David is being told, which we know is a lie (2 Samuel 1). Would David be taken in by the Amalekite's lie? Would David let himself be crowned king by this scheming Amalekite?

> 1:11 **Then David took hold of his clothes and tore them; and all the men who were with him. . . . ¹² They mourned and wept . . . for Saul and for his son Jonathan. . . . ¹³ David said to the young man who had reported to him, "Where do you come from?" He answered, "I am the son of a resident alien, an Amalekite." ¹⁴ David said to him, "Were you not afraid to lift your hand to destroy the LORD's anointed?" ¹⁵ Then David called one of the young men and said, "Come here and strike him down." So he struck him down and he died. . . .**

The lie's success is short-lived. David's initial response must have chilled the heart of the Amalekite. Why is David not celebrating? David's longtime, implacable enemy is dead. Why does David not put on the crown and armband and act like a king? Why the lament, the fasting, the weeping?

And then, why the interrogation? After the lament subsides, David calls the Amalekite back in for questioning. The first question (earlier reported as Saul's having asked, in verse 8) verifies the young man's identity as an Amalekite. The second accuses him of murder—killing the LORD's anointed.

There is no hint in the storytelling that David suspects that the Amalekite is lying. The story as told, as far as we can tell, convinces David. So far, so good. What the Amalekite has not counted on is that David is a theologian. A theologian acquires the habit of looking at people and circumstances with an eye for what God is doing. The more unlikely the person, the more unfriendly the circumstance, the more intently the theologian's discerning look. When the Amalekite saw the dead king on Mount Gilboa, he saw an opportunity to acquire an honored position in the new regime; how could he have known that David had spent half his lifetime looking at that same king and seeing God at work in him, the "anointed"?

"Amalekite" enters our common vocabulary at this point to designate the opportunistic schemer who looks at every person and every situation as a means of self-promotion. Amalekites, unlike theologians, have no concern for God's sovereignty, no sense of God's hiddenness in ordinary events. Amalekites had a history of harassing God's people, interfering with God's purposes. Two named Amalekites frame the young Amalekite who tried to use David: first, Agag the Amalekite is featured early in the Saul story (1 Samuel 15); and then near the end of the biblical story, Agag's descendant Haman, "the Agagite," appears (Esth. 3:1). Amalekites have a way of showing up at holy places at opportune times. (Attractive as opportunism is for the moment, then and now, it doesn't have a good track record. Agag was "hewed" to pieces, the young Amalekite was "struck" down, and Haman was hung.)

The Amalekite expected to set off a victory celebration with his report to David; what he precipitated was David's magnificent lament. One scholar writes of Israel's "distinctive capacity for pathos" (Brueggemann, *First and Second Samuel*, 214). In that company, David is a most distinguished poet of pathos.

1:17 **David intoned this lamentation over Saul and his son Jonathan. . . .**
 19 **Your glory, O Israel, lies slain upon your high places!**
     How the mighty have fallen!
 20 **Tell it not in Gath,**
     proclaim it not in the streets of Ashkelon;

> or the daughters of the Philistines will rejoice,
>   the daughters of the uncircumcised will exult.

Catastrophe has struck Israel, its king killed and his body desecrated. A tragedy of such dimensions must be treated with reverence, with dignity. It must not, as it surely will, become a matter of street-corner gossip, soap opera titillation. The Philistines responsible for the ravaging of Israel's royalty can be counted on to be irresponsible in the way they report and talk about it. It is bad enough that Saul and his sons are killed; it is almost worse that they should be featured in Philistine yellow journalism.

> 21 You mountains of Gilboa,
>   let there be no dew or rain upon you,
>   nor bounteous fields!
>   For there the shield of the mighty was defiled,
>   the shield of Saul, anointed with oil no more.

Mount Gilboa, the site of the final battle, was synonymous with fertility. If the Philistines cannot be counted on (as they certainly cannot) to honor the sacred dead, the land itself must do it: The very earth is called on to fast and mourn.

> 22 From the blood of the slain,
>   from the fat of the mighty,
>   the bow of Jonathan did not turn back,
>   nor the sword of Saul return empty.

Skillfully employed images provide the imagination with language to remember the simultaneous horror and honor of war. War is horrible ("blood" spilled and "fat" butchered); and war is honorable (the courageous "bow," the relentless "sword"). If either aspect is deleted, memory is defiled by either sentimentalism or meanness.

> 23 Saul and Jonathan, beloved and lovely!
>   in life and in death they were not divided;
>   they were swifter than eagles,
>   they were stronger than lions.

David's enemy and David's friend are linked as equals in the lament. Death exposes relationships and realities that are often obscured or hidden in the crossfire of daily motives and causes, agendas and projects. The funeral elegy is not an occasion for making comparisons, of assigning a grade to a

life. Every life, regardless of public opinion or personal feeling, deserves
(and requires) honest eulogy.

> 24 **O daughters of Israel, weep over Saul,**
>   **who clothed you with crimson, in luxury,**
>   **who put ornaments of gold on your apparel.**
> 25 **How the mighty have fallen**
>   **in the midst of the battle!**

Lament is a social as well as personal act. Jesus lamenting at the tomb of
Lazarus (John 11) is of a piece with David lamenting the death of Saul and
Jonathan. Lament is a gospel act. It is not sufficient to grieve alone; grieving friends are necessary too. That is why we join our grieving friends at
funerals. David calls on community help in his lament. David's loss is
everyone's loss. The "daughters of Israel," in contrast to the "daughters of
the Philistines" (v. 20), can be counted on to respond appropriately, to remember the best of Saul's life and join in the common lament.

> 25b **Jonathan lies slain upon your high places.**
> 26   **I am distressed for you, my brother Jonathan;**
>   **greatly beloved were you to me;**
>   **your love to me was wonderful,**
>   **passing the love of women.**

Saul has not been slighted in any way in the lament, but the most poignant
moment is saved for Jonathan, David's lifelong, covenanted friend.
    Friendship of the kind that David sings of is not much in evidence in our
day. We have "contacts," acquaintances, associates, teammates, roomies,
whatever. But friends? We have affairs and we "network." In contrast, C. S.
Lewis wrote that "our ancestors regarded Friendship as something that
raised us almost above humanity. This love, free from instinct, free from all
duties but those which love has freely assumed, almost wholly free from jealousy, and free without qualification from the need to be needed, is eminently
spiritual. It is the sort of love one can imagine between angels" (Lewis, *The
Four Loves*, 91).

> 27 **How the mighty have fallen,**
>   **and the weapons of war perished!**

One line—"How the mighty have fallen"—is repeated three times in the
lament (vv. 19, 25, 27). The first time it is spoken over Saul, as a witness

to catastrophe; then of Jonathan, catastrophe compounded; and now a third time in the summary couplet to form a triadic chord of harmonic beauty. Beauty. Lament is not an animal wail, an inarticulate howl. Lament notices and attends, savors and delights—details, images, relationships. Pain entered into, accepted and owned, can become poetry. It is no less pain, but it is no longer ugly. Poetry is our most personal use of words; it is our way of entering into experience, of inhabiting it as our home, not just watching it happen to us.

Lament is deeply personal; it can be embracingly public. This lament began personally with David, and locally in Ziklag, but it soon pulled in the community and ended up involving the nation. David's lament fused the personal with the public. Lament continues to be a major way by which a people nurtures and maintains its humanity socially, culturally, politically—all these aspects are included in David's lament. All wise families and cultures honor lament. Without lament, a nation is gradually but surely dehumanized into a military force or an economic function. If all a nation does is wave its flag in parade or boast of its standard of living, go to war, and make money, it ends up sooner or later a husk. Lament keeps a people in touch with leaders and friends, losses and defeats, limits and suffering—with its humanity. Lament keeps us connected with reality, with the actual—with God. That is why David not only lamented, but ordered that this lament be "taught to the people of Judah" (v. 18).

DAVID MOVES TO HEBRON (2:1–4a)

By now David has been the anointed king of Israel for many years, but not visible as such. All the years since David's anointing by Samuel (1 Sam. 16:1–13), Saul has held the throne; larger-than-life Saul has been the visible king. With Saul's death, David's royal identity becomes public for the first time.

> 2:1 **After this David inquired of the LORD, "Shall I go up into any of the cities of Judah?" The LORD said to him, "Go up . . . To Hebron." ² So David went up there. . . . ⁴ Then the people of Judah came, and there they anointed David king over the house of Judah.**

David is still in Ziklag, his wilderness headquarters, under the patronage of the Philistine King Achish during the final wilderness years of his exile from Saul. From here he has consolidated his strength, developed an appreciative and loyal following among the people of Judah by sharing the plunder from his frequent raids against the desert peoples of the south (1 Sam. 30:26–31), and married two women from that country (Carmel and Jezreel are places in the "south" in the neighborhood of Judah). He is strategically located to move onto the public stage as king.

But first he prays ("inquired of the LORD," v. 1). He prays for God's guidance; in effect, "Is this the right time to come out into the open as king?" And, "Where is the place to do it?" He receives the guidance he prays for: "Yes, this is the right time; and Hebron is the place."

Everything goes like clockwork: David moves into Hebron, a central city in Judah. Hebron, place of the ancient burial plot of Abraham and Sarah, pioneer father and mother of God's people, is a city rich in sacred tradition. This is a hallowed and fitting place for a new beginning, a site from which to launch God's kingdom rule through David over these people to whom Abraham was father. David brings with him his entire wilderness entourage, his wives Ahinoam and Abigail along with his guerrilla army and their families. It is not long before David is anointed king of his home tribe of Judah.

But only of Judah. With Saul dead, there would seem to be nothing in the way of David's proceeding immediately to rule as Saul's successor. But the eleven tribes of the north, collectively designated "Israel," are not in on this anointing, and David's earlier anointing by Samuel is not common knowledge. It is another seven and a half years before that happens. Israel's twelve tribes were a fractious bunch. Bringing them together in any kind of unity was difficult and required constant work and much patience.

Meanwhile David begins this task of bringing the northern tribes (Israel) under his rule. Two side-by-side stories set the context: Jabesh-gilead diplomacy and Abner's power play.

DAVID COURTS JABESH-GILEAD (2:4b–7)

> 2:4b When they told David, "It was the people of Jabesh-gilead who buried Saul," ⁵ David . . . said to them, "May you be blessed by the LORD, because you showed this loyalty to Saul your lord, and buried him! ⁶ Now may the LORD show steadfast love and faithfulness to you! And I too will reward you because you have done this thing. . . . "

The first thing David does to pull the north into the orbit of his influence is to court the people of Jabesh-gilead diplomatically, the people who had so courageously and compassionately rescued the bodies of Saul and his sons from the Philistine desecrations and then proceeded to give them a decent burial (1 Samuel 31). Jabesh-gilead was where, many years earlier, Saul had gotten his start. His first act as king was to deliver Jabash-gilead from the brutalities of the infamous Nahash the Ammonite (1 Samuel 11). The people who earlier had been rescued by Saul from unspeakable violations rescued Saul's body from further desecration. David blesses them for their loyalty and promises his loyalty in return. They are not yet under his rule, but they can be confident of his favor.

ABNER'S PLAY FOR POWER (2:8–11)

But while David is reaching out to bring the people of the north under his influence, Abner is busy making arrangements to continue the kingship of Saul's heirs in opposition to David.

> 2:8 **But Abner son of Ner, commander of Saul's army, had taken Ishbaal son of Saul, and brought him over to Mahanaim.** [9] **He made him king over Gilead . . . and over all Israel.** [10] **. . . But the house of Judah followed David.** [11] **The time that David was king in Hebron over the house of Judah was seven years and six months.**

Saul and three of his sons died on Mount Gilboa in the Philistine battle. But there was another son, Ishbaal. Abner, Saul's commander, having got out of the battle alive, took Ishbaal across the Jordan to the east, out of Philistine reach, and crowned him king over the parts of the country not taken by the Philistines.

Abner—as will become clear later—is not interested in Ishbaal as such. Ishbaal is merely a pretext to legitimize Abner's lust for power. Abner's move gives all those who have been associated with Saul's rule a chance at retaining power. By shoring up a "Saul party," Abner prevents David from simply stepping into Saul's shoes and proceeding with the royal vocation to which Samuel had long ago anointed him.

17. David's Civil War
2 Samuel 2:12–4:12

Three interconnecting energies, the anointing of David by the elders of Judah (2:1–4a), David's Jabesh-gilead diplomacy (2:4b–7), and Abner's Ishbaal power play (2:8–11) serve as a tripod from which to hang the story of the civil war. The three episodes are briefly reported, but in combination they provide a historical structure adequate to support the continuing narration in terms of the personal lives of a few of the people involved.

The civil-war story is told in terms of representative and named people: David, of course, then: Abner, the sons of Zeruiah (Joab, Abishai, Asahel), Ishbaal, Rizpah, Michal, Paltiel, Mephibosheth, Rechab, and Baanah— eleven names placed in settings of vivid local color and swift-paced dramatic action. (Six of David's sons are also listed, but they are not participants in the action here.)

The first battle of the war takes place with the kings themselves, David and Ishbaal, not present. Their respective generals, Joab and Abner, meet at Gibeon in central Palestine, an approximate midpoint between Ishbaal's base in the north and David's in the south. A large "pool of Gibeon," likely the same as the one designated in our text, has been excavated at this site: thirty-seven feet in diameter and eighty-two feet deep.

ABNER AND JOAB AT GIBEON (2:12–32)

2:12 **Abner son of Ner, and the servants of Ishbaal son of Saul, went out from Mahanaim to Gibeon.** [13] **Joab son of Zeruiah, and the servants of David, went out and met them at the pool of Gibeon. One group sat on one side of the pool, while the other sat on the other side of the pool.** [14] **Abner said to Joab, "Let the young men come forward and have a contest before us." . . .** [15] **So they came forward . . . , twelve for Benjamin and Ishbaal son of Saul, and twelve of the servants of David.** [16] **Each grasped his opponent by the head,**

and thrust his sword in his opponent's side; so they fell down together. . . . [17] The battle was very fierce that day; and Abner and the men of Israel were beaten by the servants of David.

Instead of taking the field against one another in an all-out battle, the generals Abner and Joab arrange for a contest of champions: Twelve men from each side are selected to represent their respective armies and fight it out, with their fellow soldiers watching and cheering them on from the sidelines. Early in his life, David himself featured in just such a contest when he was put up against Goliath in the Valley of Elah (1 Samuel 17). Our modern sports events continue the tradition, exciting similar emotions, but not with such bloody consequences.

The contest, however, doesn't turn out as expected; instead of one team beating the other, the twenty-four men on the field all kill one another—the paired opponents grab each other in a lethal embrace, each stabbing his opponent. The whole bunch of them fall in a heap, all dead. There is a kind of slapstick quality to the whole thing that we associate with Abbott and Costello routines. But nobody laughs at this one—with their champions dead, the two armies turn into a mob, pour out onto the field, and go at one another murderously, When the day is over, Joab's team has decisively bested Abner's.

2:18 The three sons of Zeruiah were there, Joab, Abishai, and Asahel.

Zeruiah is David's sister (1 Chron. 2:16). Her three sons Joab, Abishai, and Asahel, David's nephews, hold high positions in David's company. They are loyal to David and useful to him, but they are also constant trouble. Unlike David, who is portrayed as thoughtful, prayerful, and generous, these three relatives are impulsive, violent, and willful.

2:18b Now Asahel was as swift of foot as a wild gazelle. [19] Asahel pursued Abner. . . . [20] Then Abner looked back and said, "Is it you, Asahel? . . . [22] Turn away from following me; why should I strike you to the ground?" . . . [23] But he refused to turn away. So Abner struck him in the stomach with the butt of his spear, so that the spear came out at his back. He fell there, and died where he lay. . . .

[24] But Joab and Abishai pursued Abner. . . . [26] Then Abner called to Joab, "Is the sword to keep devouring forever? . . . " [27] Joab said, "As God lives, if you had not spoken, the people would have continued to pursue their kinsmen, not stopping until morning." [28] Joab sounded the trumpet and all the people stopped; they no longer pursued Israel. . . .

²⁹ Abner and his men traveled all that night through the Arabah . . . to Mahanaim. ³⁰ Joab returned from the pursuit of Abner; and when he had gathered all the people together, there were missing of David's servants nineteen men besides Asahel. ³¹ But the servants of David had killed of Benjamin three hundred sixty of Abner's men. ³² They took up Asahel and buried him in the tomb of his father. . . .

Out of the general mayhem, one incident is selected for attention—the Asahel and Abner chase.

Asahel's chase of Abner, Abner's unsuccessful appeal to let up, Abner's killing of Asahel, the continued pursuit of Abner by Joab and Abishai, Abner's appeal, this time successful, to quit the chase, the burial of Asahel, the night marches of Abner and Joab, one to the north, the other to the south—cascading action is crisply told, every detail sharply etched.

These two incidents, the contest at Gibeon and the killing of Asahel, are alive with detail: places, names, conversations, action—there is much attention to particulars. The contrast with the earlier unadorned lead sentence, "Then the people of Judah came, and there they anointed David king over the house of Judah" (2:4), is noticeable. We would like to know *how* David was made king, the negotiations involved, the terms, the key players in the process. But the storyteller's task is not to satisfy our curiosity but to involve our participation. That is accomplished with an accumulation of commonplace details rather than by making us spectators to the pomp and circumstance of the coronation. Scripture storytelling is not primarily entertainment, but is in the service of involving men and women in God's kingdom work; as it turns out, the unruly ambitions and impetuosities of Abner and Joab and Asahel provide readier access to our place in the story than the inside story of David's enthronement.

ABNER MAKES A DEAL WITH DAVID (3:1–21)

3:1 **There was a long war between the house of Saul and the house of David.** . . .

The duration of the "long war" has already been given us—seven and a half years (2:11). This summary sentence is now filled out with a cluster of stories, in which Abner and Joab are the major players.

But first there is a parenthetical aside, inserting names that will become important later in the story.

3:2 **Sons were born to David at Hebron: his firstborn was Amnon, of Ahi-
noam of Jezreel; ³ his second, Chileab, of Abigail the widow of Nabal of
Carmel; the third, Absalom son of Maacah, daughter of King Talmai of
Geshur; ⁴ the fourth, Adonijah son of Haggith; the fifth, Shephatiah son of
Abital; ⁵ and the sixth, Ithream, of David's wife Eglah. These were born to
David in Hebron.**

While the civil war rages outside Hebron, marriages are being made and
babies being born within Hebron that are significant events in the overall
story. David brings two wives to Hebron and soon acquires four more.
The six wives each bears a son during the Hebron years. Three of these
sons will emerge into prominence in the years ahead: Watch for the appearances of Amnon, Absalom, and Adonijah.

Incidentally (or not!), this listing of David's wives clashes with any romantic stereotypes that may have accrued to David in our imaginations.
The way the wives are identified suggests that politics, not love, was the
tie that bound David to a wife.

3:6 **While there was war between the house of Saul and the house of David,
Abner was making himself strong in the house of Saul. ⁷ Now Saul had a concubine whose name was Rizpah daughter of Aiah. And Ishbaal said to Abner, "Why have you gone in to my father's concubine?" ⁸ The words of
Ishbaal made Abner very angry; he said, "Am I a dog's head for Judah? Today I keep showing loyalty to the house of your father Saul . . . and have not
given you into the hand of David; and yet you charge me now with a crime
concerning this woman. ⁹ . . . For just what the LORD has sworn to David,
that will I accomplish for him, ¹⁰ to transfer the kingdom from the house of
Saul, and set up the throne of David. . . ." ¹¹ And Ishbaal could not answer
Abner another word, because he feared him.**

As a pawn to his own ambition, Abner has made Ishbaal, Saul's son, king;
now he flaunts his power by sleeping with Rizpah, Saul's concubine. In that
culture, sexual virility was evidence of political power. Abner in bed with
Rizpah is equivalant to Abner sitting on Saul's throne. Ishbaal's protest, ineffectual as it is, triggers an emotionally angry response in Abner. Then
Abner drags in theology to justify his action (vv. 9–10). His use of God-
talk to divert attention from his own self-serving actions has a long and
continuing history.

The next thing we know, Abner has abandoned his schemes for using
Ishbaal to continue the Saul monarchy and switched to David's side,

promising David that he will bring all of Israel under David's rule—northern Israel and southern Judah united under David as king. David accepts the offer, and formally validates the treaty with a feast (vv. 20–21).

As part of the negotiated deal between Abner and David, David demands that his first wife Michal, Saul's daughter, be returned to him. She has helped him flee from Saul (1 Sam. 19:11–17), but he has had to leave her behind. Now he wants her back. Is this love or politics? The political implications, at least, of his demand are obvious: Saul's daughter returned to him as his wife would be a signal to Israel that Saul's kingdom is being handed over to him as well. There is only one problem: During David's long absence in the fugitive wilderness years, she has married (or been married to) another man, Paltiel. The single-sentence description of Paltiel following his wife, weeping as she is cruelly taken from him (v. 16), is one of the most poignant in scripture.

The two women in this story, who at first appear to play minor roles, assume a larger significance when seen in parallel. Rizpah and Michal share an unhappy, but not uncommon, fate—both are reduced from person to function. In the narration, it becomes clear that both Rizpah (by Abner) and Michal (by David) are used as politically charged symbols—Rizpah as a symbol of royal virility for Abner, Michal as a symbol of royal legitimacy for David. First dehumanized, then used; this continues to happen still today.

JOAB MURDERS ABNER (3:22–38)

> 3:22 Just then the servants of David arrived with Joab from a raid. . . . But Abner was not with David at Hebron, for David had dismissed him. . . . 24 Then Joab went to the king and said, "What have you done? . . . why did you dismiss him . . . ? 25 You know that Abner son of Ner came to deceive you, and to learn . . . all that you are doing."

Joab is a fighting man and has no patience with the niceties of diplomacy. The Joab imagination is black and white, without shades or hues: Abner is the enemy, pure and simple. He is, in fact, twice an enemy—an enemy because he represents the Saul forces, and an enemy because he has killed Asahel, Joab's brother. There is only one way to treat an enemy—kill him.

David negotiates peace with Abner without Joab's knowledge. Now Joab returns the favor: He plots and carries out the murder of Abner without David's knowledge.

3:26 When Joab came out from David's presence, he sent messengers after Abner, and they brought him back . . . but David did not know about it. [27] . . . Joab took [Abner] aside in the gateway to speak with him privately, and there he stabbed him in the stomach. So he died for shedding the blood of Asahel, Joab's brother. [28] Afterward, when David heard of it, he said, "I and my kingdom are forever guiltless before the LORD for the blood of Abner son of Ner. [29] May the guilt fall on the head of Joab . . . !" . . .

[31] Then David said to Joab and to all the people who were with him, "Tear your clothes, and put on sackcloth, and mourn over Abner." . . . [33] The king lamented for Abner, saying,

"Should Abner die as a fool dies?
[34] Your hands were not bound,
    your feet were not fettered;
as one falls before the wicked
    you have fallen."

And all the people wept over him again. [35] Then all the people came to persuade David to eat something . . . but David swore, saying, "So may God do to me, and more, if I taste bread . . . before the sun goes down!" [36] All the people took notice of it, and it pleased them. . . . [37] So . . . all Israel understood that day that the king had no part in the killing of Abner son of Ner.

In the midst of war, David is not defined by war. There is more to David than getting his own way. At the death of Abner, David laments. Lament is one of the deepest and most human of responses; David is magnificent in lament. His lament over the deaths of Saul and Jonathan (2 Samuel 1), after three thousand years, continues as a highlight in the world's stories of grief. His lament over Abner displays the same depth of feeling, a similar respect for life, and a care with words that gives dignity to death.

But before he laments, David curses (vv. 28–29). He laments Abner who has so recently headed the opposition to his rule; he curses his nephew and the general of his army, Joab. Cursing is not nearly so characteristic of David as lament, but Joab's outrageous interference with David's peacemaking provokes it.

David publicly repudiates the actions of Joab and his men. He makes it clear that he has had no part in their bloody work. He goes farther: He forces the murderers to assist at the burial, to march in the funeral procession dressed in mourning. These men who get their identity from their weapons and the cultivation of violence are now humiliated and mocked for the very things in which they take pride.

David's response becomes the people's response. Hebron under the conditions of war could easily have become inflamed by murderous Joab and turned into a holocaust of brutality. Instead, because of David, Hebron is transformed into a memorial of lament. David's rule extends to far more than politics—it reaches into the emotions of the people, shaping their values, their sense of the honor, and the dignity of life itself.

> 3:38 And the king said . . . "Do you not know that a prince and a great man has fallen this day in Israel? 39 Today I am powerless, even though anointed king; these men, the sons of Zeruiah, are too violent for me. The LORD pay back the one who does wickedly in accordance with his wickedness!"

David's nephews, Joab and Abishai (and earlier, Asahel) are a thorn in David's side and will continue to be so all through this David story. All they seem to know is violence and killing. David is repeatedly exasperated.

The sons of Zeruiah are on David's side, but they are not committed to David's ways of doing things, David's way of being before God. They know and live with David, but are indifferent to David's God. It is not enough to be on the right side; it is essential also to work in the right way. These nephews, "sons of Zeruiah," through the centuries have acquired a vast progeny among those who profess to be serving God and God's cause in both the church and the world. David's descendant, Jesus, later has similar difficulties with interfering members of his family (see Mark 3:21 and John 7:1–5).

RECHAB AND BAANAH MURDER ISHBAAL (4:1–12)

> 4:1 When Saul's son Ishbaal heard that Abner had died at Hebron, his courage failed, and all Israel was dismayed. 2 Saul's son had two captains of raiding bands; the name of the one was Baanah, and the name of the other Rechab. . . .
>
> 4 Saul's son Jonathan had a son who was crippled in his feet. He was five years old when the news about Saul and Jonathan came from Jezreel. His nurse picked him up and fled; and, in her haste to flee, it happened that he fell and became lame. His name was Mephibosheth.
>
> 5 Now . . . Rechab and Baanah . . . came to the house of Ishbaal, while he was taking his noonday rest. . . . 7 . . . they attacked him, killed him, and beheaded him. . . . 8 They brought the head of Ishbaal to David at Hebron and said to the king, "Here is the head of Ishbaal, son of Saul, your enemy, who sought your life; the LORD has avenged my lord the king this day on Saul and on his offspring."
>
> 9 David answered Rechab and his brother Baanah . . . , "As the LORD lives, who has redeemed my life out of every adversity, 10 when the one who told me, 'See, Saul is dead,' thought he was bringing good news, I seized him and killed him at Ziklag—this was the reward I gave him for his news. 11 How

much more then, when wicked men have killed a righteous man on his bed in his own house! . . . " [12] So David commanded the young men, and they killed them . . . and hung their bodies beside the pool at Hebron. But the head of Ishbaal they took and buried in the tomb of Abner at Hebron.

The insertion of Mephibosheth (v. 4) is parenthetical to this part of the story. It functions like the parenthetical passage in the previous chapter (3:2–5) that lists David's wives and sons by providing data that will be needed farther along in the story. The story of Mephibosheth will be taken up later, just as the story of David's sons will be taken up later. But the names are now before us, lodged in our minds, ready for later recognition. Skilled storytellers do this, introduce out-of-context names or materials that bait our attention for a later "catch." The Russian master of the short story Anton Chekhov once wrote that if a writer puts a loaded gun on the table early in the story, it has to go off before the story ends. We anticipate: How and when will Mephibosheth (and Amnon, Absalom, and Adonijah) "go off"?

This account of Rechab and Baanah is the final episode for the civil war years. Rechab and Baanah at the end of the war repeat the miscalculation of the Amalekite, namely, that David was power-hungry and would reward anyone who furthered his ambition, whether by fair means or foul. It is beyond the understanding of Rechab and Baanah (as with the Amalekite) that David would be more interested in right than might. They have no idea that David lives in a God-alive world. This failure of imagination cost them their lives. Understanding God and his ways (theology) is practical knowledge—it can save your life. If Rechab and Baanah had known something of God, they would not have lost their heads, first metaphorically and then literally.

By now much killing has been reported: the Amalekite killed, the twenty-four combatants stabbed to death at the pool of Gibeon, followed by a body count of three hundred and seventy-nine in the battle sequel; Asahel killed, Abner killed, Ishbaal killed, and now Rechab and Baanah killed. Abner's question to Joab, "Is the sword to keep devouring forever?" (2:26), could well stand as an epitaph to this civil war part of the story (chap. 2–4)

The first and the last deaths (the Amalekite and the brothers Rechab and Baanah) are judicial executions ordered by David. But there is a certain implicit justice to all the deaths—these are unscrupulous and grasping men, scrambling to make the most of the "first come, first served" opportunities they see before them. Their fate validates the accuracy of the Psalm sentence: "Their mischief returns upon their own heads,/and on their own heads their violence descends" (Psalm 7:16). Joab comes out of it alive but cursed—his death by execution delayed for thirty or so years

(1 Kings 2:28–34). Did the Davidic observation, "The wicked are snared in the work of their own hands" (Psalm 9:16), come out of the experience of these seven and a half civil war years? Perhaps. There are also victims: the "used" women, Rizpah and Michal, the disconsolate Paltiel, the hapless Ishbaal, who is described by one scholar (McCarter) as a "thoroughly unkingly invertebrate" (McCarter, *II Samuel*, 122). There are always victims who get what they do not deserve.

Thus is shown the dark side of the civil war. But throughout, another element is being formed. In retrospect, it turns out to be the dominant element, although not nearly as dramatic in the telling: David. David praying. David waiting for the kingdom to be given to him under the sovereignty of God. David refusing to hurry. David trusting in the efficacy of his anointing to finally set him on the throne. David putting up with irritating and and disruptive associates. David fierce in his passion for honor and justice. David tender in his laments.

There are two notable aspects to this core Davidic element as the story is told to us: David does not lift a hand to take over Saul's throne; and David does not incur what he calls "bloodguilt." In contrast to the frenzy of ambition that he sees around him excited by Saul's empty throne, David conducts funerals, composes poems, marries and has children, and administers justice. In contrast to all the killing going on around him in attempts to grab power, David does not kill anyone who could be considered a rival.

It is possible to read this account of David cynically and to interpret the story as a piece of court propaganda that is designed to whitewash David of a lifetime of shrewd political manipulation that finally put him on Saul's throne. And it could very well have been written to counter the suspicions of people in Israel who were skeptical of David's motives, perhaps jealous of his success, who thought he was "too good to be true."

But reading attentively, we realize that David is not presented as too good to be true. He is very much a child of his times. The underlying plot that gives structure to this narrative is not David's goodness or innocence, but God's providence. God's sovereignty is behind David's rise to power. This is, above all, *theological* storytelling. It is not, however, theology abstracted from life, as we so often encounter it in our studies and books, but theology embodied *in* life. One of our most respected commentators on the David story gives this assessment: "The rise of David is represented not as having been a piece of chance good fortune or a wise piece of policy, but as a miraculous event disposed by a higher hand. In this way he material is brought into the larger context of all Scripture and becomes an episode in the history of God's guidance" (Hertzberg, *I & II Samuel*, 244).

18. David Consolidates Israel and Judah
2 Samuel 5–10

ISRAEL'S ELDERS ANOINT DAVID KING (5:1–5)

5:1 **Then all the tribes of Israel came to David at Hebron, and said, "Look, we are your bone and flesh. ² For some time, while Saul was king over us, it was you who led out Israel and brought it in. The LORD said to you: It is you who shall be shepherd of my people Israel, you who shall be ruler over Israel." ³ So all the elders of Israel came to the king at Hebron; and King David made a covenant with them at Hebron before the LORD, and they anointed David king over Israel. ⁴ David was thirty years old when he began to reign, and he reigned forty years. ⁵ At Hebron he reigned over Judah seven years and six months; and at Jerusalem he reigned over all Israel and Judah thirty-three years.**

This is David's third anointing: The first was by Samuel, as a youth (1 Samuel 16); the second, by the elders of Judah, his home tribe (2 Sam. 2:1–4) at the age of thirty; and now, finally, he is anointed by the elders of Israel. David is now king of the United Kingdom of Israel and Judah—all twelve tribes set under his rule. He is thirty-seven years old.

It has taken the elders a while—seven and a half years, to be exact—but they now realize that David has been on their side all along. They recognize an essential kinship with David that transcends old north-south rivalries and is unaffected by Saul's long enmity: "Look, we are your bone and flesh" (v. 1). They remember the critical role that David has played in their history: "It was you who led out Israel and brought it in" (v. 2). They are ready to make him their king.

The text makes it clear that the initiative for the anointing of David comes from the elders of Israel. Although anointed to this office early in his life by Samuel, David does not press his claim or use his Hebron-based military supremacy to impose his kingship on the tribes of the north. David knows how to wait. His waiting is not procrastination; it is not in-

E. underhill calls it a willed passivity "

dolence. It is poised submissiveness, a not-doing that leaves adequate space
and time for God's initiating actions through others. David has been waiting a long time. He has not been unoccupied during the waiting, but neither has he impatiently asserted his own claims or God-given rights. David
is a rare combination of energy and reticence, confidence and humility. He
is a leader without an ego.

The elders' approach to David is supported by a text: "The LORD said
to you: It is you who shall be shepherd of my people Israel" (v. 2). They
seem to be quoting a remembered oracle from God, although no record
of it survives. The young David entered this story as a shepherd (1 Sam.
16:11); he will retain and continue that early vocational identity now as
king. The psalm most famously associated with David (Psalm 23) applies
the shepherd metaphor to God. The prophets pick it up and use it extensively for both God and God's leaders (Isa. 40:11; Jer. 23:3–4; and Ezekiel
34 and 37:24ff.). Finally, Jesus identifies himself as a shepherd, the Good
Shepherd (John 10:11). Shepherds lead by caring and serving.

By naming David "shepherd" in the act of anointing him king, the elders subtly rehabilitate the term "king." Saul had fairly ruined the word
during his reign—he took it as a license to set himself up as sovereign in
place of God, bullying instead of blessing. But kingship in Israel was never
meant to usurp the kingship of God. The elders, whether by intention or
instinct, know the importance of words. By setting "king" in a field of
meaning dominated by "shepherd," the word king comes to be understood
as a kind of shepherd; his rule, in terms of care. The words we choose and
the way we use them affect the way we think and the lives we live: king,
yes; but in the context of shepherd.

JERUSALEM CAPTURED: "THE CITY OF DAVID" (5:6–10)

5:6 The king and his men marched to Jerusalem against the Jebusites, the inhabitants of the land, who said to David, "You will not come in here, even
the blind and the lame will turn you back"—thinking, "David cannot come
in here." [7] Nevertheless David took the stronghold of Zion, which is now the
city of David. [8] David had said on that day, "Whoever would strike down the
Jebusites, let him get up the water shaft to attack the lame and the blind,
those whom David hates." Therefore it is said, "The blind and the lame shall
not come into the house." [9] David occupied the stronghold, and named it the
city of David. David built the city all around from the Millo inward. [10] And
David became greater and greater, for the LORD, the God of hosts, was with
him.

Jerusalem, the dominant city in biblical history, now enters the story. The strategy of the choice of the place from which to rule is clear. If David is to rule a united Israel and Judah, it is important to have a central site equally acceptable to both. Jerusalem, on the border between Israel and Judah, but associated with neither, fit the bill.

What is not clear is the way in which he takes it. Jerusalem was a city occupied by a pre-Israelite tribe, the Jebusites, and had to be conquered before it could be used as the new capital. The cryptic description of the military operations and the crude language used in the account are simultaneously the delight of scholars who love puzzling out enigmatic passages and the despair of everyone else who would prefer the Bible to read plain and simple. The cryptic instruction "Get up the water shaft to attack . . . " is the puzzle. The meaning of all the key words is obscure and disputed. There was a tunnel in Jerusalem that provided access to the spring Gihon just outside the city wall. Was this tunnel used to penetrate the fortification? Scholars try out different combinations of word meanings and archaeological data to come up with a workable scenario. None of them quite works.

And crude language: Three times the phrase "the blind and the lame" is used in the passage (vv. 6 and 8) in a derogatory sense. For readers trained by these same scriptures to treat the handicapped and disadvantaged with respect, this is an offense. Again, there is no lack of ingenuity in interpretations designed to soften the language and let David off the hook of being discriminatory toward the disadvantaged. But maybe it is better simply to accept David as a child of his crude Iron Age culture, with all its built-in prejudices and insensitivities, and notice how his descendant, the "Son of David," does well what he did badly. For Matthew tells a story of Jesus, parallel to that of David, that reverses precisely what is most offensive in this David story. David and Jesus both enter Jerusalem to establish the rule of God; they both clear the place of those who defile it; but the fate of the "blind and the lame" is turned around. "Those whom David hates" are the very ones that Jesus cures.

When seen in parallel, the stories in Samuel and Matthew are a study in contrasts. Matthew, who knew the Hebrew stories well, also knew how to use them as background, whether for comparison or contrast, to give depth to his writing. When David enters the city of Jerusalem as the new king of Israel to establish a capital for his kingly rule, clearing the place of the pagan Jebusites, the blind and the lame are referred to as "those whom David hates." When Jesus, a thousand years later, enters the same city, acclaimed as both king and Son of David, he clears the area of all who defiled the holy place with their exploitative practices. His first act, after the cleanup, is to heal "the blind and the lame": "The blind and the lame came to him in the temple, and he cured them" (Matt. 21:14).

It took a thousand years, with considerable help along the way from the prophets, most notably Isaiah (29:18; 35:3–6; 42:7; 56:8; 61:1), to transform attitudes toward the disabled from denigration to dignity. This shift in attitude and sensitivity is by no means accomplished yet, but the authority for the shift (the "Son of David") is firmly established.

Still, this also must be noted: Later in the story David will deal with an actual individual who is lame—Mephibosheth (2 Samuel 9). David will bring him into the city and into his home with honor, treating him with the utmost respect. David's actions are better than his words.

Zion (v. 7) was probably a fortification within Jerusalem. The word enters the biblical story for the first time here and becomes a common synonym for Jerusalem. Over the years it develops extensive theological connotations. The root meaning of the word is not clear.

The Millo (v. 9) was a major earthen construction of some kind—wall, tower, or terracing.

17 sons – didn't count daughters → TAMAR

HOUSE AND FAMILY (5:11–16)

> 5:11 **King Hiram of Tyre sent messengers to David, along with cedar trees, and carpenters and masons who built David a house.** [12] **David then perceived that the LORD had established him king over Israel, and that he had exalted his kingdom for the sake of his people Israel.**

King Hiram, David's immediate royal neighbor to the north, welcomes David into the company of kings by building him a palace. David interprets the welcome as God's confirmation of his new leadership (as king) and work (kingdom).

> 5:13 **In Jerusalem, after he came from Hebron, David took more concubines and wives; and more sons and daughters were born to David.** [14] **These are the names of those who were born to him in Jerusalem. . . .**

Family details, supplementing the Hebron listing in 3:2–5, further confirm the solidity and legitimacy of David's rule. In addition to the six sons born in Hebron, eleven more are brought into the world in Jerusalem. Seventeen sons—an impressive progeny! (A slightly different listing is recorded in 1 Chronicles 3:1–9.) The only name in this list that will reenter the story later is that of Solomon.

These three items together—the capture of Jerusalem, recognition by King Hiram, the flourishing family—combine to say, in effect: "David is here to stay. David reigns from a firm foundation."

PHILISTINES AGAIN (5:17–25)

> 5:17 **When the Philistines heard that David had been anointed king over Israel, all the Philistines went up in search of David . . . ¹⁸ . . . and spread out in the valley of Rephaim. ¹⁹ David inquired of the LORD, "Shall I go up against the Philistines? . . . " The LORD said to David, "Go up; for I will certainly give the Philistines into your hand." ²⁰ So David came to Baal-perazim, and David defeated them there. . . . ²¹ The Philistines abandoned their idols there, and David and his men carried them away.**
>
> **²² Once again the Philistines came up, and were spread out in the valley of Rephaim. ²³ When David inquired of the LORD, he said, "You shall not go up; go around to their rear, and come upon them opposite the balsam trees. ²⁴ When you hear the sound of marching in the tops of the balsam trees, then be on the alert; for then the LORD has gone out before you to strike down the army of the Philistines." ²⁵ David did just as the LORD had commanded him; and he struck down the Philistines from Geba all the way to Gezer.**

David's firmly established and often-confirmed rule is now challenged by Israel's old enemies, the Philistines. The Philistines had brought down the kingdom of Saul; they now set out to bring David down.

David had acquired a well-earned reputation for fighting Philistines during the years he was Saul's servant. Now as king he returns to his old work. It turns out that he has not lost his touch—he is as good at defeating Philistines as ever.

Two successive battles are mentioned, both in the Valley of Rephaim, just south of Jerusalem. Both are preceded by acts of prayer: David is a king under orders; unlike Saul, he is a king who serves a King.

David is equally successful in both battles, although the strategy, under God's guidance, is different for each. Except for a glancing mention in chapter 8:1, this is the last we hear of the Philistines. David will fight other battles against other enemies in the years to come. But the Philistine threat, which has dominated for so long, is over.

Somewhere along the way "Philistine" has entered our vocabulary as a symbol-word: "Philistine" is in common use still to refer to the God-defiant person, the might-is-right spirit, the coarse and insensitive soul. But Philistines do not last. They are like crustaceans—all their armor on the outside, fierce in appearance but no match for a soft-appearing vertebrate whose bones are invisible. It is fitting, and not at all surprising, that David, with his God-attentive and prayer-formed skeletal system, gets the last word.

THE ARK (6:1–23)

The ark of God, the ancient symbol of God's presence with Israel, has been in storage for a long time now at the house of "Abinadab on the hill," in the neighborhood of the village Kiriath-jearim. The story of its capture by the Philistines, subsequent return, and decision to store it with Abinadab was told earlier (1 Sam. 4:1–7:2). That all took place previous to both King Saul and King David. Now the ark reenters the story.

> 6:1 **David again gathered all the chosen men of Israel . . .** [2] **. . . to bring up . . . the ark of God. . . .** [3] **They carried the ark of God on a new cart, and brought it out of the house of Abinadab, which was on the hill. Uzzah and Ahio, the sons of Abinadab, were driving the new cart with the ark of God; and Ahio went in front of the ark.** [5] **David and all the house of Israel were dancing before the LORD with all their might, with songs and lyres and harps and tambourines and castanets and cymbals.**

David is now firmly enthroned as king in Jerusalem; meanwhile God is "enthroned on the cherubim" (v.2) of the ark of God. The ark of God was Israel's central symbol of God's sovereign and saving presence. From the time of the conquest of Canaan under Joshua's leadership, the ark, placed in the sanctuary at Shiloh, had provided a center for Israel's worship. But it has been a long time since this ark has provided such a center. For decades it has been tucked away in an obscure village.

And then David decides to bring the ark out of exile and establish it in a place of prominence. It is a strategic act, with enormous consequences for Israel.

With the political and military dimensions of his kingdom in place, David's action—bringing the ark of God to Jerusalem—proclaims that whoever he is as king is subordinate to the kingship of God: *God* is King; God is *King*. God rules authoritatively: There is no higher court of appeal. God rules comprehensively: There is no neutral ground or no-man's-land in which to take refuge or go into exile.

God's sovereignty dominates the theology of Israel. David sees to it now that it will also dominate the imagination and politics of Israel. He does it by reestablishing the ark at the center, not at Shiloh this time, but in Jerusalem.

The action of bringing up the ark answers a question that must have been in many minds: "Will David take to himself the prerogatives of divine kingship common in the ancient East? Or will he submit his kingship to the revelation of God given to the fathers and to Moses?" Bringing up the ark is David's answer: God, revealed through revelation, salvation, and providence, is the ruling center of Israel's life. The ark is placed where it can immediately shape the way Israel thinks and lives, regarding both God (theologically) and government (politically).

There is persistent and insidious pressure to assimilate the biblical revelation to the culture, constantly reinterpreting God in terms of the assumptions and needs of current affairs. In David's time, the danger was that God's rule would be understood in terms of the numerous myths of the surrounding king-gods. In our time, the danger is understanding God's rule in terms of voter preferences tabulated by pollsters. The biblical story and the way it is told exerts a continuous counterpressure on those who read it: The world must be brought under the politics of God, not God put to the service of the world's politics.

Worship is the single sufficient and appropriate response to the reality of God's sovereignty; it also implicitly exposes the illusion of the many countersovereignties. Nothing else will substitute for worship.

The ark of God is brought to Jerusalem in an act of worship (v. 5) to provide a center for worship. The means (worshiping) and the end (worship) are perfectly congruent. Biblical worship requires this congruence. It is false to use manipulative means to bring people to worship God. It is fatal to use the worship of God as a "cover" to legitimize human causes. It is always difficult for the worshiping community to arrive at this congruence, and the failures to do it are more conspicuous than the achievements. But this story at least puts the parts (the means and the end) on the same page together.

6:6 **When they came to the threshing floor of Nacon, Uzzah reached out his hand to the ark of God and took hold of it, for the oxen shook it. ⁷ The anger of the LORD was kindled against Uzzah; and God struck him there because he reached out his hand to the ark; and he died there beside the ark of God. ⁸ David was angry because the LORD had burst forth with an outburst upon Uzzah; so that place is called Perez-uzzah, to this day. ⁹ David was afraid of the LORD that day. . . . ¹⁰ So David was unwilling to take the ark of the LORD into his care in the city of David; instead David took it to the house of Obed-edom the Gittite. ¹¹ The ark of the LORD remained in the house of Obed-edom the Gittite three months; and the LORD blessed Obed-edom and all his household.**

But there is one person in this grand worshiping entourage who is not worshiping. His name is Uzzah.

At first appearance, Uzzah's death seems arbitrary, but a second look reveals something else. The clue is in verse 3: "They carried the ark of God on a new cart. . . . " That sentence catches the attention of the person who knows the origin and meaning of the ark. Moses had given explicit instructions on how the ark was to be transported: it was not to be touched by human hands, but reverently carried by Levites on poles inserted through rings attached to the ark (Exod. 25:13–14 and 1 Chron. 15:14–15). Uzzah and Ahio, the priests assigned to care for the ark in David's time, ignore the Mosaic instructions. Instead of carrying the ark on poles, they substitute advanced Philistine technology, an oxcart (see 1 Samuel 6). The oxcart was certainly more efficient, but it was also decidedly impersonal— the replacement of consecrated persons by a laborsaving machine, the impersonal eliminating the personal. Uzzah is the patron saint of those who uncritically embrace technology without regard to the nature of the Holy.

As the Christian imagination over the centuries has reflected on Uzzah's death, one insight reappears over and over: It is fatal to take charge of God. When the oxen stumble and Uzzah reflexively reaches out to keep the ark from sliding off, it is not an isolated act; it is Uzzah's *habit* to manage the ark, and supposedly along with it God-in-the-ark. The eventual consequence of this kind of obsessional management of God is death, whether slow or sudden. God will not be put and kept in a box, whether the box is constructed of crafted wood or hewn stone or brilliant ideas or fine feelings. We do not take care of God; God takes care of us. Uzzah is the person who, instead of losing himself in the worship of God, has God in a box and officiously assumes responsibility for keeping God safe from the mud and dust of the world. Men and women keep showing up in religious precincts who take upon themselves the task of protecting God from the vulgarity of sinners and the ignorance of commoners.

At the time, David is not in a position to take all this in; he sees the sudden death, not the life that led up to the death. Afraid to proceed, he calls off the parade and places the ark in storage again, this time with Obed-edom the Gittite in charge. "Gittite" probably means "a man from Gath," that is, a Philistine.

This is the third named Philistine to enter the David story: first Goliath, whom David killed, then Achish, who gave him protection, and now Obed-edom, whom he entrusts with a dangerous assignment. So much for the stereotype "Philistine." Philistines can also be used by God.

In the preceding chapter, which gave us the story of the fight against the

Philistines in the Valley of Rephaim, David named the place Baal-*perazim* (5:20). Here at the site of Uzzah's death, David names the place *Perez-uzzah* (6:8). The *paraz* in both place names links the two stories. It is the Hebrew verb that means "burst forth" or "break out" or "erupt." In both instances, it refers to God's action, divine energy erupting into the scene, but there is also a contrast: The first name is David's exclamation of delight at his salvation by God from a dangerous evil (the Philistines); the second name is David's burst of anger at God's judgment against supposedly safe religion (the priest). God arrives, but in his own way. His action is not always congenial to our expectations or desires. God is on David's side, but not "in his pocket."

> 6:12 **It was told King David, "The LORD has blessed the household of Obed-edom and all that belongs to him, because of the ark of God." So David went and brought up the ark of God from the house of Obed-edom to the city of David with rejoicing; . . . [15] with shouting, and with the sound of the trumpet.**
>
> [16] **As the ark of the LORD came into the city of David, Michal daughter of Saul looked out of the window, and saw King David leaping and dancing before the LORD; and she despised him in her heart.**

David's "leaping and dancing before the LORD" stands in stark contrast to his wife Michal's cool contempt from the sidelines (see also vv. 20 and 23). The contrast serves as both warning and rebuke to all who are more interested in the protocol of worship than in worshiping God.

> 6:17 **They brought in the ark of the LORD, and set it in its place, inside the tent that David had pitched for it; and David offered burnt offerings and offerings of well-being before the LORD. [18] . . . David . . . blessed the people . . . [19] and distributed food among all the people. . . . Then all the people went back to their homes.**
>
> [20] **David returned to bless his household. But Michal the daughter of Saul came out to meet David, and said, "How the king of Israel honored himself today, uncovering himself . . . as any vulgar fellow might shamelessly uncover himself!" [21] David said to Michal, " . . . I have danced before the LORD. . . . "**
> [23] **And Michal the daughter of Saul had no child to the day of her death.**

By his action, bringing the ark to Jerusalem, and by his manner, dancing before the Lord, David establishes worship at the center of the life of the people over whom he rules as God's king. If God is the central reality of existence in general and human life in particular, worship is our "real work." Nothing we do is more basic; nothing we do is an advance beyond it.

Biblical worship is rhythmic, comprising two elements: divine revelation and human response. There is a profound simplicity to worship, but it is an achieved simplicity, for many things are involved and much can go wrong. It is extremely important to get this right. But, as usual, the biblical account, instead of giving us a precise definition that we can use, provides us with a story in which we are invited to participate. When we listen well, this story shapes our imaginations to the nature and dangers of worship.

This story of David bringing the ark to Jerusalem is a skillful weave of the intricate threads that make up the tapestry of worship; entering this story, we become aware of both the intricacy and the simplicity.

Worship begins in divine revelation: Who God is, and what God does and how, is the first element. The ark of God provides a focus for this. In Israel, the ark gave visual witness to God in specific terms: salvation at the Red Sea (Moses' staff), revelation at Sinai (the stone tablets), providence in the wilderness (the jar of manna), the overarching sovereignty (the cherubim throne). "God" has a history; "God" is not a generalized abstraction, but a divine being with experienced content. The people's response in dancing and singing and feasting as they process to Jerusalem is the second element. The people let themselves be defined by the reality of God, and then respond appropriately.

But there is more to it than that. There always is in worship. Three names are prominent: David himself, Uzzah, and Michal. David holds the center: He leads the worship and worships; he both begins and concludes the story. Uzzah and Michal also hold prominent places, but negatively: In the context of worship they do *not* worship. Uzzah does not worship; he fussily *functions*—he manages a religious business. Michal does not worship; she critically *observes*—she evaluates performance by appearance. To be present at the place of worship and not to worship is both common and dangerous: refusal to worship the living God results in loss of life—death (Uzzah) and barrenness (Michal).

But David worships. The word "worship" does not occur here; instead, the metaphor "dancing" is used—and repeated four times (vv. 5, 14, 16, 21). Dancing as a metaphor for worship gives the sense that our response to God takes us out of ourselves, sets us free from the plod of merely getting across the street, pulls us into a divine dance.

David's primary orientation is to God, and his primary influence in history has been in worship. His work as king was soon over and his political (though not his theological) influence at an end. But his work in worship continued and flourished. The example he set and the psalms that he composed and modeled have a huge heritage and flourish still. Aside from

Jesus, David is the single most important influence on worship in Judaism and the church. David has influenced far more people by his worship than he ever did by his politics.

As this story, David bringing the ark to Jerusalem, has entered the life of Israel and church, it has given structure and insight and warning to the worshiping people of God. Christians sometimes pick up an echo of this leaping and dancing David story in Luke's account of the embryonic John leaping in Elizabeth's womb in the presence of Mary, newly pregnant with Jesus (Luke 1:41).

COVENANT AND PRAYER (7:1–29)

The pace and mood of the narrative change abruptly at this point. From the moment David is anointed king in Hebron (2:1–4), the story plunges from one dramatic episode to the next in breathless succession, a narrative equivalent of whitewater rafting. And then, suddenly, nothing. Still waters. The action stops.

But only apparently. What happens is that the action moves inward: David prays. There is plenty going on still, but it cannot be told in the same way. If we are impatient with anything other than fast-paced, emotion-evoking prose, we are in danger of missing the crisis-pivot implicit here. Walter Brueggemann names this chapter "the dramatic and theological center of the entire Samuel corpus. Indeed, this is one of the most crucial texts in the Old Testament for evangelical faith" (Brueggemann, *First and Second Samuel*, 253).

> 7:1 Now when the king was settled in his house, and the LORD had given him rest from all his enemies around him, ² the king said to the prophet Nathan, "See now, I am living in a house of cedar, but the ark of God stays in a tent." ³ Nathan said to the king, "Go, do all that you have in mind; for the LORD is with you."

Things are finally coming together for David. After the years of danger and struggle and waiting, fulfillment: "settled in his house" and "rest from all his enemies" (v. 1). But David is not ready for retirement—he is at the height of his ability and energy, and the momentum is up. He looks for the next thing to be done. He does not have far to look—he has just brought the ark of God to Jerusalem; he will now build a sanctuary for it, a place of worship. He will give architectural expression to the centrality and importance of the worship of God in Israel. He has established *his* place in Jerusalem; now he will establish *God's* place.

He announces his building plans to his pastor, the prophet Nathan, and gets his approval and blessing. There are times when circumstances are so clear and obvious and our motives so selfless and pure, that it hardly seems necessary to pray. And so, of course, neither David nor Nathan prays. What could be more appropriate at this point in Israel's history and David's life for bringing glory to God? At that moment, the sanctuary is as good as built.

> 7:4 **But that same night the word of the LORD came to Nathan: ⁵ Go and tell my servant David: Thus says the LORD: Are you the one to build me a house to live in? ⁶ I have not lived in a house since the day I brought up the people of Israel from Egypt to this day, but I have been moving about in a tent and a tabernacle. ⁷ . . . did I ever speak a word . . . saying, "Why have you not built me a house of cedar?" ⁸ Now therefore thus you shall say to my servant David: . . . ¹¹ . . . the LORD will make you a house. ¹² When your days are fulfilled and you lie down with your ancestors, I will raise up your offspring after you. . . . ¹³ he shall build a house for my name, and I will establish the throne of his kingdom forever. . . .**

After a night of prayer, Nathan withdraws the building permit. What looked so wonderful in the daylight of enthusiastic but prayerless good intentions is now seen to be quite inappropriate. God shows Nathan that David's building plans for God will get in the way and distract from God's building plans for David. God's word to David through Nathan is essentially this:

"You want to build me a house? Forget it, I'm building you a house. The kingdom that I am shaping here is not what you do for me but what I do through you. I'm doing the building here, not you. I'm not going to let you confuse things by launching a building operation on your own. If I let you fill Jerusalem with the sights and sounds of your building project—carpenters' hammers, masons' chisels, teamsters' shouts—before long everyone will be caught up in what *you* are doing, and not attentive to what *I* am doing. This is a *kingdom* that we are dealing with, and I am the king. I've gotten along without a so-called "house" for a long time now; where did you ever come up with the idea that I need or want a house? If there is any building to be done, I'm doing it. I've been working with you since your shepherd days, building a kingdom—a place where salvation and justice and peace can be realized. That is why you are here, to give visibility and representation to what I am doing, not to call attention to what you are doing. We have just had one such failure in Saul, and we are not going to have another. There will come a time when it is appropriate to build something like what you have in mind—your son, in fact, will do it—but this is not the time. First we have to get the concept of *my* sovereignty established in the people's imagination and practice—your kingship a witness to my kingship, not an obscuring of it. *That* is the house I am building—your kingship as witness and representation of my sovereignty. First things first."

This message of God through Nathan to David is dominated by a recital of what God has done, is doing, and will do. God is the first-person subject in twenty-three verbs in this message, and these verbs carry all the action: *God's* action. David, full of what he is about to do for God, is now subjected to a comprehensive rehearsal of what God is doing for David. Nathan's message continues to be incorporated into the life of contemporary praying communities of faith through Psalm 127: "Unless the LORD builds the house,/those who build it labor in vain."

> 7:18 **Then King David went in and sat before the LORD, and said, "Who am I, O Lord GOD, and what is my house, that you have brought me thus far? 19 And yet this was a small thing in your eyes, O Lord GOD; you have spoken also of your servant's house for a great while to come. May this be instruction for the people, O Lord GOD! . . . 22 Therefore you are great, O LORD God; for there is no one like you. . . . 23 Who is like your people, like Israel? . . . 25 And now, O LORD God, . . . confirm it forever; do as you have promised. . . . 27 For you, O LORD of hosts, the God of Israel, have made this revelation to your servant, saying, 'I will build you a house'; therefore your servant has found courage to pray this prayer to you. . . . 29 now therefore may it please you to bless the house of your servant, . . . with your blessing shall the house of your servant be blessed forever."**

"Then King David went in and sat before the LORD" (v. 18). David *sits.* This may be the most critical act that David ever does, the action that puts him out of the action. It is critical because this is the test that will qualify him for the kingship to which he has been anointed. By sitting down, David renounces royal initiative. He takes himself out of the driver's seat and deliberately places himself prayerfully before God the King. Some of the most significant prayers in the Psalter are the ones that announce and respond to God as King. David strikes the posture from which these prayers must be prayed. Psalm 93 is representative of several psalm prayers that worship God as king:

The LORD is king, he is robed in majesty;
    the LORD is robed, he is girded with strength.
He has established the world; it shall never be moved;
    your throne is established from of old;
    you are from everlasting.

The floods have lifted up, O LORD,
    the floods have lifted up their voice;
    the floods lift up their roaring.
More majestic than the thunders of mighty waters,
    more majestic than the waves of the sea,
    majestic on high is the LORD!
Your decrees are very sure;
    holiness befits your house,
    O LORD, forevermore.

As David sits before God and prays, his prayer shows that he has listened most carefully to God's word as delivered by Nathan. Nathan's sermon is a rehearsal of God in action—God the first-person subject across the board (twenty-three first-person verbs). The evidence that David has been listening shows up in the grammar of his prayer: He has been converted from talking about God as an impersonal object (v. 2) into addressing God in the second person. Seventeen times in this prayer David refers to God by name: God, LORD God, LORD, God of Hosts; he uses the personal pronoun for God over forty more times. From being full of himself and his plans for God, David has become fully attentive to God's plans for him. The prayer makes explicit a radical reversal from doing something for God to letting God do something for him: "For you O LORD of hosts, the God of Israel, have made this revelation to your servant, saying, 'I will build you a house'; therefore your servant has found courage to pray this prayer to you" (v. 27). And courage it did take, immense courage, to relinquish control and leave the initiative to God.

What we do not do for God is often far more critical than what we in fact do. God is the beginning, center, and end of the world's life—of existence itself. But we are often unaware of God's action except dimly and peripherally. Especially when we are in full possession of our powers—our formal education complete, our careers in full swing, people admiring us and prodding us onward—it is hard not to imagine that we are at the beginning, center, and end of the world, or at least that part of the world in which we are placed. Ambitious building projects, whether architectural or moral or programmatic, are dear to the religious spirit. But it is precisely at these moments that we are likely to need prophetic interference—we need a Nathan. We need to quit whatever we are doing and sit down. In sitting down, we let the dust raised by our furious activity settle; the noise generated by our building operations goes quiet; we become aware of the real world, *God*'s world.

Christians are characteristically afraid of being caught doing too little for God. But there are moments, far more frequent than we suppose, when doing nothing is precisely the gospel thing to do. Every once in a while an old heresy reappears that distorts this pregnant and worshipfully obedient "nothing" into an ill-conceived and irresponsible "nothing doing." Wrongheaded teachers emerge from time to time, telling us that since God does everything, we must train ourselves to do nothing, cultivating a kind of pious sloth: "The less we do for God, the more God can do for us." Others counsel stoic resignation to whatever happens, since all that happens is "the will of God." Still others misconceive a life of prayer and faith as acquiescence to the inevitable. But biblical and Davidic not-doing is neither sloth nor stoicism; it is a strategy.

When David sits down before God, it is the farthest thing from passivity or resignation—it is prayer. It is entering into the presence of God, becoming aware of God's word, trading in his plans for God's plans, letting his enthusiasm for being king with authority and strength to do something for God be replaced with zeal to become a king who would represent truly the sovereignty of God, the High King.

There is little danger that in such inaction we will end up with nothing to do. David did much before he sat down, and he did much afterward: God commands and we obey; God sends and we go. The Christian life is a gloriously active life as the Holy Spirit does the work of Christ in and through us; so there is no danger that in sitting before the Lord our legs will atrophy and we'll never be able to get up again. But there is great danger in getting so caught up in our God-plans that we will forget all about God. When David sat down, the real action started: not David making God a house, but God making David a house.

MORE FIGHTING (8:1–14)

8:1 Some time afterward David attacked the Philistines and subdued them; David took Metheg-ammah out of the hand of the Philistines.

As it turns out, this is the last mention of Philistines. It is hard to believe—this barbaric enemy, which dominated the life of Israel for so long, is now history. But the concept has continued—"Philistine" as a metaphor for the godless, the insensitive, the soul-defying life of the person who "in control" continues to live either ignorant of God or indifferent to God.

> 8:2 **He also defeated the Moabites. . . .** [3] **David also struck down King Hadadezer son of Rehob of Zobah. . . .** [6] **. . . and the Arameans became servants to David and brought tribute. The LORD gave victory to David wherever he went.** [7] **David took the gold shields that were carried by the servants of Hadadezer, and brought them to Jerusalem. . . .**
>
> [9] **When King Toi of Hamath heard that David had defeated the whole army of Hadadezer,** [10] **Toi sent his son Joram to King David, to greet him and to congratulate him. . . . Joram brought with him articles of silver, gold, and bronze;** [11] **these also King David dedicated to the LORD, together with the silver and gold that he dedicated from all the nations he subdued,** [12] **from Edom, Moab, the Ammonites, the Philistines, Amalek, and from the spoil of King Hadadezer son of Rehob of Zobah.**
>
> [13] **David won a name for himself. When he returned, he killed eighteen thousand Edomites in the Valley of Salt. . . .**

Most of David's fighting up until now has been defensive. Here he goes on the offensive. He expands the borders of Israel in every direction. Six nation groups (Philistia, Moab, Aram, Edom, Ammon, Amalek) and two kings (Hadadezer and Toi) are listed.

The writer understands this expansion as an expression of God's rule, in giving God's people space to live out the many dimensions of the covenant life: "The LORD gave victory to David wherever he went" is repeated twice (vv. 6 and 14).

Details from the Edomite war (vv. 13–14) found their way into the superscription of Psalm 60.

GOVERNMENT APPOINTMENTS (8:15–18)

> 8:15 **So David reigned over all Israel; and David administered justice and equity to all his people.** [16] **Joab son of Zeruiah was over the army; Jehoshaphat son of Ahilud was recorder;** [17] **Zadok son of Ahitub and Ahimelech son of Abiathar were priests; Seraiah was secretary;** [18] **Benaiah son of Jehoiada was over the Cherethites and the Pelethites; and David's sons were priests.**

David's foreign affairs are primarily military operations. On the domestic front he administers "justice and equity to all his people" (v. 15). The two words, justice and equity, are fundamental to God's sovereign rule.

David is as attentive to waging peace as to waging war. The security that resulted from military victories is put to the use of justice. But although these words are embedded in Israel's prayers (the Psalms) and social conscience (the Prophets), this kind of work never gets as much attention as war.

Administration is not as exciting as battle, but it is more important and the effects are more enduring. The list of names and offices shows the careful attention that David gave to helping his people live well. The flash of swords in battle catches most of the headlines, but the headlines do not last; the tedious decision making that takes place in meetings is largely unremarked, but the decisions enter the daily routines of people's lives and affect the ways we love and care for our neighbors.

MEPHIBOSHETH SHOWS UP (9:1–13)

> 9:1 **David asked, "Is there still anyone left of the house of Saul to whom I may show kindness for Jonathan's sake?"** [2] **Now there was a servant of the house of Saul whose name was Ziba, and he was summoned to David. . . .** [3] **. . . Ziba said to the king, "There remains a son of Jonathan; he is crippled in his feet." . . .** [5] **Then King David sent and brought him. . . .** [6] **Mephibosheth . . . fell on his face and did obeisance. David said, "Mephibosheth!" He answered, "I am your servant."** [7] **David said to him, "Do not be afraid, for I will show you kindness for the sake of your father Jonathan; I will restore to you all the land of your grandfather Saul, and you yourself shall eat at my table always."** [8] **He did obeisance and said, "What is your servant, that you should look upon a dead dog such as I?"**
> **. . .** [11] **. . . Mephibosheth ate at David's table, like one of the king's sons.** [12] **Mephibosheth had a young son whose name was Mica. And all who lived in Ziba's house became Mephibosheth's servants.** [13] **Mephibosheth lived in Jerusalem, for he always ate at the king's table. Now he was lame in both his feet.**

Some people when they become successful use all their energy and resources protecting and guarding their success. Others go out of their way looking for ways to share what they have, extending the realm of blessing. David went looking for ways to be generous.

The name of Mephibosheth was introduced to us as an aside in the account of Ishbaal's assassination (4:4); Mephibosheth was lame, his feet ruined when his nurse dropped him in her panicked escape from the Philistines after the defeat of Saul and Jonathan, as the household servants ran for refuge to the safety of a small village across the Jordan, Lo-debar. He was five years old. Mephibosheth was never again able to walk. He grew up in obscurity, lame. That much we can piece together from that single verse of introduction in chapter 4. Now we get the story.

His birth name was probably Meribbaal (see 1 Chron. 9:40). Mephibosheth may have been a nickname ("Seething Dishonor") that others gave him, calling attention to his victimized life. But this is conjecture.

When David asks if there is anyone left of Saul's family "to whom I may show kindness for Jonathan's sake" (v. 1), he is asking, in effect, "Is there any one left in the enemy camp that I can love?" David is not looking for a replacement for the rare and exquisite love that he and Jonathan enjoyed for too short a time (see 1 Samuel 20); he is looking for an *enemy* to love.

For there are still people loyal to Saul who do not like David. After Saul's death, Abner had tried to pull the Saul forces together by making Ishbaal king and running the kingdom from behind scenes. With Abner's death and Ishbaal's assassination, that attempt collapsed, but Saul loyalists did not disappear. Any Saul descendant was a potential king, offering a possibility, however remote, for a restoration of the Saul monarchy. David is not so secure that he can afford to ignore such threats. And it is just such a threat that he invites into his home.

The word translated "kindness" in our text is one of those large Hebrew words that radiates a spectrum of meanings like a rainbow of colors from a diamond in the sunlight: kindness, love, steadfast love, covenantal friendship, loyal love, and justice. It is a favorite word among the psalmists to convey God's characteristic relationship with us; it is a favorite word of prophets to designate our most appropriate relationship with one another. The story of David and Mephibosheth conveys many of these meanings; the story is better than a definition.

In his place of secure power, David exercises that power by looking for a way, and ways, to love. At the time that he and Jonathan made their friendship-covenant, neither knew which of them would end up king of Israel—what they promised each other, though, was that whoever ended up king, love, not power, would characterize their relationship; love, not vengeance; love, not convenience.

David's first word to Mephibosheth is the speaking of his name (v. 6). Mephibosheth is recognized as a person. He is not a nameless exile; he is not a subcategory of victim. He has a name, and David goes to the trouble to learn it: Mephibosheth. If there was any shame or dishonor associated with this name through the years, as some conjecture—a name that he was called rather than a name by which he was addressed—it is wiped clean of ignominy as David addresses him in loyal-love. The name is used seven times in this story of their meeting, without a hint of denigration in the usage. From now on, Mephibosheth will be defined by covenant (the Jonathan and David covenant), not etymology. He will get his identity not from a lexicon, but from love.

The nature of loyal-love is clarified in David's words of reassurance, "Do not be afraid." It is a phrase common in biblical narrative. It is frequent because there is much to fear in life. We constantly meet up with people who have more power than we have. How will they use that power, that authority? Will they diminish us, exploit us, use us, get rid of us? We learn to be cautious and put up defenses.

I was standing in line in a pharmacy one day with my five-year-old grandson. I picked up a conversation with the man ahead of me. We talked amiably until our turn to be served by the pharmacist. Later, as we were driving away, my grandson asked, "Did you know that man, Granddad?" I said that I did not. "Well, you shouldn't have talked to him then—it's dangerous to talk to strangers." My grandson had been carefully coached by his parents: It *is* dangerous to talk to strangers. We do well to be cautious, protective. David takes a risk when he invites Mephibosheth into his home; but it is also risky for Mephibosheth. He does well to be fearful.

And then we come before God, a God of power and mystery. How will God treat us? Will he punish us, destroy us, take away our freedom? Based on our previous experience, any of that is certainly possible, maybe even probable. That is why we need so much reassurance: "Do not be afraid." Relax, it's going to be all right. The phrase is often on the lips of angels, the emissaries of God's good news. It was often on the lips of Jesus, who regularly brought frightened and bewildered men and women into the very presence of God. Here it is on David's lips.

Mephibosheth has every reason to be deathly afraid of David at that moment. He has no reason to think that David is not out to get rid of him, the last vestige of Saul's family and therefore a potential rival to David's claim to the throne. And then he is disarmed and prepared for inclusion into the friendship-covenant that his father Jonathan and David had made before his birth.

David puts content into the word loyal-love when he turns over to Mephibosheth all the lands of his grandfather Saul so that he will have an independent income, assigns Ziba, once servant to Saul, to manage the farms and take care of his affairs, and then brings Mephibosheth into his household as one of the family. The love that germinates in covenant with a friend now issues mature in a search for an obscure heir, the restoration of confiscated lands, and daily hospitality at the royal table. Loyal-love is not greeting-card sentiment; it has the substance of the good earth beneath it and the regularity of three square meals a day to reinforce it.

In our culture in which love is so extensively romanticized and privatized, the Mephibosheth story provides stabilizing ballast to counter the stormy emotions that the weather of our times lets loose daily on our ideas and experiences of love. Emotions, of course, *are* an essential component of love—but not only ecstatic emotions, not exclusively sexually oriented emotions. There are also emotional dimensions to concern and compassion, to responsibility and kept promises. *Loyal-love* is a way of life that works for the good of another, brings out the best in the other, sees behind or beneath whatever society designates a person to be (disabled, inconvenient, a rival, worthless, dysfunctional), and acts to affirm a God-created identity. One of the ways in which the Christian community can contribute to the atrophied understandings and declining capacities for love in our society is to install the David and Mephibosheth story in the canon of the world's great love stories.

Mephibosheth reenters the story in chapters 16–19 in radically altered circumstances.

STILL MORE FIGHTING (10:1–19)

10:1 **Some time afterward, the king of the Ammonites died, and his son Hanun succeeded him. ² David said, "I will deal loyally with Hanun son of Nahash, just as his father dealt loyally with me." So David sent envoys to console him concerning his father. . . . ⁴ . . . Hanun seized David's envoys, shaved off half the beard of each, cut off their garments in the middle at their hips, and sent them away. ⁵ When David was told, he sent to meet them, for the men were greatly ashamed. . . .**

⁶ When the Ammonites saw that they had become odious to David, the Ammonites sent and hired the Arameans. . . . ⁷ When David heard of it, he sent Joab and all the army with the warriors. . . .

⁹ . . . [Joab] chose some of the picked men of Israel, and arrayed them against the Arameans; ¹⁰ the rest of his men he put in the charge of his brother Abishai, and he arrayed them against the Ammonites. ¹¹ He said . . . ¹² "Be strong, and let us be courageous for the sake of our people, and for the cities of our God; and may the LORD do what seems good to him." . . . ¹⁴ When the Ammonites saw that the Arameans fled, they likewise fled. . . .

¹⁵ But when the Arameans saw that they had been defeated by Israel, . . . ¹⁹ . . . they made peace with Israel, and became subject to them. . . .

War with the Ammonites began in an act of Davidic loyalty (v. 2). This act is virtually identical with the sentence that opens the Mephibosheth story: "Is there still anyone left of the house of Saul to whom I may show kindness for Jonathan's sake?" (9:1).

"Deal[ing] loyally" (10:2) and "kindness" (9:1) are the same word in the Hebrew text and link chapters 9 and 10 as expositions of David's character. This is the most comprehensive word in the Hebrew language for God's love. David aggressively looks for ways to express God's kindness, God's generous loyalty, God's compassionate care. David, working from a position of kingly strength, is intent on demonstrating his King's strength, God's strength, as a positive energy that helps, not a negative force that hurts. David is in the business of enlarging life, not shrinking it. Both persons targeted for his concern are connected with David's longtime enemy Saul: first Mephibosheth, Saul's grandson (chapter 9), and now Hanun, Nahash's son.

Nahash entered the biblical story as a brutal oppressor; King Saul defeated him (1 Samuel 11). The war against Nahash the Ammonite was Saul's first military venture. But during the years that followed, years in which Saul was obsessed with David as his enemy, Nahash apparently had befriended David, his motive along the lines of the proverbial "the enemy of my enemy is my friend." So at the death of King Nahash, David sends condolences to the king's son, Hanun, not forgetting Nahash's kindness to him and intending to express his loyal gratitude. But Hanun treats the messengers as spies, crudely and publicly humiliates them, and provokes David into an act of war. David's capacity for love has not matured to the level his descendant Jesus teaches and demonstrates. Instead of turning the other cheek, David goes to war.

The narrative is taut and tense. The words are few, but the resulting story is alive. At one level, the story is a historical chronicle of one of David's many wars. But two substories within the story give it dramatic energy that fuels reflection and memory, namely, Hanun's insult (vv. 4–5) and Joab's strategy (vv. 9–14).

Suspicious that David's emissaries, who are bringing bereavement condolences, are in fact spies, Hanun shaves off half of each man's beard, making them look ridiculous, and cuts off their garments at the hip, exposing their genitals. They entered Hanun's presence as respected members of David's royal court; they leave looking like clowns, figures of fun to be mocked and jeered by everyone on the street. There is an adolescent quality to Hanun's insult—the kind of hazing we associate with college pranksters.

Father and son, Nahash and Hanun, make quite a pair. Nahash made his mark in history by threatening to gouge out the right eyes of Israelites, his son joining him in the ranks of the infamous by his outrageous humiliation of David's men. Like father, like son, cruelties and indignities pass from one generation to another. Hanun inherits his father's mean streak.

Joab's strategy is the balancing counterstory. Joab is apparently outnumbered ("the battle . . . set against him both in front and in the rear," v. 9), but he gains a victory by his superior strategy, skillfully splitting his forces, leading one attack himself and putting his brother Abishai at the head of the other. The description is sketchy, but enough detail is given to present Joab as a canny military strategist.

The attention given to David's part in this particular military affair brackets David's rule with Saul's early leadership: Injustice and indignities are violations of God's ways, and God's king is responsible for restoring the order of the creation.

The story is tersely told. The basic war escalates as the Ammonites bring in the Arameans as allies. But by now David is far stronger militarily than either the Ammonites or Arameans have supposed, and these old border enemies of Israel are defeated. The Arameans become subject to Israel in a peace treaty. The Ammonites withdraw from the battle, but continue to be a threat. This continuing Ammonite hostility sets the stage for the approaching Bathsheba and Uriah scene (chaps. 11 and 12).

It may be good to pause at this point in the story and reflect on one of the continuing difficulties for us in reading this David story: the whole question of ethical behavior. David is responsible for a lot of killing. We fondly remember David as the man whom God called "a man after my heart" (Acts 13:22). We honor him as the "sweet psalmist of Israel" (2 Sam. 23:1, King James Version). He is a stock figure in the moral examples we set before our children. But the unavoidable fact is that he engaged in an enormous amount of killing. He comes to public notice in Israel by killing Goliath. He makes his mark in Saul's army by killing Philistines. He survives in the wilderness years by killing Amalekites and assorted border enemies. He summarily executes the assassins of Saul and Ishbaal. Large numbers of Ammonites and Arameans are enrolled in the death counts. To complicate the moral landscape still further, he marries many women, has a harem of concubines, and will soon add adultery to his dossier.

How do we maintain our moral equilibrium in all of this? How do we keep this story coherent with Moses and Jesus and Paul? In an age of diminishing respect for life and accelerating violence on all fronts—child abuse, spousal abuse, tribal wars, international conflicts, abortion, euthanasia, suicide, sexual harassment, the nuclear threat—what do we make of the seemingly unembarrassed inclusion of David in the story of our salvation?

This is a question that cannot be left unanswered. Various attempts are made from time to time to deal with it. But overall what helps most, so that we do not interfere with or distort the story, is simply to accept and appreciate the conditions in which it is given.

This is quite obviously not a story of moral uplift. The story of David is not provided to show us how to live. David is not a moral example. There is a long history in the church of "pious" reading that overlooks or suppresses any behavior that doesn't fit our ethical norms. But there is no hint of this in the narrative itself. This is "unlaundered history" (Brueggemann, *First and Second Samuel*, 3). These are the men and women with whom God works. They turn out to be no better or worse than the people with whom he works still, the very ones we face in the mirror every morning and rub shoulders with every day.

Holy history is not utopian history—the age of the Bible was not a "golden age" that we are trying to reproduce in utopian terms. It is rather an affirmation that *these* are the conditions and people that provide the stuff of salvation. The biblical story, from beginning to end, is told in terms of the social, cultural, political, and ethical world as it is. God's revelation is not imposed from without, the rendition of a moral and spiritual utopia that descends into our midst, which we can then enter. God's kingdom works from the inside, taking whatever is given at any one time as stuff to reveal God's presence and will. Morality is not a precondition for holiness or salvation.

The surprising thing in all this is that a fine ethical and moral conscience is capable of asserting itself in culturally uncongenial conditions: Iron Age assumptions regarding war and polygamy and power provide the conditions, but do not control the outcome: In these conditions, David can act honorably with his enemy, be rebuked by his pastor, and pray for forgiveness for his sins. It is hard to imagine a culture less congenial to God's program than Canaanite society.

God embraces us, sin and all, in the act of shaping our salvation. God is not scrupulous in choosing men and women in the work of establishing and developing the kingdom among us. God uses flawed David just as David will use mean Joab.

The entire biblical story—and this story within the story, the David story, never lets us forget it—is primarily a *God* story, not a human story. This is the narrative of what God does to save us, not what we do to please

God. We are always wanting to take over this story, to find ways of doing it on our own so that God becomes a pleased spectator to our finely wrought lives. This, of course, does not mean that there is nothing we can do to please God; there is much—our human believing and obedience are insistently and constantly worked into the story of what God is doing. But it is also quite clear that nothing we do is either the first or the last word in this world of God's sovereignty and salvation.

It is particularly important at this point in the story to understand the theological structure of the story that we are reading, namely, that this is a revelation of the ways of God among us and not a moral handbook with illustrated lessons on how to behave. David's behavior at this point takes a precipitous descent into actions that are particularly unattractive and even abhorrent. But even at its human worst, David's life continues to provide the material that reveals God at God's best.

19. David's Sin with Bathsheba and Uriah
2 Samuel 11–12

BATHSHEBA (11:1–27a)

The Ammonite war, set off earlier by the demeaning insult by Hanun (10:4–5), now resumes. This war provides the background setting for David's infamous adultery.

Two names are unforgettably linked with David: Goliath and Bathsheba. The two names are well established in the memory of even casual readers of the Bible. The physical forms attached to the names could hardly be more different: Goliath—the ugly, cruel giant; Bathsheba—the beautiful, gentle woman. Goliath, an evil tyrant; Bathsheba, an innocent victim. But different as Goliath and Bathsheba are in character and appearance, there is a similarity in the place they hold in David's life. Both bring him into places of testing. The giant and the woman enter David's life at contrasting times. In the meeting with Goliath, David is young, unknown, and untested. In the meeting with Bathsheba, David is mature, well known, and thoroughly tested and tried. In the first meeting, David emerges triumphant; in the second meeting, he goes down in defeat. The common element in the two meetings is God. For this story too, for all its moral and human pathos, is primarily a story of God's purposes worked out in David's life.

> 11:1 **In the spring of the year, the time when kings go out to battle, David sent Joab with his officers and all Israel with him; they ravaged the Ammonites, and besieged Rabbah. But David remained at Jerusalem.**
>
> ² **It happened, late one afternoon, when David rose from his couch . . . that he saw from the roof a woman bathing; the woman was very beautiful.** ³ **David sent someone to inquire about the woman. It was reported, "This is Bathsheba daughter of Eliam, the wife of Uriah the Hittite." ⁴ So David sent messengers to get her, and . . . he lay with her. . . . Then she returned to her house. ⁵ The woman conceived; and she sent and told David, "I am pregnant."**

⁶ So David sent word to Joab, "Send me Uriah the Hittite." . . . ⁷ When Uriah came to him, David asked how Joab and the people fared. . . . ⁸ Then David said to Uriah, "Go down to your house, and wash your feet." . . . ⁹ But Uriah slept at the entrance of the king's house with all the servants of his lord, and did not go down to his house. ¹⁰ When they told David, "Uriah did not go down to his house," David said to Uriah, "You have just come from a journey. Why did you not go down to your house?" ¹¹ Uriah said to David, "The ark and Israel and Judah remain in booths; . . . shall I then go to my house, to eat and to drink, and to lie with my wife? . . . I will not do such a thing." ¹² Then David said to Uriah, "Remain here today also, and tomorrow I will send you back." . . .

¹⁴ In the morning David wrote a letter to Joab, and sent it by the hand of Uriah. ¹⁵ In the letter he wrote, "Set Uriah in the forefront of the hardest fighting, and then draw back from him, so that he may be struck down and die." ¹⁶ . . . [Joab] assigned Uriah to the place where he knew there were valiant warriors. ¹⁷ . . . some of the servants of David among the people fell. Uriah the Hittite was killed as well. ¹⁸ Then Joab sent and told David all the news about the fighting; ¹⁹ and he instructed the messenger, "When you have finished telling the king all the news about the fighting, . . . ²¹ . . . you shall say, 'Your servant Uriah the Hittite is dead too.'"

²² So the messenger went, and came and told David . . . ²³ . . . , "The men gained an advantage over us, . . . ²⁴ . . . some of the king's servants are dead; and your servant Uriah the Hittite is dead also." ²⁵ David said to the messenger, "Thus you shall say to Joab, 'Do not let this matter trouble you, for the sword devours now one and now another; press your attack on the city, and overthrow it.' And encourage him."

²⁶ When the wife of Uriah heard that her husband was dead, she made lamentation for him. ²⁷ When the mourning was over, David sent and brought her to his house, and she became his wife, and bore him a son.

It is spring. David's army has gone to finish off the Ammonites, the war that Joab had begun earlier (chap. 10). David stayed behind. He is by now well established as king, with no need to prove himself in battle. But as we see him withdrawing from front-line participation with his people in battle, a shadow darkens the page. Is staying at home symptomatic of an anemia of soul? Is he pulling back from life itself? We do not have to wait long for an answer.

One afternoon while walking on the palace roof, positioned so that he can see into the courtyards of nearby houses, he sees a woman bathing. She is extraordinarily beautiful. He sends for her, takes her to his bed, and then discards her, sending her home. Her name is Bathsheba. Her husband is off fighting in the Ammonite war. A month or so later Bathsheba learns that she has conceived and sends word to David, "I am pregnant" (v. 5).

David, masterful at dealing with problems, handles this one by sending for Uriah, giving him a few days off under the pretext of getting his first-hand report on how the war is going. He expects him to go immediately to his wife and the marital bed, so that he will think he is responsible for the pregnancy. ("Wash your feet," v. 8, is a euphemism for sexual intercourse.) But Uriah is a loyal soldier who does not feel right about enjoying his wife while his fellow soldiers are roughing it out on the battlefield, so he spends the night on the porch of the palace. Uriah's moral restraint is an implicit rebuke to David's immoral indulgence. David tries again, but finding that Uriah cannot be manipulated, sends him back to the battlefield with a letter to his general, Joab, instructing Joab to place Uriah in the thick of the fighting, where he will be certain to get killed. Joab, an old hand at intrigue, falls in with David's scheme. Uriah is killed in the next day's battle. Word comes back to David reporting the death. After her requisite time of mourning is complete, David sends for Bathsheba and marries her.

We are not prepared for such a David. What began as a lustful whim developed into an enormous sex-and-murder crime. How does such sin happen? As with most sins, gradually and unobtrusively.

This one, it turns out, can be traced along the tracks left by a seemingly amoral verb, *send*. But as we read the story, we gradually realize that this is not a morally neutral word; it signals the impersonal exercise of power. By following the use of this verb we can trace David's descent from love and obedience into calculation and cruelty. Verb by verb, we watch David remove himself from compassionate listening and personal intimacy with others to taking a position outside and above others, giving orders, exercising power.

The passage begins with the curt phrase "David *sent* Joab (v. 1). We notice nothing amiss at this point; it is David's work to give assignments to his officers, to send them off with orders. But two verses later (v. 3), David *sent* to inquire about Bathsheba; this is an exercise of the same authority, but not exactly now in the line of his work. By the time the word occurs the third time (v. 4), as "David *sent*" and got Bathsheba in order to go to bed with her, we know that something has changed: the power that David legitimately employs to govern the kingdom is now being used to indulge a personal whim. The power that so notoriously corrupts those who have it has corrupted David. The corruption is evident in a cluster of three "sendings" in a single verse (v. 6): "So David *sent* word to Joab, '*Send* me Uriah the Hittite.' And Joab *sent* Uriah to David." The repeated verbs are employed to exhibit a ruthless use of bare power, cut free from the constraints of morality or responsibility or personal relationship. There is now nothing holding David back; the adrenaline of power is surging in his veins. We learn that he instructed Joab to have Uriah killed in battle and *sent* Uriah on his way to deliver his own death warrant (v. 14). After he had accomplished his cover-up, "David *sent*" for Bathsheba a second time and married her (v. 27).

Two other occurrences of "send" in the story subtly prepare us for the truth that David, despite his seemingly successful venture into the exercise of depersonalized royal power, was not so nearly in control as he supposed: Bathsheba "*sent* and told David, 'I am pregnant' " (v. 5); Joab "*sent* and told David all the news about the fighting" (v. 18), letting him know that he understood exactly what he was up to. The operations of Bathsheba's fertile womb and Joab's conniving mind both eluded David's control.

There is a final and decisive use of "send" in this story: "And the LORD *sent* Nathan to David" (12:1). Now *God's* sovereignty comes into play. And that is the end of David's detour into "playing god" with people's lives. God and only God is sovereign.

Such is the story. It is a story repeated with variations over and over and over through the centuries. Sin stories, after a while, tend to sound pretty much alike—virtually all sins ring changes on the theme of wanting to be gods ourselves, taking charge of our own lives, asserting control over the lives of others. Since there are only a finite number of ways to do this, no one of us reading this story has any difficulty finding himself or herself in it. Nor does finding ourselves in this story, whether in fact or imagination, surprise us. We are sinners. The precise details of our sin may not correspond to David's, but the presence and recurrence of sin does. The moment we recognize our common sin bond with David, we are ready for the only real surprise in this story, the forgiveness story that develops out of the sin story.

NATHAN (11:27b–12:15a)

11:27b **But the thing that David had done displeased the LORD,** 12:1 **and the LORD sent Nathan to David. He came to him, and said to him, "There were two men in a certain city, the one rich and the other poor.** 2 **The rich man had very many flocks and herds;** 3 **but the poor man had nothing but one little ewe lamb, which he had bought. He brought it up, and it grew up with him and with his children; it used to eat of his meager fare, and drink from his cup, and lie in his bosom, and it was like a daughter to him.** 4 **Now there came a traveler to the rich man, and he was loath to take one of his own flock or herd to prepare for the wayfarer who had come to him, but he took**

the poor man's lamb, and prepared that for the guest who had come to him."
[5] Then David's anger was greatly kindled against the man. He said to Nathan, "As the LORD lives, the man who has done this deserves to die; [6] he shall restore the lamb fourfold, because he did this thing, and because he had no pity."

[7] Nathan said to David, "You are the man! Thus says the LORD, the God of Israel: I anointed you king over Israel, and I rescued you from the hand of Saul; [8] I gave you your master's house, and your master's wives into your bosom, and gave you the house of Israel and of Judah; and if that had been too little, I would have added as much more. [9] Why have you despised the word of the LORD . . . ? You have struck down Uriah . . . and have taken his wife to be your wife. . . . [10] Now therefore the sword shall never depart from your house. . . . [11] Thus says the LORD: I will raise up trouble against you from within your own house. . . . "

The story takes a radical turn for the better when David's pastor, Nathan, shows up and preaches a sermon. At the moment David has no idea that he is listening to a sermon, for he is not sitting in a pew and Nathan is not standing in a pulpit. It is a sermon without a biblical text and there is not a single explicit reference to God in it. How could David have known what was going on?

Nathan is good at this. He stalks his prey. He tells an artless, simple story about a rich man with large flocks of sheep who needed a lamb for a dinner he was giving. Instead of taking a lamb from his own ample flocks, he cruelly and arrogantly took the pet lamb of a poor man living down the street. He killed the lamb and served it up to his guests.

David, drawn into the story and outraged at such cruelty, unsuspectingly takes up his role as a righteous judge and pronounces a death sentence on the rich man.

Nathan pounces, "You are the man!" (v. 7).

Since the first telling and writing of this sentence, there can hardly be a generation in which it has not been heard as personal address: "*You* are the man!" "*You* are the woman!" God's word, however it begins, and however long it takes to get there, always ends up direct and personal: me, you. The word of God is not about somebody else. It is never a general, abstract truth, but always personal address. The biblical revelation is never a commentary on ideas or culture or conditions; it is always about actual persons, actual pain, actual trouble, actual sin: you, me; who you are and what you have done; who I am and what I have done.

It is both easy and common to lose this personal focus and let the biblical story blur into generalized pronouncements, fuzzy cosmic opinions, and religious indignation. That is, in fact, what David does: He listens to Nathan preach a sermon about (he thinks) somebody else and gets all worked up over this unnamed person's terrible sin. This is the religion of the dormitory bull session, the TV spectacular, the talk-show gossip. It is the religion of moral judgmentalism, self-righteous finger-pointing, the religion of accusation and blame.

With each additional word in Nathan's sermon, David becomes more religious—he feels sorry for the poor man who lost his pet lamb, he seethes with indignation over the rich man who stole the lamb. Pitying and judging are religious sentiments that can be indulged endlessly, making us feel vastly superior to everyone around us, but not making a particle of difference in our lives. Like David: pitying and judging, becoming more religious by the minute, absorbed in a huge blur of moral sentimentality.

And then the sudden, clear focus: You are the one—*you!*

Nathan is the patron of all who break through the barriers of detachment and sentiment and address the person. The task of all Christian discourse, whether in word or music or image, is to get around third-person defenses and compel a second-person recognition, which enables a first-person response. Nathan is master of this art.

> **12:13 David said to Nathan, "I have sinned against the LORD." Nathan said to David, "Now the LORD has put away your sin; you shall not die. ¹⁴ Nevertheless, because by this deed you have utterly scorned the LORD, the child that is born to you shall die." ¹⁵ Then Nathan went to his house.**

Addressed personally, David answers personally, "I have sinned against the LORD" (v. 13). He abandons the pretentions of power. He quits giving out opinions on other people's lives (the poor man and the rich man). He realizes who he is before God—a sinner, a person in trouble, a person who needs help, a human being who needs God.

One of the frequent misunderstandings of the biblical story by outsiders is that a confession of sin is a groveling admission that I am a terrible person, a tactic sometimes described as "beating yourself up." Insiders to the story soon learn that the sentence "I have sinned against the LORD" is full of hope. It is full of hope because it is full of God.

The Latin phrase *felix culpa*, usually attributed to Augustine, puts the hope in a slogan: "O happy sin!" Only when we recognize and confess our sin are we in a position to recognize and respond to the God who forgives our sin.

Psalm 51 has traditionally been inserted into the David story at this point. The prayer that begins in a realization of sin develops into a joyful

participation in God's creation and salvation. Six other psalms have also
been identified and grouped with this one as "penitential" (Psalms 6, 32,
38, 102, 130, 143). When Augustine was dying and confined to his bed, he
had these seven "sin" psalms inscribed on the walls of his room so that he
could have them before him as his "last words." Some have supposed this
to have been morbid, but it was not—it was an exercise of lively joy in what
God does best: graciously forgive sins, gloriously save sinners.

There is a remarkable verbal resonance to this story of David standing
before Nathan in the later story of Jesus standing before Pilate. They are
both passion stories—David's passion for Bathsheba, Jesus' passion for us.
Pilate said of Jesus, "Here is the man!" (John 19:5), a clear echo of what
Nathan said to David: "You are the man!"

The sentences are alike in that they focus on a single, named person. It
is not by an outside idea or cause or law or dream or vision or organiza-
tion that we come to our senses and get our feet on the ground of reality,
but in *person*.

The sentences are at the same time unlike. Nathan's sentence brings
David (and therefore us) to the brink of God. David realizes who he is, not
as a power-wielding king in control of himself and others, but simply as
himself before God: It is God with whom he has to do. Pilate's sentence,
in contrast, brings Jesus to the brink of who we are, the ones with whom
God has to do, God for and with us.

These parallel sentences, separated in time by a thousand years, focus
the good news: The place of sin is not a place of accusation or condemnation, but of salvation. They effect recognition: In David before Nathan, I
recognize myself as the one in whom a sense of sin arouses a sense of God.
And they invite us: In Jesus before Pilate I'm invited by one who presents
God to me—I did not know God was that close, that kindly, that inviting.

The subtlety of sin is that very often it does not feel like sin when we
are doing it; it feels godlike, religious. It feels fulfilling and satisfying, a re-
play of the episode in Eden when the tempter said, "You will not die; . . .
you will be like God" (Gen. 3:4–5). David did not feel like a sinner when
he sent for Bathsheba; he felt like a lover, and what can be better than that?
David did not feel like a sinner when he sent for Uriah; he felt like a king
in control, and what can be better than that? Somewhere along the line he
had withdrawn from a life of obeying God; adoration of God had receded,
and obsession with self had moved in. When Nathan–*sent* by God!–walked
into the room that day, he recovered for David an awareness of God. Simultaneously he aroused David's sense of sin with his parable-sermon, and

David's heart was roused. In that double awareness of God and sin, David prayed, was forgiven, and took up his life again as God's king.

BATHSHEBA'S TWO CHILDREN (12:15b–25)

12:15b **The LORD struck the child that Uriah's wife bore to David, and it became very ill. ** [16] ** David therefore pleaded with God for the child. . . . ** [18] ** On the seventh day the child died. . . .**

[20] ** Then David rose from the ground, washed, anointed himself, and changed his clothes. He went into the house of the LORD, and worshiped. . . . ** [22] ** He said, "While the child was still alive, I fasted and wept; for I said, 'Who knows? The LORD may be gracious to me, and the child may live.' ** [23] ** But now he is dead; why should I fast? Can I bring him back again? I shall go to him, but he will not return to me."**

[24] ** Then David consoled his wife Bathsheba, and went to her, and lay with her; and she bore a son, and he named him Solomon. The LORD loved him, ** [25] ** and sent a message by the prophet Nathan; so he named him Jedidiah, because of the LORD.**

Not all sincere prayers are answered on our terms. David, the most notable pray-er in the history of faith (the Psalms provide the documentation), does not get what he asks for in his prayer. David prays for the healing of his sick child. It is a prayer soaked in repentance for his sin; it is a prayer undergirded and intensified with seven nights of fasting; it is prayer supported by "the elders." And the child dies.

With this prayer, we are in the company of other notable prayers of puzzling outcome: Job's prayer for an answer to his suffering, Jesus' Gethsemane prayer (Mark 14:36), Paul's prayer for the removal of his "thorn" (2 Cor. 12:8–10). It is not quite accurate to say that these prayers were not answered; they *were* answered—Job's "out of the whirlwind"; Jesus' in "what you [Father] want"; and Paul's in "My grace is sufficient for you." Magnificent answers, each one, but not exactly what was asked for. And David? The death of his prayed-for baby sends him devoutly "into the house of the LORD," where he worships (v. 20), and then in compassion to his wife Bathsheba, whom he "console[s]" (v. 24). He has just emerged from an episode in which he has been all but oblivious of God, attempting to assert his own mastery of life, and in which he has been cruelly indifferent to the people around him: Bathsheba was an object; Uriah an obstruction; Joab a tool. The "answer" to David's prayer is his rehabilitation into a person capable of humble prayer before God and tender love for others, qualities that he had "loved long since, and lost awhile" (John Henry Newman quoted from *The Hymnbook*, 1955 edition, no. 331, "Lead Kindly Light").

The birth of Solomon, briefly mentioned (vv. 24–25), is the occasion for another message from Nathan. The prophet who brought the message of God's judgment now delivers a message of God's love. The message, as so often among our Hebrew ancestors, is compressed into a name—Jedidiah, "Beloved of the LORD." The naming is timely, for David is about to be plunged into a sea of troubles (most of them of his own making—see 2 Samuel 12:10–12), which will last for the rest of his life. The named presence of Jedidiah/Solomon in the household keeps Nathan's love message accessible to David during those long and difficult years in which the judgment message is being worked out in the lives of his other children.

THE AMMONITES AGAIN (12:26–31)

12:26 **Now Joab fought against Rabbah of the Ammonites, and took the royal city. . . .** [30] **[David] brought forth the spoil of the city, a very great amount.** [31] **. . . Thus he did to all the cities of the Ammonites. Then David and all the people returned to Jerusalem.**

David's war with the Ammonites is now over. Except for historians, contemporary readers of the Bible are not much interested in the Ammonites. But it is important to note how significant they are in the telling of this part of the story (even as the Philistines were earlier). This most poignant and dramatic of all the David stories (Bathsheba and Uriah and Nathan) is bracketed by accounts at its beginning and end of war with the Ammonites. This juxtaposition of outside world events with internal person-to-person relations is not arbitrary—what goes on in the world is no less a part of the Christian life than what takes place in the soul. There is a widespread, nonbiblical, understanding of the spiritual life that attempts to develop faith in God quite apart from the conditions of culture and politics. But we never get the biblical revelation in a vacuum, isolated from the society in which it occurs. And so this nation of Ammon plays a more significant role in our understanding of the Christian life than we are used to giving it.

It is easy, and common, to concentrate exclusively on the David given to us in the dramatic and insight-filled encounters with Samuel, Saul, Goliath, Jonathan, Achish, Abigail, Mephibosheth, Bathsheba, and Nathan, to name only the obvious. But all the time these soul-revealing episodes are being told us, wars are being fought and a government is being administered. Biblical history is unrelentingly personal, but personal never means private or individualistic. In the biblical revelation the culture and its conditions are just as much a part of the story as prayer and grace—and just as ambiguous. For the outside world is no more suited to sorting out into "good guys and bad guys" than the inside world of sin and grace, judgment and salvation. Wonderful David is flawed; Joab is a mixed bag. Israel is not all good; Ammon is not all bad. As we read these narratives, we learn not to "take sides" too quickly, but rather to discern God's presence coming into view and God's will being worked out all over the place, and sometimes in persons and places where we least expect it. In the case of Ammon, we have already been told that the very evil King Nahash once befriended David when he was in need (10:2); later in this story the nation of Ammon will supply yet another helper for David when he was in desperate straits (17:27). We learn to be cautious about demonizing the outsider or enemy; we never know who might show up from the enemy camp as God's messenger.

20. David's Troubles with Sons and Others
2 Samuel 13–20

It is easy to exaggerate David; it takes considerable restraint *not* to. In his lifetime, he excited extravagant admiration, an admiration that has only increased in the subsequent centuries of holy history. He was (and is) a charismatic figure, who very quickly looms larger than life in the eyes of his admirers. Michelangelo sculpted in marble what most Jews and Christians have carved in their imaginations—a flawless David, the spirited human body in perfection.

But the biblical text does not give us a flawless David; this final stretch of storytelling has him plunged into a cataract of troubles, many of them of his own making. The narrator of this story refuses to idealize David, to set him above our common humanity in any way. Putting people on pedestals is a way of not having to deal with them (and the God who is working in them) in regular life. Telling a story theologically (as this story is told) does not mean dressing it up in Sunday best. It is absolutely essential that we acquire a sense of our common God-created, Jesus-saved, and Spirit-blessed selves that is unedited, unabridged, and unblinking. These final episodes in the David story make sure that we get the whole story, not just the so-called "inspiring" parts.

THE RAPE OF TAMAR (13:1–22)

13:1 **Some time passed. David's son Absalom had a beautiful sister whose name was Tamar; and David's son Amnon fell in love with her.** [2] **Amnon was so tormented that he made himself ill because of his sister Tamar.** .... [3] **But Amnon had a friend whose name was Jonadab, the son of David's brother Shimeah; and Jonadab was a very crafty man.** [4] **He said to him, "O son of the king, why are you so haggard . . . ?" Amnon said to him, "I love Tamar, my brother Absalom's sister."** [5] **Jonadab said to him, "Lie down on your bed, and pretend to be ill; and when your father comes to see you, say to him, 'Let my** sister Tamar come and give me something to eat. . . . " ⁶ So Amnon lay down, and pretended to be ill; and when the king came to see him, Amnon said to the king, "Please let my sister Tamar come and make a couple of cakes in my sight, so that I may eat from her hand."

⁷ Then David sent home to Tamar, saying, "Go to your brother Amnon's house, and prepare food for him." ⁸ So Tamar went to her brother. . . . She took dough, kneaded it, made cakes in his sight. . . . ¹¹ But when she brought them near him to eat, he took hold of her . . . "Come, lie with me, my sister." ¹² She answered him, "No, my brother, do not force me. . . . " ¹⁴ But he would not listen to her; . . . he forced her and lay with her.

¹⁵ Then Amnon was seized with a very great loathing for her. . . . Amnon said to her, "Get out!" ¹⁶ But she said to him, "No, my brother; for this wrong in sending me away is greater than the other that you did to me." But he would not listen to her. ¹⁷ He called the young man who served him and said, "Put this woman out of my presence. . . . " ¹⁸ . . . So his servant put her out. . . . ¹⁹ But Tamar put ashes on her head . . . and went away, crying aloud as she went.

²⁰ . . . So Tamar remained, a desolate woman, in her brother Absalom's house. ²¹ When King David heard of all these things, he became very angry, but he would not punish his son Amnon, because he loved him, for he was his firstborn. ²² . . . Absalom hated Amnon, because he had raped his sister Tamar.

This is the first installment of Nathan's prophesied consequences of David's sin against Bathsheba and Uriah: "I will raise up trouble against you from within your own house" (12:11). Trouble indeed: David's virgin daughter violated; David's firstborn son a rapist. David's violation of Bathsheba is now played out before his own eyes in his own home in Amnon's violation of Tamar; soon his murder of Uriah will be reproduced in Absalom's murder of Amnon.

The story is succinctly told without moralizing comment, the drama tense and impelling as one sin follows another in rapid succession.

The four names that dominate the story are all introduced in the first sentence: David and three of his grown children, Absalom, Tamar, and Amnon. Absalom and Tamar are by his wife Maacah; Amnon, his firstborn son, by Ahinoam.

The action begins in Amnon's lust for his half sister Tamar. It is a cultivated lust, meditated, imagined, nurtured, a lust that becomes an obsession. But Tamar is out of bounds to Amnon; he can see no way to get to her. As one of the virgin daughters of the king, she is kept under some kind of protective custody. Her very inaccessibility fuels Amnon's lust.

It so happens that Amnon's cousin, Jonadab, notices his behavior, and when he finds out the cause, comes up with a plan that will enable Amnon to consummate his lust. ("Shimeah" in v. 3 is the same as the "Shammah" of 1 Samuel 16:9, David's third oldest brother.) Jonadab is described as a "very crafty man" (v. 3). Amnon is not smart enough on his own to get to Tamar; he needs an accomplice, and Jonadab is more than ready to help. The world is full of people like this, eager to put their wits to the service of other people's evil. The intelligence and imagination that is generated daily in the cause of assisting others to acquire illegitimate power and indulge wrongful pleasure is astounding. By now "Jonadab" enterprises have sprung up all over the world, dedicated to helping men and women satisfy their sinful desires.

The Jonadab plan is ingenious. First, get King David involved. With David playing a leading role, no one will suspect anything amiss, least of all David himself, who as father and king, responsible for the moral and physical well-being of his family and kingdom, provides a respectable front for the "smoke-filled back room" maneuvering. Amnon is to involve his father by pretending to be sick, and then recruit his father to send Tamar to his bedside to comfort him with food. David, without the slightest suspicion that he is being used to further his son's raging lust, does what he is asked. Tamar is sent to Amnon.

And Tamar, also unsuspecting, does what she is told. She prepares food for Amnon. But more than simple nourishment is involved—she is not just to bring in a casserole and drop it off. She prepares a meal in his presence, and the food preparation itself seems to serve as a kind of ritual of comfort, elaborate and time-consuming. The word for the dish she prepares, here translated "cakes," has a sense of "soul food"—as nurturing emotionally as it is nutritionally. The loving attention Tamar gives to the meal is to provide leisurely solace to her sick brother. Meanwhile, tension builds in the narrative: We sense that while Tamar innocently and affectionately is serving her brother, he is calculating how to get her into his bed.

With an atmosphere and setting of intimacy well established, Amnon orders the servants out of the room. Amnon now has his sister where he wanted her, and proceeds to pull her into bed with him. She refuses, protesting, "Don't make me do this! Don't hurt me! This kind of thing isn't done among our people. You'll ruin us both. Where would I ever show my face? And you—you'll be out on the street in disgrace. Please, please! Ask our father; he'll let you marry me."

The last plea, for Amnon to go to David and request marriage with her, is probably a desperate attempt to buy time, for Israel had traditions and regulations prohibiting such a marriage (Lev. 18:9, 11; 20:17; Deut. 27:22), although Abraham and Sarah had just such a marriage (Gen. 20:12).

At any rate, it does not work. Amnon is not listening. Tamar has long since ceased being a person to be listened to or a sister to be treated with love. She has been depersonalized into a target for his lust. As far as Amnon is concerned, Tamar is nothing but a piece of pornography. Once she is depersonalized into a sex object, he can do whatever he wishes. Amnon rapes Tamar.

And then, "seized with a very great loathing" (v. 15), he hates her. Amnon throws her out of the house into the street and locks the door against her. First rape, then hate. And the hate is worse by far than the rape. It is possible (though not probable) to account for the rape as the result of out-of-control sexual desire. But hate is not merely physical, a matter of glands and hormones; it requires mind and emotions devoted to destruction. Internalized, the rape escalates into hate. Amnon has violated her body; now he violates her *soul*. This is sacrilege on a grand scale.

Violated Tamar now laments on a grand scale. What has taken place in the privacy of Amnon's room, Tamar proceeds to broadcast publicly through the streets of Jerusalem. She tears her beautiful virgin's robe, covers her head with ashes, and demonstrates her violation by dramatic gesture and loud weeping. (The "hand on her head," v. 19, was a customary expression of grief in those times, similar to our wringing of hands; see Jer. 2:37.) Tamar entered Amnon's house invited, expecting to express compassionate love, intending to help and heal; after an hour or so, she leaves the same house rejected and hated, her life in ruins, a "desolate woman" (v. 20). We never hear of Tamar again. She is not, though, forgotten—Absalom keeps her name and the reminder of her beauty alive by naming his beautiful daughter after her (see 14:27).

Absalom finds his sister, takes her home, and cares for her. His first response is to control the damages—minimize Amnon's rape as a family matter, keep it quiet, and, as we would say, "try to get over it."

When David learns of the rape he is angry, but his anger does not amount to anything. Anger that is provoked by arriving at a scene like this, anger that is an outrage over the desecration of life, can become a powerful fuel for justice, for setting things right, for getting wrongdoers back on the right path and helping the wronged. But nothing comes of David's anger. The reason given for his inaction, which amounted to a failure to pursue justice, is that he "loved" Amnon. The word love strikes a sour note in this setting, for we remember that this episode began with the observation that Amnon loved Tamar (vv. 1, 4). Now we are told that David loved Amnon. What kind of love is this? Amnon's "love" provides the impetus for rape; David's "love" is a mask for injustice.

Every time we read or hear the word "love," we do well to be alert to what is going on. It is a most glorious word and signals the best of which men and woman are capable; but it is also frequently used to hide violence and excuse indulgence. No word in our language is in more need of probing and testing of the kind that this story gives it, and that much later Paul gives it in 1 Corinthians 13. If subjected to Paul's vocabulary test on love, Amnon and David would both flunk.

David's anemic anger leaves Amnon unpunished and Tamar ignored. But that is not the end of it, for it starts Absalom on a path of violence. Absalom's first reaction to Tamar's rape is to keep it within the family and make the best of a bad situation (v. 20). But when his father fails to respond adequately, the injustice enters Absalom's soul; it seethes and rankles there. If David will not act justly, he will. He begins plotting vindication for Tamar and vengeance against Amnon. After two years of planning, he finds a way to pull it off.

THE MURDER OF AMNON (13:23–38)

13:23 **After two full years Absalom had sheepshearers at Baal-hazor, which is near Ephraim, and Absalom invited all the king's sons.** [24] **Absalom came to the king, and said, "Your servant has sheepshearers; will the king and his servants please go with your servant?"** [25] **But the king said to Absalom, "No, my son, let us not all go." . . .** [27] **But . . . he let Amnon and all the king's sons go with him. Absalom made a feast like a king's feast.** [28] **Then Absalom commanded his servants, "Watch when Amnon's heart is merry with wine, and when I say to you, 'Strike Amnon,' then kill him. . . . "** [29] **So the servants of Absalom did to Amnon as Absalom had commanded. Then all the king's sons rose, and each mounted his mule and fled.**

[30] **. . . the report came to David that Absalom had killed all the king's sons, and not one of them was left.** [31] **The king rose, tore his garments, and lay on the ground. . . .** [32] **But Jonadab . . . said, " . . . Amnon alone is dead. This has been determined by Absalom from the day Amnon raped his sister Tamar. . . . "**

[37] **But Absalom fled, and went to Talmai son of Ammihud, king of Geshur. David mourned for his son day after day.** [38] **Absalom, having fled to Geshur, stayed there three years.** [39] **And the heart of the king went out, yearning for Absalom; for he was now consoled over the death of Amnon.**

The setting for Absalom's murder of Amnon is not geographically certain—it is anywhere from four to twelve miles north of Jerusalem—but the occasion is clear: sheepshearing. Sheepshearing time in that culture was festival time, a time for celebration and feasting, a year of hard work rewarded with relaxed eating and drinking (we saw an earlier instance of this at Nabal's sheepshearing, 1 Sam. 25:2–8). Absalom uses his father to get Amnon to the feast where he will be killed. (Do we catch an echo here of Amnon using this same father to get Tamar to make him a meal so he could rape her?)

We are not used to seeing David "used." We are used to seeing David take the initiative in prayer and action, leading Israel decisively. But no longer. Absalom has moved into the power vacuum left by David's failure to execute justice, his failure to "act like a king."

But Absalom is no improvement over David. Stepping into the gap left by David's failure to carry out justice, Absalom displays none of David's wilderness virtues. There is nothing in Absalom equivalent to the years of disciplined patience through which David, though maligned by Saul, continued to honor him. Absalom is impetuous. Absalom waits, but he waits like a cat, ready to pounce. During the wilderness years we saw David wait for God, submitting his sovereignty to God's sovereignty. There is no evidence in Absalom of this patience of soul, and as the story develops none will appear. Absalom knows nothing of God's sovereignty. Absalom takes things into his own hands, oblivious that God's hands have anything to do with the affairs of the kingdom.

Absalom's long-brooded vengeance is quickly executed: He waits until the sheepshearing celebration is well under way, all the brothers having a good time eating and drinking, enjoying the brotherly camaraderie that the party provides. It is easy to imagine this large family of brothers and half-brothers making the most of this occasion to catch up on family gossip. When Absalom observes that Amnon is sufficiently drunk, he signals his servants to kill him. The murder is a bombshell. In the confusion, all the brothers quite naturally assume that they also are marked for assassination and run for their lives, escaping on their royal mules. When the report of Amnon's murder arrives in Jerusalem, it has expanded to the dimensions of a massacre—all the king's sons killed by Absalom in a royal bloodbath!

At this point, Jonadab shows up again in the story. Jonadab, Amnon's cousin (David's nephew), who provided the insider counsel that led to Amnon's rape of Tamar, is apparently also an insider to Amnon's murder by Absalom. He reassures the king that only Amnon had been marked for death at the sheepshearing festival. This is not wholesale, mindless violence, it is targeted vengeance. Absalom is simply carrying out justice. Has the king so soon forgotten about his daughter's rape? (Jonadab has a way of being in on the action without taking any responsibility for what happens. Earlier he provided the scheme that made the rape possible; here he seems to know all about the plans for the murder. He is the kind of person who shows up so often in areas of religion and politics—a parasite on persons in power. People like this do nothing creative or responsible, but always seems to be on hand with insider gossip or information that may be of use).

As his brothers are running for their lives—unnecessarily as it turns out—Absalom runs for *his* life. Absalom has no assurance that his father will be as lenient with him as he was with Amnon, and he does not hang around to find out: "Absalom fled" (vv. 34 and 37) to the east, across the Jordan River to his maternal grandparents. His grandfather Talmai was king of the small country of Geshur. His mother, Maacah, had grown up there; Absalom will spend the next three years in asylum with his grandparents.

There is no explicit evidence in the text that Absalom has anything more in mind in the murder of Amnon than avenging his sister's rape. And that has now been accomplished. The cost to Absalom is exile. Some readers of the text, though, suspect that Absalom's later attempt to replace his father on Israel's throne is already being considered. They interpret the sheepshearing banquet as a setup to kill his father and his brothers, leaving him as sole heir to the throne. But when his father declines the invitation, he has to settle for vengeance on Amnon.

We do not know whether Absalom has ambitions to the throne at this point, but if he does not, he soon will. The two years of Amnon-hate that went into planning the assassination banquet, plus the three years in exile from his father, have provided ample time to conceive himself as the rightful replacement for this king, delinquent as David has been in carrying out essential matters of justice in the kingdom. Later, Absalom will openly call into question the king's ability to manage his affairs (15:1–6). This has been a five-year gestation period for what will emerge in Absalom's later takeover of the government.

THE RETURN OF ABSALOM (14:1–33)

> 14:1 Now Joab son of Zeruiah perceived that the king's mind was on Absalom. ² Joab sent to Tekoa and brought from there a wise woman. He said to her, "Pretend to be a mourner. . . . ³ Go to the king and speak to him as follows." And Joab put the words into her mouth.
>
> ⁴ When the woman of Tekoa came to the king, she . . . said, "Help, O king! ⁵ . . . Alas, I am a widow. . . . ⁶ Your servant had two sons, and they fought with one another in the field . . . and one struck the other and killed him.

⁷ Now the whole family has risen against your servant. They say, 'Give up the man who struck his brother, so that we may kill him. . . . ' Thus they would quench my one remaining ember. . . . "

. . . ¹¹ . . . He said, "As the LORD lives, not one hair of your son shall fall to the ground."

. . . ¹³ The woman said, " . . . in giving this decision the king convicts himself, inasmuch as the king does not bring his banished one home again. . . . "

. . . ¹⁹ The king said, "Is the hand of Joab with you in all this?" The woman answered and said, "As surely as you live, my lord the king, one cannot turn right or left from anything that my lord the king has said. For it was your servant Joab who commanded me. . . . " . . .

²¹ Then the king said to Joab, "Very well, I grant this; go, bring back the young man Absalom." . . . ²³ So Joab set off, went to Geshur, and brought Absalom to Jerusalem. ²⁴ The king said, "Let him go to his own house; he is not to come into my presence." So Absalom went to his own house, and did not come into the king's presence.

Joab observes David's change of heart regarding Absalom (13:39) and decides to do something about it. If David cannot figure out a way to bring Absalom back from exile, Joab will figure it out for him. But how? Joab, blunt, direct, and impetuous, a man of action, is not ordinarily given to subtleties, but this situation seems to call for delicate handling. David's emotional need for Absalom and his kingly responsibilities to represent justice are not easily reconciled. Joab needs an accomplice. He finds just the person he needs in Tekoa.

Tekoa is south of Bethlehem, the birthplace of David. Presumably Joab, as part of David's extended family (he was David's nephew, the son of his sister Zeruiah), grew up there also and would know the country well, including outstanding people who lived there. This unnamed "woman of Tekoa" had a reputation as a "wise woman," and Joab sent for her. (A couple of hundred years later the shepherd Amos would come out of Tekoa and make his prophetic mark on the life of God's people.)

Joab coaches the woman in how to dress and act and what to say. She follows his directions and appears before David as a widow in mourning. Joab "put the words into her mouth" (14:3), and she speaks them as her own. It is a cooked-up, parablelike story designed to involve David in working out the impasse in which he has found himself with Absalom.

The prophet Nathan a few years earlier used this same story method to great effect in David's life, in the affair of Bathsheba and Uriah. A thousand years later, Jesus will become the world's most famous teller of stories as a way to involve his listeners in recognizing and dealing with God in their lives. Story is not the only verbal way to draw a person into intimacies of soul and God, but it is the method of choice in our Holy Scripture. This biblical way contrasts with our contemporary preference for information. We typically gather impersonal (pretentiously called "scientific") information, whether doctrinal or philosophical or historical, in order to make decisions. And we commonly consult outside experts to interpret the information for us. But we don't live our lives by information; we live them in relationships in the context of a community of men and women, each one an intricate bundle of experience and motive and desire, and of a personal God who has designs on us for justice and salvation. Information gathering and consultation of experts leaves out nearly everything that is uniquely *us*—our personal histories and relationships, our sins and guilt, our moral character and obedience to God. Telling a story is the primary verbal way of accounting for life the way we live it in actual day-by-day reality. There are no (or few) abstractions in a story—story is immediate, concrete, plotted, relational, personal. And so when we lose touch with our lives, with our *souls*—our moral and spiritual, our God-personal lives—story is the best verbal way of getting us back in touch again. Which is why God's Word is given for the most part in the form of story.

David has lost touch with what is essential to his life: Matters of affection and matters of justice are all tangled and muddled right now in the person of Absalom. Absalom is stuck in exile; David is stuck in loneliness. Joab gets things moving again with a story.

The "wise woman" of Tekoa tells the story by posing as a widow with two sons, one of whom has just killed the other. Her family, she says, is now insisting that she give up the one remaining son to be executed in punishment for murdering his brother. But they don't care for *her* in this; all they are concerned with is an abstract principle, "justice." This remaining son is all she has left—her husband is dead, one son is dead, and now "they would quench my one remaining ember" (v. 7).

In a most poignant way, she expresses the conflict between the family's impersonal insistence on justice and her personal need for a relationship with her only son, "my one remaining ember."

David is moved by her story and promises to protect her son from the impersonal machinery of justice: "Not one hair of your son shall fall to the ground" (v. 11). David does not yet notice that the story is about him and Absalom, his fatherly "yearning" for Absalom conflicting with his kingly duty to punish Absalom for the murder of his brother. He does not yet notice that he has just made a choice that will bring Absalom home as a son, and not as a murderer.

Then the wise woman of Tekoa (as Nathan the prophet had done earlier) *makes* David notice: "The king convicts himself" (v. 13).

David also notices something else—the parable-story is perhaps a little *too* customized to David's circumstances. David suspects that the Tekoa woman is not on her own in telling this story; he suspects Joab. He confronts the woman with his suspicion, and she readily admits it.

But by now the story has done its work; David is both convicted and convinced. He sends Joab off to bring Absalom back from exile, from David's in-laws in Geshur.

The story now takes an odd turn: Absalom is back in Jerusalem. The story of the woman of Tekoa (and Joab), by affirming the claims of his fatherly heart over his kingly responsibilities to justice, has prodded David to bring Absalom back from exile. But now he refuses to see Absalom. Absalom is not permitted to come into David's presence. The "yearning" for Absalom, which Joab used to plot the story that roused David to bring his son home, does not result in reunion and restoration. David shuns Absalom. David gives the curt order, "He is not to come into my presence" (v. 24). What do we make of this "yearning" that results in shunning?

Careful students of biblical narratives make a distinction between "blanks" and "gaps." "Blanks" are insignificant omissions, teasing our curiosity, perhaps, but not affecting the story; "gaps" are significant deletions that raise the ante of our attention, forcing notice not by what is said, but by what is not said. This is a gap. And what we notice is that David's emotions are not congruent with his actions. Earlier (13:21) David's emotional anger over the rape of Tamar did not result in dealing appropriately with either Tamar (in compassion) or Amnon (in justice). Now David's emotional affection for Absalom fails to result in a personal meeting. The narrator supplies no motive for David's refusal to see Absalom, but he makes sure we notice the immense chasm between what David feels and what he does, between his yearning for Absalom and his shunning of Absalom.

14:25 **Now in all Israel there was no one to be praised so much for his beauty as Absalom; . . . there was no blemish in him.** [26] **When he cut the hair of his head (for at the end of every year he used to cut it . . .), he weighed the hair of his head, two hundred shekels by the king's weight.** [27] **There were born to Absalom three sons, and one daughter whose name was Tamar; she was a beautiful woman.**

By now, Absalom has become the central character in the story. It is time to take a good look at him, for he will continue on center stage for some time to come. "Beauty" is the word that characterizes him, a beauty that captures the admiration of the whole country. It is the same word that was used to describe his father David's first appearance in the story (1 Sam. 16:12). The beauty appears again in Absalom's daughter, Tamar (v. 27). Absalom both receives and passes on David's beauty.

Absalom's striking good looks are epitomized in his hair. This massive and luxurious head of hair, which he cuts once a year, will later play a role in his doom (see 18:9). The prominence of Absalom's hair is emphasized in the detail that the annual haircut produced two to three pounds of hair—"Quite a lot of hair," notes McCarter, "especially if it was washed regularly!" (McCarter, *II Samuel*, 349).

> 14:28 **So Absalom lived two full years in Jerusalem, without coming into the king's presence.** [29] **Then Absalom sent for Joab to send him to the king; but Joab would not come to him. He sent a second time, but Joab would not come.** [30] **Then he said to his servants, "Look, Joab's field is next to mine, and he has barley there; go and set it on fire." So Absalom's servants set the field on fire.** [31] **Then Joab rose and went to Absalom at his house, and said to him, "Why have your servants set my field on fire?"** [32] **Absalom answered Joab, "Look, I sent word to you: Come here, that I may send you to the king with the question, 'Why have I come from Geshur? It would be better for me to be there still.' Now let me go into the king's presence; if there is guilt in me, let him kill me!"** [33] **Then Joab went to the king and told him; and he summoned Absalom. So he came to the king . . . and the king kissed Absalom.**

Absalom's praised position in Jerusalem (v. 25) is at variance with the continued shunning he gets from his father. Everybody, it seems, loves Absalom extravagantly, except for his own father. Absalom chafes under David's deliberate and continued refusal to see him.

David, in his refusal to see Absalom (vv. 24 and 28), contributes to his own soon-to-erupt troubles. Now it becomes obvious: David's pardon of Absalom was impersonal; his forgiveness was a judicial act, not a fatherly embrace. He lets Absalom return to his own city and provides him with a place to live but does not greet him by name, will not permit him into his presence—not so much as a look.

Sin feeds on sin. The rape of Tamar feeds the murder of Amnon feeds the hardheartedness of David. Absalom responded to Amnon's sin by sinning. Now David responds to Absalom's sin by sinning. Absalom got rid of Amnon by killing him. David gets rid of Absalom by shunning him. David lost his son Amnon because of the sin of Absalom. David loses his son Absalom by his own sin.

Absalom stews in banishment. He is home, but he is not home. This is no life, just to be permitted to exist. He wants acceptance, a personal word of forgiveness. He wants his father's love. He needs more than food and drink and a house to live in; he requires grace and mercy in order to live. At first he is simply glad to be back, but gradually comes to realize that he needs far more than a piece of royal legislation in his favor; he needs a father.

We pause and reflect on how differently this story would have turned out if David had anticipated the story Jesus told about the father whose son went into a far country, lived a life of self-indulgence, and returned having disgraced his father's house (Luke 15). Even though he had done a terrible thing, the father never quit looking for him, looking for a way to forgive him and restore him to full sonship. When he did come, finally, the father ran to greet and embrace him, welcoming him home with a huge banquet. What if David had been that father? What if Absalom had been allowed to sit with his father, tell the story of his affection for Tamar, his anger at Amnon, and the purgatory of his exile? The father would once more have had a son, the son would once again have had a father.

But David does not do that. David turns hard on Absalom. We are not privy to David's reasons. Does he think that what he is doing is good for Absalom, punishing him until he feels the full weight of responsibility and pain for the murder? After his conspicuous failures in administering justice in his kingdom, is he trying to make up for it in one fell swoop with Absalom? Whatever line David is using to rationalize his position, underneath there is a bedrock refusal to forgive, a withholding of grace, a denial of mercy.

This is the third monumental sin of David's life, the most inexcusable, and the one for which he will pay the highest price. The adultery with Bathsheba was the affair of a passionate moment. The murder of Uriah was a royal reflex to avoid detection. But the rejection of Absalom is a steady, determined refusal to give his son what God has given David himself. Day by day he hardens in this denial of love. This is sin with a blueprint. This is sin that requires long-term commitment, comprehensive strategy. Jerusalem is a small city—scrupulous care is necessary to avoid seeing or being seen by Absalom.

Absalom sends messages to Joab asking for help in seeing his father, but Joab ignores him. Joab is not well known for his sensitivity to intimacy needs. Well, then, if words do not work, maybe action will. Absalom sets fire to Joab's barley field, and *that* gets his attention. Absalom is not asking for pardon, he is not demanding restoration, he is desperate for a *father*, no matter what the terms. He is quite ready to accept a death sentence, so long as his *father* gives it. But he is tired of being ignored. Joab, who two years before had used the woman with a story to get Absalom back in Jerusalem, is now pressured to intervene directly; he goes to David and asks the father to receive his son. David gives in. He receives his son Absalom and kisses him.

But the kiss comes too late. It has been far too long in coming. By now Absalom has changed his identity; he is no longer David's son, longing to be received by his father, but David's rival, ambitious to replace his father.

The story does not make it clear just when Absalom got it into his head (and heart!) to get rid of his father and take over the throne of Israel. The ambiguity is no doubt intentional. But it was probably a long time in the making. It is the way evil works—conceived in obscurity, it has a long, silent, often unconscious incubation, and then a violent outbreak, an epidemic of violence ravaging family, community, and nation.

THE COUP OF ABSALOM (15:1–12)

> 15:1 **After this Absalom got himself a chariot and horses, and fifty men to run ahead of him.** [2] **. . . when anyone brought a suit before the king for judgment . . .** [3] **Absalom would say, "See, your claims are good and right; but there is no one deputed by the king to hear you.** [4] **. . . If only I were judge in the land! . . . I would give them justice."** [5] **Whenever people came near to do obeisance to him, he would put out his hand and take hold of them, and kiss them.** [6] **. . . so Absalom stole the hearts of the people of Israel.**
>
> [7] **At the end of four years Absalom said to the king, "Please let me go to Hebron. . . .** [8] **For your servant made a vow while I lived at Geshur in Aram: If the LORD will indeed bring me back to Jerusalem, then I will worship the LORD in Hebron."** [9] **The king said to him, "Go in peace." So he . . . went to Hebron.** [10] **But Absalom sent secret messengers throughout all the tribes of Israel, saying, "As soon as you hear the sound of the trumpet, then shout: Absalom has become king at Hebron!"** [11] **Two hundred men from Jerusalem went with Absalom; they were invited guests, and they went in their innocence, knowing nothing of the matter.** [12] **While Absalom was offering the sacrifices, he sent for Ahithophel the Gilonite, David's counselor. . . . The conspiracy grew in strength, and the people with Absalom kept increasing.**

Absalom spends two years plotting the murder of his brother and waiting for the right opportunity (13:23); he spends four years preparing to kill his father.

Murder ranks as the highest crime in most (all?) societies. Not once, but twice, Absalom carefully premeditates a murder. But it is unlikely that Absalom *felt* like a murderer, or even thought of himself as a murderer. Both of his murder plots were conceived and carried out under the guise of doing good. Most sin is. One of the surprising characteristics of sin is its capacity to appear as good and to convince the sinner that he or she is doing something that is both necessary and good.

Both of Absalom's murder plots were conceived as acts of justice. In the murder of Amnon, Absalom was avenging the honor of his violated sister and dealing with a matter of justice that his father had failed to tend to. As far as Absalom was concerned, he was doing something right; that he was forced to use violent means was David's fault—if King David had been doing his job as both king and father, Absalom would not have been forced by his outraged conscience to kill his brother.

And it turns out that Absalom's murder of Amnon was more or less a dress rehearsal for the attempted murder of his father. The plot to kill his father and take over the kingdom is nurtured in a setting of "justice vacuum"—people are coming to Jerusalem from all over the kingdom, bringing their complaints and justice needs to the king, and the king turns out to be not available. David is proving grossly lax with regard to acting as judge in matters of right and wrong, protecting the weak from exploitation, upholding right against mere "might." These are obviously his responsibilities as a ruler, and he is not doing them.

King David's failure to do his job fuels Absalom's indignation—indignation over the widespread lack of concern for the weak and the needy, anger at the growing injustice in the city. Absalom knows that he himself would never let matters degenerate like this: "If only I were judge in the land! Then all who had a suit or cause might come to me, and I would give them justice" (v. 4). It may be that from the outset Absalom was cynically using the needs of the people for his own political ambition; more probably he really did feel the injustices, and only in the course of time did they become incorporated into his strategy for overthrowing his father. Most sin begins small and insinuates itself in subtle ways.

So even though David's failure in matters of justice may not be the origin of Absalom's plot to become king, it certainly provides the setting in which it could develop self-justifying and righteous reasons for carrying it out. Absalom would reason, "It is not fair that all these people have no one to stand up for them; a competent king is necessary for the good of the country; and here I am in a God-given position to do something about it."

David's inaccessibility to Absalom's need to be treated justly during the two years of his shunning provides plenty of personal and emotional content to Absalom's public concern for reforming the justice system in Israel. Or maybe the personal experience is all that mattered to Absalom, and the public concern is all pretense. At any rate, the text gives us ample material to see Absalom developing a self-image as a prophet committed to the cause of justice. He is not planning a murder; he is working for justice.

Absalom is skilled and patient and "good" in his four years of plotting. First, he cultivates an image of competent leadership—his chariot and horses with fifty men running before him is sheer image building. People want leaders who look and act like leaders. Absalom, with his charismatic good looks and extravagant entourage, looked like a king long before he attempted the takeover as king. Second, he cultivates a reputation for knowing and caring for people's needs. His daily greeting of needy people at the gate, getting to know them and letting them know how much he cares, is a strategy as meticulously planned and carried out as any modern public-relations firm could have pulled off. Third, he employs the setting of a religious banquet as a launching pad for his revolt to depose David as king and get himself enthroned in his father's place. Absalom has a flair for the dramatic; he knows how to stage dramatic events that suit his purpose. The sheepshearing banquet out in the country served his purpose well enough in the murder of Amnon; but the stakes are higher now. Earlier he only needed to provide an unsuspicious setting where he could kill Amnon and get away quickly; this time he needs to convert an entire populace from simply admiring him as a prince to serving him as their king, and quickly. He needs the trappings of approval as well as religious sanction and authoritative endorsement. The holy city of Hebron would serve nicely.

When Absalom is sure that his glamorous image and compassionate reputation are well established, he plans a religious banquet in Hebron. To the considerable trappings of popular approval, he now adds religious sanction and authoritative endorsement. The banquet is set up as an act of worship: Absalom made a vow (he said) while in exile that if God would bring him home he would "worship the LORD in Hebron" (v. 8) in gratitude to God for his safe homecoming. Two hundred invited guests from Jerusalem, innocent of what is really going on, provide the legitimacy of numbers to the worship (all these people can't be wrong). He also gets the famous Ahithophel to be present. Ahithophel is King David's counselor, with a reputation for wisdom. The two hundred guests plus Ahithophel, popularity capped with expertise, is a most impressive endorsement.

With everything in place, Absalom employs the element of surprise to create a sudden sense of completed action: Messengers dispersed secretly all over the country on signal simultaneously would shout the news, "Absalom has become king in Hebron!"

If David's reign as king is, in fact, failing, as Absalom's carefully orchestrated campaign is designed to make evident, the headline news will sound like good news in the people's ears. A new regime! A fresh start! But it will also be possible for alert Israelites to hear in the announcement an implicit denial of God's sovereignty, of which David is the representative, however inadequate and flawed.

The phrase "God has become king" was a standard acclamation of faith in Israel's prayers and hymns. The psalms, which document so much of Israel's worship life, repeat the phrase "God is become king" or "God is king" (either translation is possible) in several settings. Many scholars have concluded that it is *the* characteristic proclamation of Israel's worship at this time in its history (Psalms 47, 93, 97, and 99 are the most prominent witnesses). God's sovereign rule centers the life of Israel, and in worship Israel gives witness to it. Jesus confirms this centrality and witness by picking up the proclamation and making it the defining mark in his preaching: "The time is fulfilled, and the kingdom of God has come near; repent, and believe in the good news" (Mark 1:15).

That proclamation gives us the term "gospel," the good news that there has been a change of government and that God is king. This proclamation, at the center of Israel's faith, the center to which David's kingship gives witness, is parodied in Absalom's claim to the throne. The sentences are nearly identical, only one word has changed—"Absalom" replaces "God." *Absalom has become king!*

It is impossible for us from this distance in time and place to assess the impact of the parody on the people's ears. Would they have been so impressed by the religious language they had become accustomed to in their worship, " . . . become king," that they wouldn't notice that Absalom's name had been substituted for God? This is common enough among religious people, especially when the accompanying emotions and atmosphere are sufficiently dazzling. Or would the substitution have been obvious but welcome, since David's witness to God's kingship was so faulty and intermittent? This is also common, for there are many people who, impatient with God's vast tolerance of human inefficiency and seemingly infinite patience with human sin, jump at the chance for a ruler who will make everything better quickly. (Most authoritarian governments, whether fascist or communist, have low crime rates.) Or would the proclamation have been heard for what it is, as shocking blasphemy?

At any rate, we know how it sounds to us who have a long schooling in the nature of God's rule, complete with a graduate course in Christ the King: It is blasphemy bold and simple. We read this story of God's sovereignty being worked out, even if badly (in Saul) and imperfectly (in David). We know the reluctance with which Samuel sanctioned the "king" venture in the first place. We are aware all along of David's disciplined patience in refusing to get rid of Saul, even when Saul is at his worst, and take over as king—Saul was God's "anointed" and David will not interfere. We are aware of David's reticence in putting forth any personal claims to sovereignty—he is made king by others: Samuel's anointing, the Hebron elders, the Israel elders. The writer has provided detail after detail to show that David never claims the throne himself or personally does anything to displace Saul. One motive for telling the story this way is obviously political; it allays any suspicion among the storyteller's original readers that David is an illegitimate usurper to the throne. But the deeper motive is certainly theological, showing that David never for a moment considers his leadership as a position of personal power: *God* rules, *God* has become king and David is only a witness and servant to God's sovereignty. We never find the phrase "David has become king" in this story. That acclamation is made only in the worship of God (Psalms 47, 93, 96–99). And it is *this* about David that makes him central to the story of faith: not that he is a great king, for he is not—his failures, both moral and political, are conspicuous and glaring—but that he never puts himself forward as a replacement for God as king, ever. Certainly, one of the reasons that the narrator insists on telling us everything bad about David, refusing to idealize or glamorize him, is in order to show how God's sovereignty is worked out through just such a mixed bag of human failure and sin.

It is essential at this place in the story to reflect on the fundamental and much verified truth that sin is a *religious* act: It presents itself and is carried out as a way of doing good either for God or as a god. To support this insight, the biblical narrator does not "demonize" Absalom, but quite the opposite. He is presented most attractively: his handsome beauty, his reputation for caring (for the violation of Tamar and for injustice among the people), his courtesy and attentiveness as he takes the time to get acquainted with their needs, two hundred innocent guests happy to accept his invitation to the banquet in Hebron, the famous counselor Ahithophel supporting him. We can see why people are drawn to him. *We* are drawn to him.

At the same time that the narrative refrains from demonizing Absalom, it also does not piously pretend that David is any better than he is. David is not given to us as a "role model." His faults are not headlined, but it does not take much reading between the lines to realize that he has been a lousy king. The revolt that Absalom mounts "seems . . . to have fed on a mass of indefinable grievances" (Bright, *A History of Israel*, 188). There is a sense that David deserves all the trouble Absalom brings him.

What we are given is far better and more satisfying than a cartoon caricature of "good David" or "bad Absalom"—we are immersed in the story of God's gracious sovereignty being worked out through the lives of frail, willful, disobedient, sometimes repentant and sometimes not, men and women who are created to live to God's glory. *That* is what keeps us reading this story over and over again and finding it "good news."

THE FLIGHT OF DAVID (15:13–16:14)

Travel narrations, ranging in style and content from Homer's *Odyssey* to Chaucer's *Canterbury Tales*, are well suited to keeping a heterogeneous company of people and a diverse assortment of motives together in a coherent and comprehensible plot. David's flight from and return to Jerusalem is among the best of the world's travel stories, second only to the "way" that Jesus walked from Gethsemane to Golgotha. The journey that begins here will conclude in chapter 20; it is the most intense and detailed portion of the entire David story.

> 15:13 **A messenger came to David, saying, "The hearts of the Israelites have gone after Absalom."** [14] **Then David said . . . , "Get up! Let us flee, or there will be no escape for us from Absalom. Hurry. . . . " . . .** [17] **The king left, followed by all the people; and they stopped at the last house.** [18] **All his officials passed by him; and all the Cherethites, and all the Pelethites, and all the six hundred Gittites who had followed him from Gath, passed on before the king.**

The earlier phrase, "Absalom stole the hearts of the people . . . " (v. 6), now comes up for elaboration: The theft (stealing the hearts), accomplished on the sly, is now brought into the open and used to mount a public revolt against David's rule. Absalom, after years of working behind the scenes, steps onto the center of the stage and claims to be king. David is forced to abandon his throne and palace and flee for his life.

Many of the people (but not all) go over to Absalom's side; David escapes Jerusalem with only his household servants and personal bodyguard. The Cherethites and Pelethites are foreign mercenaries, not blood Israelites, and so are under David's personal authority. The six hundred Gittites would have been Philistines that David brought with him to Hebron and Jerusalem from his fugitive period in Ziklag, those years that he was under the patronage of the Philistine King Achish of Gath (see 1 Samuel 27–30). Even though haste is required, a certain ceremonial decorum seems to have been preserved: The king waits at the outskirts of the city ("the last house" v. 17) until all these people pass on ahead of him. There is a hint here of the later seafaring tradition in which the captain is the last to leave the sinking ship. David is still king; he is not reduced to running frantically to save his own skin. David is dignified in his leaving, caring for the people who go with him. That small detail ("the last house") interrupts the action sufficiently to let us see David not simply reacting to Absalom, but being responsible to the people left in his care and, cool under pressure, making strategic decisions.

In reading the account of David's flight, it helps to have a picture of the flight path. The route begins on the heights in Jerusalem and descends to the Jordan River near to where it enters the Dead Sea. Jerusalem is set at the highest point in that part of Palestine, and the Jordan at the lowest. It is about twenty-six miles from the city to the river. David descends roughly the same route that Joshua had ascended a couple of hundred years earlier when he led the Hebrew people into possession of their promised land. That detail would not have been lost on the first readers of this story. The geographical features of the road are embedded in the narration and serve the drama. Leaving Jerusalem, there is first a brief descent into a valley, the Wadi Kidron, then a short ascent up the Mount of Olives. Not far past the crest of Olives is the village of Bahurim, mentioned twice in the flight (chaps. 16:5 and 17:18), and then the long descent through wilderness to the River Jordan near the city of Jericho. This is the famous "Jericho Road" that provides the setting for Jesus' story of the good Samaritan and the lyrics to the gospel song of that name.

Ten individuals are singled out for David's personal attention during the flight and located at points along the way: Ittai at the "last house" of Jerusalem (vv. 17–23); Abiathar and Zadok, with their sons Ahimaaz and Jonathan, just across the Wadi Kidron (vv. 24–29); Ahithophel on the ascent of the Mount of Olives (vv. 30–31); Hushai at the summit of the Mount of Olives (vv. 32–37); Ziba just past the summit (16:1–4); and Shimei and Abishai at the village of Bahurim just a mile or so farther on (16:5–13). It is quite a company that David deals with as he is forced to leave home and work, family and security. How much contemporary experience of faith and trouble are compressed into this crisis event! The ten names keep the story personal and dramatically alive. Storytellers love names.

15:19 Then the king said to Ittai the Gittite, "Why are you also coming with us? Go back, and stay with the king; for you are a foreigner, and also an exile from your home." . . .

Ittai is a bright spot in this dark story. He is a Philistine from Gath, the hometown of the giant Goliath. David made his early mark on Israel's life by killing Philistines; now in his later life one of them, Ittai, joins his company and helps him. Unlike the Cherethites and Pelethites, who were paid to be there, Ittai is there out of personal loyalty, and perhaps spiritual conviction. Was Ittai a convert to David's God? Quite possibly, for theological terms are used in their conversation: David blesses Ittai with God's "steadfast love and faithfulness" (v. 20), and Ittai uses Israel's confessional language ("As the LORD lives . . . ," v. 21) in his response. David started out killing Philistines; he ends up converting them!

We notice the contrast: David, fleeing from his son who has betrayed him, is befriended by a stranger willing to risk his life for him. We also notice that Ittai's loyalty to David is an echo of the loyalty of David's great-grandmother Ruth (also a foreigner!) to Naomi (Ruth 1:16–18).

15:24 Abiathar came up, and Zadok also, with all the Levites, carrying the ark of the covenant of God. They set down the ark of God. . . . ²⁵ Then the king said to Zadok, . . . ²⁷ . . . "Look, go back to the city in peace, you and Abiathar, with your two sons, Ahimaaz your son, and Jonathan son of Abiathar." . . .

Abiathar and Zadok are next, priests carrying the ark of the covenant with them, this ark which David brought to Jerusalem in a parade of festive worship (2 Samuel 6) and which is such a powerful symbol of God's presence and power in Israel. David orders both the priests and the ark back to Jerusalem. David refuses to "use" God to his advantage. That had been attempted by an earlier generation (see 1 Samuel 4) with disastrous results. David is fleeing for his life, but he is not trying to hang on to his kingship by any means at hand. He is aware that being king is not something he can or should engineer. David is that rarity among leaders, a person who is not obsessed with power, with being in control, with using everyone and anyone around him (including God) as a support system to his rule. He is also quite aware that there is more to Absalom's rebellion than politics and family dynamics; there is God's judgment. So even while he is escaping from Absalom, he is submitting to God's judgment.

But the deeply moral refusal to use the holy ark to his advantage in combination with the penitential submission to God's judgment does not

preclude considerations of self-interest. It occurs to David that back in
Jerusalem the two priests and their sons could be of use to him as infor-
mants. Piety and practicality are not mutually exclusive; they can be quite
comfortable bedfellows.

> 15:30 **But David went up the ascent of the Mount of Olives, weeping as he
> went, with his head covered and walking barefoot; and all the people . . . ,
> weeping as they went. [31] David was told that Ahithophel was among the con-
> spirators with Absalom. And David said, "O LORD, I pray you, turn the coun-
> sel of Ahithophel into foolishness."**

Ahithophel is a big name in David's government, maybe the biggest. He
is David's trusted counselor, with a reputation among the people as a wise
man: "In those days the counsel that Ahithophel gave was as if one consulted the oracle of God" (16:23). As insiders to the story, we know that
Ahithophel is already in on the Absalom conspiracy (15:12); but David did
not yet know it. Now David knows. When David receives the report that
Ahithophel has joined the Absalom forces, the effect is devastating—if
Ahithophel believes in and supports Absalom, the popular mind will conclude that God is on Absalom's side. Ahithophel, simply by being present
in Jerusalem with Absalom, will give the Absalom rebellion sanction and
legitimacy.

David's response to the bulletin on Ahithophel is to pray: "O LORD, I
pray you, turn the counsel of Ahithophel to foolishness" (15:31). We commonly think of David as a person of prayer—the psalms, many of them ascribed to David, document his vigor in prayer. But this is the first reference
to David praying since his seven days of fasting and prayer for the life of
the child conceived in his adultery with Bathsheba (12:16–18). We have
considerable evidence that David has not been tending the store during
these years—both family and governmental responsibilities are in a state
of disarray. He probably was not being attentive to God either. But the
Ahithophel crisis puts him on his knees again. He prays. Isaac Bashevis
Singer, the Nobel Prize–winning novelist, once said in a radio interview,
"I only pray when I'm in trouble; but I'm in trouble all the time, so I pray
all the time." David is in trouble; David prays.

> 15:32 **When David came to the summit, where God was worshiped, Hushai
> the Archite came to meet him. . . . [33] David said to him, " . . . [34] . . . return
> to the city and say to Absalom, 'I will be your servant, O king. . . .'" [37] So
> Hushai, David's friend, came into the city, just as Absalom was entering
> Jerusalem.**

Hushai the Archite is designated as "David's friend" (v. 37). The term "friend" has a meaning beyond what we give it in our ordinary speech. We have learned from old Egyptian texts that there were official, honorific overtones to the word as used in that culture. Hushai is not merely the king's "buddy"; he is the king's trusted adviser. As such he has both position and authority to match Ahithophel. David sends him back to Jerusalem to serve as his spy. It looks as if Absalom now has the two most prominent "wise" men in Jerusalem on his side, Ahithophel and Hushai—powerful endorsements. What he doesn't know is that one of them is secretly David's spy. Now David has five men—Abiathar, Zadok, Jonathan, Ahimaaz, and Hushai—strategically placed in Jerusalem, serving his interests.

16:1 When David had passed a little beyond the summit, Ziba the servant of Mephibosheth met him. . . .

Ziba is Saul's servant from the old days and now the steward of Mephibosheth, Jonathan's lame son (see 2 Samuel 9). It is not entirely clear why he shows up. The story he gives is that he is bringing provisions of bread and fruit and wine to David's company. He also reports that his ward, Mephibosheth, has abandoned David with the hope that in the governmental shake-up he, as Saul's only surviving heir, will become king. The storyteller doesn't make it clear to us whether Ziba is telling the truth or making it up. Later, Mephibosheth will present a different version of what happened (2 Sam. 19:24–30). But for now David believes Ziba, accepts his help, and turns over all of Mephibosheth's possessions to him. We do not have to decide whether Ziba is telling the truth or not to see that he is bent on using the David-Absalom crisis to his own advantage. There always seem to be people like this in times of trouble. Hurt people, troubled people, suffering people, rejected people are vulnerable people. The number of individuals in the so-called "helping professions" who help themselves by exploiting others in times of trouble is appalling. Ziba was the spiritual ancestor of Charles Dickens's character Fagin (in *Oliver Twist*), who succinctly articulated the creed: "Some conjurers say that number three is the magic number, and some say number seven. It's neither, my friend, neither. It's number one. . . . Ha! Ha! Number one for ever."

16:5 When King David came to Bahurim, a man of the family of the house of Saul came out whose name was Shimei son of Gera; he came out cursing. 6 He threw stones at David. . . .

Shimei takes up the post of doomsday prophet. He has a vested interest in David's disgrace, for he is related to Saul. It now appears that the kingdom was not quite as united under David as we had thought. All this time there has been a party of dissidents who maintained their identity as Saul loyalists, waiting, hoping, watching for weakness in David that they could exploit and use to bring about their return to power. We caught a hint of that in Ziba's accusation that Mephibosheth, as an heir of Saul, still had aspirations to becoming king (2 Sam. 16:3). Shimei now sets himself up as a prophet, interpreting current events as acts of God in support of the Saul party. Later Sheba will try, unsuccessfully, to restore a Saul monarchy (2 Samuel 20). So we know that Shimei is not a lone voice; he is representative of a faction that all through David's reign continues to consider David as an unlawful usurper to Saul's throne. As Shimei steps forward and speaks as a prophet who discerns God's hand in the events of the day (v. 8), David is fleeing Jerusalem in disgrace; obviously God is judging him. Shimei curses David in God's name. He is a self-appointed prophet of doomsday judgment.

Shimei, hurling rocks and shouting curses, delivers his hellfire and brimstone sermon; in effect, "Get out of town, you worthless old man. Murderer! Dirty old man. Murderer!" Then more rocks, more curses. The curses must have hurt more than the rocks did: "Corrupt and stupid king! Killer king!"

This kind of ad hoc prophecy continues to be popular in the field of religion: Newspapers and news bulletins provide the texts for many a contemporary Shimei-prophet, stridently announcing God's intervention in human affairs. There is always enough sin and corruption at hand to lend plausibility to the tirades. But they do not come from a careful and devout reading of either God's Word or current events; these voices are formed from a poison brew of resentment and envy and lust for power.

16:9 Then Abishai son of Zeruiah said to the king, "Why should this dead dog curse my lord the king? Let me go over and take off his head." ¹⁰ But the king said, "What have I to do with you, you sons of Zeruiah? If he is cursing because the LORD has said to him, 'Curse David,' who then shall say, 'Why have you done so?'" ...

Abishai, one of David's military leaders, is the tenth and final name to play a part on the Jericho Road. Abishai proposes to kill Shimei for his blasphemous and brutal sermon. Abishai and his brother Joab (the Zeruiah brothers) were loyal associates of David and served him zealously. But they were dubious allies—they had a history of impetuously taking things into their own hands. They were for David's cause without understanding David's God. David was also a person of action, but his actions, as evidenced in the psalms, were characteristically (but not always!) rooted in prayer and a life with God. The Zeruiah brothers are all action and no prayer. They are on the side of righteousness without any rootage in righteousness.

Abishai, characteristically, proposes a quick and obvious solution to the Shimei problem: "Let me go over and take off his head—nobody is going to talk to my king this way." But David restrains him. We can summarize David's response in these words: "Shimei is right; he is telling the truth about me. He is preaching God's word to me this night. God commanded him to curse me. Shimei is only a mouthpiece for God's curses. Let him alone—his sermon of curses is God's word preached to me."

A bad sermon can still tell the truth. David is able to hear God's word in Shimei's rants, and what he hears brings David to himself. He faces what he has become—all the wrongs he has committed, all the people he has failed, are brought to awareness by Shimei's curses. David could have taken a defensive and vengeful posture. But he does not. He faces the truth about himself. He faces the truth that his basic identity has not been "king" but "sinner," and that he can only live by God's mercy. Shimei's curses peel the royal veneer off David and expose his soul. David lets Shimei's curses become the word of God to him—kerygmatic Shimei.

16:14 **The king and all the people who were with him arrived weary at the Jordan; and there he refreshed himself.**

The descent is over; the flight is complete. David has escaped. Meanwhile Absalom has arrived in Jerusalem. At the very time that David flees down the "Jericho Road," Absalom enters Jerusalem and plots the strategy that will, he thinks, finish David off for good.

ABSALOM'S WAR (16:15–18:18)

16:15 **Now Absalom and all the Israelites came to Jerusalem; Ahithophel was with him.** [16] **When Hushai the Archite, David's friend, came to Absalom, Hushai said to Absalom, "Long live the king! Long live the king!"** [17] **Absalom said to Hushai, "Is this your loyalty to your friend? Why did you not go with your friend?"** [18] **Hushai said to Absalom, "No; but the one whom the LORD and this people and all the Israelites have chosen, his I will be, and with him I will remain.** [19] **. . . Just as I have served your father, so I will serve you."**

The first thing that happens in Absalom's council of war is that Hushai, following David's instructions, establishes himself in Absalom's confidence. Knowing of Hushai's relationship with his father, Absalom is surprised to find Hushai on his side—and suspicious. He questions him: "I thought you were my father's friend—is this how you treat your friend?" Hushai claims to be committed to a higher loyalty, loyalty to God. He allays Absalom's suspicions by telling him that since he, Absalom, is both God's choice and the people's choice, he has decided to join God and the people and throw in his lot with Absalom. It is all barefaced flattery, of course, but Absalom falls for it: When a man of Hushai's solid standing reminds Absalom that he is both God's choice and the people's choice, and now Hushai's choice, Absalom knows without a doubt that he is in the presence of a wise man. Vain people are highly susceptible to flattery, and Absalom is nothing if not vain. Getting past Absalom's suspicions and gaining his confidence prove embarrassingly easy for Hushai.

Hushai now shares equal status with Ahithophel as Absalom's advisers. The strategy for establishing the new regime proceeds; Ahithophel's advice is given first.

16:20 Then Absalom said to Ahithophel, "Give us your counsel; what shall we do?" 21 Ahithophel said to Absalom, "Go in to your father's concubines." . . . 23 Now in those days the counsel that Ahithophel gave was as if one consulted the oracle of God; so all the counsel of Ahithophel was esteemed, both by David and by Absalom.

17:1 Moreover Ahithophel said to Absalom, "Let me choose twelve thousand men, and I will set out and pursue David tonight. 2 I will come upon him while he is weary and discouraged, and throw him into a panic. . . . " 4 . . . The advice pleased Absalom and all the elders of Israel.

5 Then Absalom said, "Call Hushai the Archite also, and let us hear too what he has to say." 6 When Hushai came to Absalom, Absalom said to him, "This is what Ahithophel has said; shall we do as he advises? If not, you tell us." 7 Then Hushai said to Absalom, "This time the counsel that Ahithophel has given is not good." 8 Hushai continued, "You know that your father and his men are warriors, and that they are enraged, like a bear robbed of her cubs in the field. . . . 11 . . . my counsel is that all Israel be gathered to you . . . and that you go to battle in person. . . . "

The respective counsels of Ahithophel and Hushai are set side by side before Absalom. Ahithophel and Hushai are both respected and wise counselors, but the advice they give could not be more different.

Ahithophel's counsel is two-pronged. The first element is sheer public

relations: Absalom is to enter his father's harem and sleep with the concubines. This would dramatically establish Absalom's replacement of David
in the public mind. (In the ancient world, even more than in ours, sexual
potency and political power were linked.) The event was to be staged so
that no one in Jerusalem would miss either the act or its significance. And
so Absalom orders a tent to be pitched on the palace roof—everyone in the
streets (and the streets were no doubt crowded that day) watches the concubines file in, followed by Absalom. The tent, while preventing people
from actually seeing him in bed with the women, also served to arouse the
imaginations of everyone gathered around. As in the sideshow tents of our
traveling circuses, what goes on in the minds of the crowds who look at the
tents from the outside far exceeds what actually takes place inside. That
tent, conspicuously placed on the royal palace roof, holds the attention of
the whole city. Looking at the tent and listening for the sounds coming
from it is everyone's occupation. The longer Absalom is in the tent, the
more his reputation grows—his royal virility and youthful glamour a contrast to David's disgraced and impotent flight.

The second element in Ahithophel's counsel is that he himself,
Ahithophel, will leave that very night, go after the fleeing David, and run
him down. He will catch him at his weakest, exhausted from the flight and
disheartened over his son's betrayal, and kill him. But there will be no
war—only David will die. Ahithophel will then lead all David's company
back to the city in triumph and present them to Absalom "as a bride comes
home to her husband" (17:3). No one will lose husband or son in battle—
Absalom will be a peace hero. And Absalom will not have to lift a hand;
Ahithophel will do it all for him.

Ahithophel's counsel has all the appearance of irresistibility: All Absalom has to do is indulge himself sexually with the concubines while
Ahithophel gets rid of David, with the result that Absalom ends up both
charismatically popular and in undisputed power.

Can Hushai top this? He does. But he does it not with a more attractive
option, but with a more difficult one. There are two parts to his counsel.
First, he reminds Absalom that David and those with him are fierce warriors. All their fighting instincts and skills are aroused—"like a bear robbed
of her cubs" (17:8). Ahithophel, he says, has badly underestimated what
Absalom is up against: David is not only fierce but famously shrewd. He
has spent years in situations like this, chased and hunted in the wilderness.
There is no way that he can be disposed of so easily. Hushai faces Absalom
with the hard reality of *fact*, the fact of David, Philistine-killing, Saul-
surviving David. The second part of Hushai's counsel is his insistence that

Absalom himself must lead the campaign against David, and he is going to need every fighting man available to bring it off. He can't delegate this to someone else. This is not a minor chore to be tended to by an aide, even if the aide is as eminent as Ahithophel. Only a huge fighting force ("like the sand by the sea for multitude," 17:11), with Absalom at its head, is adequate for this task. If Absalom takes the time to be thoroughly prepared, David won't stand a chance.

With the Ahithophel and Hushai plans before him, side by side, Absalom chooses Hushai's. We readers who are insiders to the story know that Ahithophel's counsel is without doubt the better and, if followed, would likely have succeeded. How could Hushai possibly offer an alternative counsel that would be strategically convincing and still save David? He knows that what he must do is buy time—keep Absalom from attacking immediately; give David time to get things together and organize a fighting force. But how? He does it by appealing (again!) to Absalom's vanity. He paints a picture of David built up from actual facts but, in the circumstances of that night, larger than life—a wildly fierce, preternaturally canny David. And then he launches Absalom into the possibility of being even larger. Ahithophel's counsel involved the humiliation and denigration of David ("This is going to be easy, Absalom, so easy I'll do it for you"); Hushai's counsel presented a proud and wildly raging David ("This is the hardest thing you'll ever do, Absalom—are you up to it?"). Vain Absalom takes the bait, hook, line, and sinker.

17:14 Absalom and all the men of Israel said, "The counsel of Hushai the Archite is better than the counsel of Ahithophel." For the LORD had ordained to defeat the good counsel of Ahithophel, so that the LORD might bring ruin on Absalom.

Abruptly, but briefly, the narrator steps outside the story itself and makes an explicitly theological statement about the story: God is quietly and behind the scenes sovereign throughout and within all the details of the story. In this intricate tangle of vanity and deceit, cunning and betrayal, God is at work using these unlikely people, and means to bring about divine judgment ("bring ruin on Absalom") and confirm divine promise ("Your house and your kingdom shall be made sure forever before me," 7:16). Had we forgotten that a page or so earlier in the story David had prayed, "O LORD, I pray you, turn the counsel of Ahithophel into foolishness" (15:31)? Well, here is the answer. And this is the *way* of the answer: sovereignty hidden in the mess of history, God alive and present in the tangle of human sin and need. "There are hidden, powerful purposes from God that operate through Hushai, but they are not dependent on him or on any other human agent, because in the end the outcome was 'commanded.' Such a view of the historical process, alien to our modernity, can only be articulated by way of narrative, which allows for the hiddenness" (Brueggemann, *First and Second Samuel*, 314).

As a culture we are a people impatient of story, at least if it goes on very long. We prefer the anecdote, the sound bite, the slogan. We want digested "truth." Bare facts—information, whether doctrinal or scientific—and skip the mystery. But our impatience is a piece with our unwillingness to submit to the long processes of God's ways of working with us. It is also evidence of an unwillingness to share the extended and extensive workings of God with imperfect men and women who make up the company of redemption. We prefer depersonalized shortcuts. We want an interventionist God; we want an obvious God with no mystery; we want to know it all and to know it now, with no loose ends.

We want God quickly, on our terms: "Bypass the processes of creation and redemption and get this over with!" And we want God vertically, without the inconvenience of other people, flawed, imperfect other people.

Story, and the longer the better (and the Bible *is* long), forces us to inhabit the community of sinners and saints, with no one exempt from the process. Story prevents us from assuming that we can get God coming down a rope ladder and pulling us out of history. Storytelling, and especially biblical storytelling, trains us in patient submission to the processes of holy history. Von Hugel, one of the preeminent spiritual guides of this century, used to say that when we get to the heart of life, things are "not clear, but vivid" (von Hugel, *Essays & Addresses*, 145). Luminosity, not clarity, is the distinctive mark.

This single sentence of theological luminosity ("For the LORD had ordained . . . ") gives us our bearings; and then we are plunged back into the story.

17:15 **Then Hushai said to the priests Zadok and Abiathar, "Thus and so did Ahithophel counsel Absalom and the elders of Israel; and thus and so I have counseled. ¹⁶ Therefore send quickly and tell David, 'Do not lodge tonight at the fords of the wilderness, but by all means cross over; otherwise the king and all the people who are with him will be swallowed up.'" ¹⁷ Jonathan and Ahimaaz . . . ²¹ . . . went and told King David. They said to David, "Go and cross the water quickly; for thus and so has Ahithophel counseled against you." ²² So David . . . crossed the Jordan; by daybreak not one was left who had not crossed the Jordan.**

While we readers of the story know that Absalom has opted for Hushai's plan, Hushai, within the story, doesn't yet know it. So he prepares David for the worst, for the execution of Ahithophel's plan.

There are now five men in Jerusalem who are secretly on David's side; all five now go into action. Hushai tells the priests Zadok and Abiathar of the possibility of immediate pursuit if Ahithophel's strategy is followed. They send word to their two sons, Jonathan and Ahimaaz, who are hidden just outside the city ready to courier messages to David. As the two sons leave, despite their precautions they are spotted and reported to Absalom. With Absalom's servants in pursuit, they are forced to hide. They are helped by a friendly accomplice in Bahurim, a village a short distance along the way, and climb into his well; the man's wife camouflages their hiding place by throwing a blanket over the well and spreading grain over it. When Absalom's men show up, she throws them off the scent by misdirecting them another way. As soon as the coast is clear, the priests' sons proceed on their mission, find David, and warn him of the impending danger. David gets everyone with him across the river to safety. By daybreak David's company has the Jordan River as protection against the possibility of a sudden assault by Absalom and Ahithophel.

The action is fast-paced, taut with suspense. The bold lies of the woman at the well in Bahurim, in combination with the dangerous espionage work of Jonathan and Ahimaaz, are taken up into this weave of providence that is being crafted for David's salvation through the hours of this memorable night.

17:23 **When Ahithophel saw that his counsel was not followed, he saddled his donkey and went off home to his own city. He set his house in order, and hanged himself; he died and was buried in the tomb of his father.**

Ahithophel's suicide unmasks the emptiness of his life. For a long time, he was David's trusted adviser with a vast reputation among the people ("as if one consulted the oracle of God," 16:23). But his betrayal of David exposes his true character: "Even my bosom friend in whom I trusted,/who ate of my bread, has lifted the heel against me" (Psalm 41:9). For all his so-called wisdom, he badly misjudged the David and Absalom affair. He had concluded that the future of the kingdom was with Absalom. All the smart money seemed to be on Absalom at that moment, and Ahithophel is nothing if not smart. Ahithophel, it turns out, has been an opportunist all along. Behind that suave, sage reputation, Ahithophel has been looking out for himself. When David was the best bet, he bet on David. Of course he served David well over those years—David was the brightest star on the horizon—but the moment it appeared that David's star was in eclipse, Ahithophel went for the next sure thing: good-looking, ambitious, charismatic Absalom. It turns out that there was no character to the counselor, no moral substance, no spiritual muscle—a hollow man, pasted over with scraps of slogans and graffiti. The moment political fortunes changed in the wind of Absalom's rebellion, Ahithophel set his sails to catch the new winds of power. And he ends up a shipwreck.

Is there also an element of old but disguised anger fueling the betrayal? Maybe. Ahithophel is the grandfather of Bathsheba. Smoldering resentment over David's treatment of his granddaughter may have been an element in his betrayal. Many have thought so.

There is a long tradition among the readers of this story to identify Psalm 55 as the prayer that expresses David's experience of Ahithophel's betrayal, most explicitly in verses 12–14:

> It is not enemies who taunt me—
> I could bear that;
> it is not adversaries who deal insolently with me—
> I could hide from them.
> But it is you, my equal,
> my companion, my familiar friend,
> with whom I kept pleasant company;
> we walked in the house of God with the throng.

Ahithophel's betrayal of David is somewhat eclipsed in the Christian imagination by Judas Iscariot's betrayal of Jesus. The two betrayers are similar in that each is a trusted companion who at a moment of crisis turns on his leader in anticipation of personal gain. And they both end in suicide. Each thinks that he is going to better himself. They kill themselves when they realize that they have miscalculated, for they had been living, most probably for a long time (betrayal is rarely an impulsive act; it is habit of life exposed by a crisis), for nothing other than "self," and now with the "improved self" exposed as a delusion, there is nothing more to live for. So—suicide. Ahithophel and Judas share the epitaph: "Those who want to save their life will lose it" (Mark 8:35).

The two betrayals, set side by side, post a warning: Whenever we are dealing with matters of relationship, whether with persons or with God, betrayal is the sin above all sins "lurking at the door" (Gen. 4:7). Betrayal is common and difficult to detect as a sin, at least in its early stages, because it nearly always originates in a desire to improve our lives in what seem to be justified ways: Our leader or friend (parent or child, associate or spouse—in the long run, God) disappoints us, fails to deliver what we suppose is our human right, and so we "turn in" what we judge has become a liability in favor of an asset. It happens a lot in human relationships. It happens even more in relations with God. God doesn't deliver what we had counted on, and so we find a god or goddess who will. We would do well not to distance ourselves from Ahithophel by vilifying him as the archvillain—he is one of us. His betrayal and suicide are not nearly as remote from our common lives as we might suppose.

> **17:24 Then David came to Mahanaim, while Absalom crossed the Jordan with all the men of Israel. [25] Now Absalom had set Amasa over the army in the place of Joab.... [26] The Israelites and Absalom encamped in the land of Gilead.**
>
> **[27] When David came to Mahanaim, Shobi ... and Machir ... and Barzillai ... [28] brought beds, basins, and earthen vessels, wheat, barley, meal, parched grain, beans and lentils, [29] honey and curds, sheep, and cheese from the herd, for David and the people with him to eat; for they said, "The troops are hungry and weary and thirsty in the wilderness."**

In rejecting Ahithophel's counsel and following Hushai's, Absalom gives David much-needed time to get his dispirited and disheveled company ready for war.

And Absalom himself has time to organize his troops under a new commander. David's commander, Joab, went with David; Absalom picks Joab's nephew to lead his forces.

Both armies are now across the Jordan River to the east, East Israel, sometimes named Transjordan. The generic name for this country is Gilead, a forested hill country full of Hebrew stories (among them Jacob, Sihon and Og, Gideon, Jephthah, Jair, Elisha). In earlier wars of deliverance, David had won the hearts of the non-Israelites of east Israel; now he consolidates his position at one of its important cities, Mahanaim, making the city his headquarters. It is about twenty miles to the north of where he crossed the Jordan. Three men of substance, grateful for David's help in those earlier years, establish a generous food supply for David's troops. Their names are Shobi, Machir, and Barzillai. Rejected by his own people, David finds himself graciously welcomed by these non-Israelites.

Mahanaim is the place where Abner crowned Ishbaal in an attempt (unsuccessful as it turned out) to maintain the Saul dynasty in the face of the rising threat of David after he had just come to power in Hebron (2 Sam. 2:8–11). Now it is the place where David attempts (successfully) to maintain his kingship against the rising threat of Absalom. Early and late in David's rule, Mahanaim is a place of importance.

> 18:1 **Then David mustered the men who were with him. . . .** [2] **And David divided the army into three groups: one third under the command of Joab, one third under the command of Abishai son of Zeruiah, Joab's brother, and one third under the command of Ittai the Gittite. The king said to the men, "I myself will also go out with you."** [3] **But the men said, "You shall not go out. . . . you are worth ten thousand of us; therefore it is better that you send us help from the city."** [4] **The king said to them, "Whatever seems best to you I will do." So the king stood at the side of the gate, while all the army marched out. . . .** [5] **The king ordered Joab and Abishai and Ittai, saying, "Deal gently for my sake with the young man Absalom." And all the people heard when the king gave orders to all the commanders concerning Absalom.**

David is now ready for battle. Thanks to Hushai's counsel to Absalom, he has ample time to organize his soldiers, pick up allies who will provide food for his soldiers, and settle on his strategy. Absalom unknowingly handed his father, as if on a platter, everything David needed to bring about Absalom's defeat.

It is the old Philistine-fighting David that we now see in action here: crisp orders, generous support from others, courageous and energetic readiness to fight. He has to be restrained by his own men from leading them out onto the field of battle in person. In their intervention, we catch a sense of the affection in which he is held by those loyal to him.

All this is no more than we would expect. The surprising element is the final order David gives to his three commanders, Joab, Abishai, and Ittai: "Deal gently for my sake with the young man Absalom" (v. 5). We read these words and are startled. How did a sentence like this manage to come out of David's mouth? David has just been catapulted from a comfortable throne into a harsh wilderness. Only days before he was dealt the biggest shock of his life when he learned that Absalom for years and behind his back had been undermining David's rule—Absalom plotting all these years to kill his father and take over as king! And David all the time oblivious to it. Any moment now, in this unforgiving wilderness, Absalom's plot might succeed. And at the very moment David tells his commanders to "deal gently" with Absalom, Absalom is hunting him down—David hunted by his son as years before he had been hunted by Saul. But he was young during those Saul years; he is no longer young. Amazingly, he is still compassionate—as compassionate with this son who hates him as he was with Saul who hated him. The worst rejection David has experienced precipitates this extraordinary love command: "Deal gently for my sake with the young man Absalom."

> 18:6 So the army went out . . . and the battle was fought in the forest of Ephraim. [7] The men of Israel were defeated there by the servants of David, and the slaughter there was great on that day. . . .
> [9] Absalom happened to meet the servants of David. Absalom was riding on his mule, and the mule went under the thick branches of a great oak. His head caught fast in the oak, and he was left hanging between heaven and earth, while the mule that was under him went on. [10] A man saw it, and told Joab. . . . [14] Joab . . . took three spears in his hand, and thrust them into the heart of Absalom, while he was still alive in the oak. [15] And ten young men, Joab's armor-bearers, surrounded Absalom and struck him, and killed him.
> [16] Then Joab sounded the trumpet, and the troops came back from pursuing Israel. . . . [17] They took Absalom, threw him into a great pit in the forest, and raised over him a very great heap of stones. . . . [18] Now Absalom in his lifetime had taken and set up for himself a pillar that is in the King's Valley . . . ; he called the pillar by his own name. It is called Absalom's Monument to this day.

In the widespread general slaughter of that day's battle, one death is singled out for attention—Absalom. In deliberate defiance of David's command, Joab kills him. He not only kills him, he violates him.

The actual site of the battle, "the forest of Ephraim," cannot be located precisely, but it is obviously a forested area of tangled undergrowth and loose rock, which is characteristic of the land as we see it today.

The scene is dramatic: As Absalom rides his mule through the tangle of forest, his magnificent head of hair, of which he is inordinately proud, catches in the branches of a huge oak tree. The mule keeps going and Absalom is left hanging by his hair from the tree. His hair, his famous hair, symbol of his beauty and virility, is now the means by which he is rendered helpless, defenseless in the midst of the fighting. The first person to find him honors David's command of nonviolence and simply reports back to Joab. But Joab has no patience with David's values and, arriving on the scene, without hesitation spears him, not just once but three times. Joab's ten armor-bearers join in, compounding the violence. They all want a part of the action of killing Absalom. Killing Absalom turns into a frenzy. But that is not the end of it; the violence is extended by throwing the corpse into a pit and pelting it with stones. No state funeral for Absalom—his violated body is not so much buried as pelted into oblivion in an orgy of stone-throwing. First David's command violated; now Absalom's body violated.

The narrator emphasizes the anarchic meanness of Absalom's "last rites" by inserting here a mention of "Absalom's Monument," the vanity pillar that he had set up for himself near Jerusalem to assert his importance. The two monuments are set parallel in our imaginations: the haphazard heap of angrily thrown rocks, memorial to his final vanity, and the self-erected stone pillar, memorial to his early vanity. Vanity compounded: "vanity of vanities" (Eccl. 1:2)—Absalom's memorial. The double meaning of vanity, vanity as pride and vanity as emptiness, is expressed in the contrasting monuments.

DAVID'S MOURNING (18:19–19:8a)

18:19 Then Ahimaaz son of Zadok said, "Let me run, and carry tidings to the king. . . . " 20 Joab said to him, "You are not to carry tidings today . . . because the king's son is dead." 21 Then Joab said to a Cushite, "Go, tell the king what you have seen." The Cushite bowed before Joab, and ran. 22 Then Ahimaaz son of Zadok said again to Joab, "Come what may, let me also run after the Cushite." . . . 23 . . . So he said to him, "Run." Then Ahimaaz ran by the way of the Plain, and outran the Cushite.

24 Now David was sitting between the two gates. The sentinel went up to the roof of the gate by the wall, and when he looked up, he saw a man running alone. . . . 26 Then the sentinel saw another man running. . . . 27 The sentinel said, "I think the running of the first one is like the running of Ahimaaz son of Zadok." The king said, "He is a good man, and comes with good tidings."

28 Then Ahimaaz cried out to the king, "All is well!" . . . 29 The king said, "Is it well with the young man Absalom?" Ahimaaz answered, " . . . I saw a great tumult, but I do not know what it was." 30 The king said, "Turn aside, and stand here." . . .

31 Then the Cushite came; and the Cushite said, "Good tidings for my lord the king! For the LORD has vindicated you this day. . . . " 32 The king said to the Cushite, "Is it well with the young man Absalom?" The Cushite answered, "May the enemies of my lord the king, and all who rise up to do you harm, be like that young man."

We last saw Ahimaaz, along with Jonathan, delivering a message to David that an attack from Absalom was imminent: David was in danger of his life and needed to get across the Jordan to safe ground—and quickly (2 Sam. 17:15–22). Now Ahimaaz delivers a very different message to David: The danger is over, the war is over; David can relax.

But this is a good news/bad news message. The good news is that the

Absalom rebellion has been put down, the civil war is over and won. The bad news is that Absalom, whom the king explicitly ordered to be treated "gently," is dead. The two elements, and the tension that builds up between them, are conveyed by separate messengers, Ahimaaz with the good news and an unnamed "Cushite" with the bad news.

Joab tries to restrain Ahimaaz from going to David. Calculating Joab does not want David to hear the news from a trusted friend of the family. A personal messenger would deliver a personal message, and Joab, personally implicated in the bad news part of the message, does not want to be mentioned. So he sends an outsider, a "Cushite," to deliver the news impersonally: "Go, tell the king what you have seen" (v. 21). He would be more likely to provide an objective battle report, with Joab's insubordinate murder of Absalom laundered out. Joab tells Ahimaaz that he doesn't want him to go because he wants to protect him from David's response to the news of Absalom's death. But the person he really wants to protect is himself. Ahimaaz won't be restrained, and Joab finally relents with a curt, "Run."

Joab's attempted restraint of Ahimaaz heightens the tension inherent in the news. Ahimaaz gets a late start, but is a faster runner and gets there first. He is not only faster; he is smarter. The Cushite apparently takes the most direct route, through the tangled forest of Ephraim, back to Mahanaim, where David sits waiting for news at the city gates. Ahimaaz "ran by the way of the Plain," the longer but smoother route that goes along the river valley of the Jordan. We get a sense of Ahimaaz, personally involved in this mission, using all his wits and energy; in contrast, the Cushite is doggedly doing his job, obediently but impersonally following orders.

The two messengers divide the message between them, first the good news and then the bad news: Ahimaaz is first with the good news of the victory; the Cushite follows with the bad news of Absalom's death.

When David presses Ahimaaz for Absalom details, Ahimaaz falters and says, in effect, "I don't know about that part." Some interpret his shuffling as cowardice, fearing David's response; after all, he had once killed a messenger of bad news (2 Sam. 1:11–16). But it is more likely that he is simply and compassionately giving the bad news gradually and gently. David is father as well as king, and Ahimaaz is as sensitive to the personal as to the official dimensions of the message he is delivering.

If asked the question "Who would you rather have bring the news of your child's murder, a close friend or a police officer?" we would most certainly choose a friend. Ahimaaz is such a friend. The Cushite was the designated messenger of Joab, the "policeman."

By the time the Cushite arrives with his bad news of Absalom's death,

Ahimaaz is already compassionately there, a personal presence at David's side to help absorb the shock of the bad news of Absalom's death.

This detailed and extended narration of how Joab, Ahimaaz, and the Cushite play their respective parts in reporting Absalom's death to David provides a way for us as readers to become participants in David's response. We experience in some measure the ambiguities of love and justice. The death of Absalom serves the cause of justice triumphantly; the death of Absalom exposes the pain of unrequited love tragically: David's throne is saved; David's heart is broken.

The art in this narration consists in refusing to set the emotional and personal qualities of Ahimaaz and David on one side and the impersonal and official world of Joab and the Cushite on the other, and then to insist that we choose one over the other, as if one were more godly or "spiritual" than the other. Ahimaaz and the Cushite share the same reality. In this life, under the conditions in which we live it, we must not (in reality we cannot) attempt to eliminate either messenger in this complex history of sin and salvation that we inhabit.

In our desire to live more personally, to live out of our souls and not merely perform assigned functions, it is easy to vilify the official, institutional, bureaucratic world represented by Joab and the Cushite, treat them as subspiritual, and suppose that we can fashion a spiritual life that is pure and unsullied by pragmatism. But it cannot be done. David is as much in need that day of the blunt Cushite as of sensitive Ahimaaz. And of Joab. Despite all Joab's impulsive activism and coarse opportunism, David *needs* Joab. David, with his "heart after God," and Joab, who is never happier than when wielding his sword, belong to the same people of God.

There is a long history of reflection on these matters, on the deep and unresolvable conflict in all matters of spirit—the competing claims of love and justice, value and necessity, and matters of conscience and affairs of the state. Can abstractly formulated and enforced social and political justice coexist with the unpredictable idiosyncrasies of personal integrity? Can the free spirit maintain itself within the structures of ordered righteousness? Half-formed Christians are often heard to express the tension stated in the sentence, "I love Jesus but hate the church." In the course of history, first one and then the other achieves dominance, but even in extreme cases (totalitarian regimes or anarchic communes) the "other" never simply goes away. In our personal lives, there is a steady pressure to adopt one way and treat the other as the enemy. The biblical story, however, has David and Joab coexisting alongside each other. The personal and spontaneous David is far more attractive than the impersonal and institutional

Joab. And they do not have an easy time with each other. But the fact is that they are both necessarily part of the story. Love and war do not take place in separate or separated worlds. The death of Absalom is an exposition of love and of war simultaneously.

> 18:33 **The king was deeply moved, and went up to the chamber over the gate, and wept; and as he went, he said, "O my son Absalom, my son, my son Absalom! Would I had died instead of you, O Absalom, my son, my son!"**

David's words of mourning rank among the saddest, most heart-rending words ever spoken. They are wrenched out of David's gut when the Cushite's words sink home: his son murdered in the forest of Ephraim. David is no stranger to death, no stranger to tears, no stranger to murder, no stranger to disappointment, no stranger to sin. But no event in his life combines all these elements with such intensity, such ferocity, as does the matter of Absalom.

It is a bitter cup to drink. Will he drink it? This David who experienced so many blessings, entered into such exuberant joys, gave us words that we use still to express the generosity of God in our lives ("My cup runneth over," Psalm 23:5, King James Version), and characteristically lifted what he called "the cup of salvation" (Psalm 116:13) to toast God's goodness and blessing in the world and in his life—will he drink this cup? Will he take in the full measure of rejection, alienation, and rebellion and experience it in the depths of his being? At this moment, immersed in the experience of betrayal and ruin, we can almost hear the words spoken a thousand years later by Jesus, "Remove this cup from me; yet, not my will but yours be done" (Luke 22:42).

The cup is not removed. David, like our Lord after him, drinks it to the last drop, empties the cup. He tastes the bitterness, takes in the full reality of sin-sourced suffering. He speaks the name "Absalom" three times; he says "my son" five times. He experiences and then expresses in his lament the tangle of love and hate, righteousness and sin, good and evil that come to a head in Absalom.

At the farthest descent from Jerusalem, deep in the wilderness forest of Ephraim, David's story most clearly anticipates and most nearly approximates the Gospel story, the story of Jesus that extends into our stories, passion stories, stories of suffering, but suffering that neither diminishes nor destroys us, but makes us more human, prayerful, and loving.

There is a form of Christian meditation on Jesus that is structured along the route from Pilate's judgment seat where he is condemned to death to the hill, Golgotha, where he is killed on a cross to the garden tomb where he is buried. . . . The meditation formed on the fourteen "stations of the cross," fourteen events (some real, some imagined) that occur on the last day of his preresurrection life, from his condemnation to his burial, is a way of praying our way into and through suffering.

Our Christian ancestors have sometimes read this story of David's flight from Jerusalem as an anticipation of Jesus' route along the Via Dolorosa (the "road of sorrows") from Pilate's judgment seat to the cross on Golgotha, ending at Joseph's tomb. The parallels are not exact, and there are more differences than continuities, yet the theme is approximate: Both David and the "Son of David" are rejected and leave Jerusalem accompanied by both friends who help and foes who mock; at the darkest place both utter cries of dereliction; the rejection of each "David" is a revolt against God's anointed leader, and the rejections in both instances are unsuccessful—David is returned to Jerusalem to resume his rule, and Jesus, raised from the dead, ascends to the "right hand of the Father" to rule forever.

DAVID'S RETURN (19:1–43)

19:1 It was told Joab, "The king is weeping and mourning for Absalom." ² So the victory that day was turned into mourning for all the troops. . . . ⁵ Then Joab came into the house to the king, and said, "Today you have covered with shame the faces of all your officers who have saved your life today. . . . ⁶ . . . I perceive that if Absalom were alive and all of us were dead today, then you would be pleased. ⁷ So go out at once and speak kindly to your servants." . . . ⁸ Then the king got up and took his seat in the gate. The troops were all told, "See, the king is sitting in the gate"; and all the troops came before the king.

David is both king and father, but in the moment of his grief, "king" recedes into the shadows and "father" takes center stage. David gives himself to his grief. In the years preceding, it is probable that he let the "king" part of his life eclipse the "father" part. Now it goes the other way, "father" eclipses "king." He is absorbed in his grief, isolated in his loss.

But not for long. Joab unceremoniously jerks David back into being king. By this time we are used to Joab's style—unfeeling, business-as-usual, abrupt. Joab invades David's grief and scolds him into a public appearance; he must assure the people and the troops that everything is in order, that the king is in control, that *their* lives have meaning and dignity. Joab, of course, is right; but he is also, as so often, right in the wrong way. Personal intimacies are no part of Joab's world; Joab takes on the task, a little too vigorously it would seem (possibly because he was responsible for Absalom's death), of getting David back into royal harness. David accepts Joab's direction and takes up his work of king again. King and kingdom are saved.

> 19:8b **Meanwhile, all the Israelites had fled to their homes.** [9] **All the people were disputing throughout all the tribes of Israel, saying, "The king delivered us from the hand of our enemies. . . .** [10] **But Absalom, whom we anointed over us, is dead in battle. Now therefore why do you say nothing about bringing the king back?"**

The outcome of the battle is clear-cut, but it also plunges the country into confusion. The people had been thoroughly captivated by Absalom—intoxicated by his charisma and seduced by his charm. Excited by his promises and glamour, by the infusion of new energy into their lives, they had anointed Absalom king, probably without a second thought regarding David. David was used up. And now it turns out that old David is very much alive and young Absalom is a mutilated corpse. They cannot be ruled by a corpse—but do they want the old man back?

In the vacuum of power resulting from Absalom's death, anti-David and pro-David elements assert themselves. As long as David was firmly in control of the kingdom, anti-David elements were kept quiet. And when Absalom seemed such a sure thing, the pro-David elements kept a discreetly low profile. But now both voices clamor for attention: The pro-David and anti-David factions compete for prominence. One party wants him back right now, no questions asked (v. 10b). But other voices are strong enough to keep David's return from being a sure thing. David has put down Absalom's rebellion; he has yet to recover his kingdom.

Pulled away from his intense, but too brief, season of mourning, David now takes on the demanding diplomatic work of recovering his kingdom. His descent from Jerusalem to exile is now reversed and becomes an ascent along the identical road back home. And just as his descent was marked by meetings with significant people along the way, the ascent is also marked by personal encounters, some of them the same as those encountered on the descent to the wilderness. Five names or sets of names mark the intinerary: Zadok and Abiathar, Amasa, Shimei, Ziba and Mephibosheth, and Barzillai.

> 19:11 **King David sent this message to the priests Zadok and Abiathar, "Say to the elders of Judah, . . .** [12] **'You are my kin, you are my bone and my flesh; why then should you be the last to bring back the king?'"**

On leaving Jerusalem, David sent Zadok and Abiathar back. They carried out much-needed espionage work in the court of Absalom, serving as David's eyes and ears there. Their undercover intelligence work was critical in providing David with the information crucial to his survival. Now they are used as David's spokesmen to the ambivalent "elders of Judah," who had joined the Absalom rebellion and are now leaderless. David, through the priests, reminds them that they are the very ones who at Hebron made him king in the first place (2 Sam. 2:1–4), an act that was later seconded by the "elders of Israel" (2 Sam. 5:3). What are they waiting for? Isn't it clear, both through their early decision and now through this decisive victory, that David is their uncontested sovereign? The priests push the vacillating elders to act and act now to welcome David back as king.

19:13 **"And say to Amasa, 'Are you not my bone and my flesh? So may God do to me, and more, if you are not the commander of my army from now on, in place of Joab.'"** [14] **Amasa swayed the hearts of all the people of Judah as one, and they sent word to the king, "Return, both you and all your servants."** [15] **So the king came back to the Jordan; and Judah came to Gilgal to meet the king and to bring him over the Jordan.**

Amasa is a newcomer in the lineup. Amasa was the commander of Absalom's troops in the rebellion. He held a parallel position in Absalom's chain of command to Joab's position in David's. Amasa is also, as is Joab, David's nephew.

And now, working to recover his throne, David appoints Amasa as commander of his army and dumps Joab. What does this mean? At first reading it seems wrong: The rebel Amasa is rewarded and the loyal Joab sacked. But a second look at the text, reading this time "between the lines," furnishes discernible motives. First, "loyal" Joab had just murdered David's son in open defiance of David's explicit orders. There is nothing in the text telling us that David knew of that act of insubordination, but it was done in the open, with many witnesses. It is hardly conceivable that David did not soon learn of it. All during his rule, David had sometimes tolerated and other times used Joab's ruthless ways; this time Joab went too far; David has had it with Joab. He fires him and replaces him with Amasa.

A second probable motive has to do with recovering popular support. The general populace would still be emotionally attached to Absalom. Amasa, as a prominent leader in the Absalom rebellion, and now at the head of David's troops, will provide powerful pragmatic reasons for the people to fall into line behind David. So for reasons both personal (his anger at Joab) and public (his need for popular support), it makes sense to appoint Amasa as his new military commander.

The combination of the appeal to the elders and the appointment of Amasa works. It is not long before the people of Jerusalem troop down to the Jordan to welcome David and bring him back to the city as king.

> 19:16 **Shimei . . . hurried to come down with the people of Judah to meet King David;** [17] **with him were a thousand people from Benjamin. And Ziba, the servant of the house of Saul, with his fifteen sons and his twenty servants, rushed down. . . .**

We know by now that the cursing of Shimei in the course of David's flight from Jerusalem (2 Sam. 16:5–13) was not a merely personal thing; Shimei was spokesman for a strong anti-David segment of the population. Shimei had earlier supposed that he was delivering the final judgment on the rejected king and that David would soon be no more. But now David is back and in power. Shimei is the first in line to repent and ask for mercy, as well he should be.

> 19:18b **Shimei son of Gera fell down before the king, as he was about to cross the Jordan,** [19] **and said to the king, "May my lord not hold me guilty or remember how your servant did wrong on the day my lord the king left Jerusalem. . . .** [20] **. . . I have sinned." . . .** [21] **Abishai son of Zeruiah answered, "Shall not Shimei be put to death for this, because he cursed the LORD's anointed?"** [22] **But David said, "What have I to do with you, you sons of Zeruiah, that you should today become an adversary to me?" . . .** [23] **The king said to Shimei, "You shall not die." And the king gave him his oath.**

On the descent from Jerusalem, Abishai wanted to kill Shimei but was prevented by David; now on the ascent back, he again wants to kill him, and again he is restrained by David. On the flight out, David accepted Shimei's curses as the word of God's judgment on him; now he accepts Shimei's repentance and forgives him.

The "sons of Zeruiah," Abishai and Joab, have no sense of God; the only language they know is that of the sword and violence. Early in David's reign, exasperated over Joab's murder of Abner, David says, "These men, the sons of Zeruiah, are too violent for me" (2 Sam. 3:39); now late in his reign, following Joab's murder of Absalom and Abishai's move to murder Shimei, he is saying virtually the same thing: "What have I to do with you, you sons of Zeruiah, that you should today become an adversary to me?"

The "sons of Zeruiah," and they are legion in the world of religion, are always more than eager to do God's work, but they refuse to do it in God's way. They are vehemently on God's side, but have no interest in God's methods. Mercy, compassion, forgiveness, and grace are alien to them. But violence is not a means of grace.

Jesus also had his "sons of Zeruiah" to deal with. In a story that echoes this one, Luke tells of the time that James and John, the "sons of Zebedee" whose bellicosity had earned them the name "Sons of Thunder" (Mark 3:17), were rebuked by Jesus for wanting to kill the Samaritans who were unwelcoming to Jesus (Luke 9:51–56).

There is also a political dimension to David's forgiveness of Shimei. Shimei is a leader among the old Saul loyalists. Shimei killed (as Abishai wanted) would make a martyr of him for the Saul party—and dissidents thrive on martyrs. But Shimei forgiven would demonstrate David's continuing commitment to the welfare of the family and followers of Saul (see David's covenant with Jonathan, 1 Sam. 20:42). By bringing Shimei and his thousand Benjaminites (Saul's tribe) into his victory parade in the ascent back to Jerusalem, David shows himself king of *all* the people, not just those who had fought with him—"Do I not know that I am this day king over Israel?" (v. 22).

19:24 **Mephibosheth grandson of Saul came down to meet the king. . . .**

This is the fourth, and final, mention of Jonathan's son Mephibosheth in the David story. The first mention is a brief note telling us that in the confusion following Saul's death he was dropped by his nurse and crippled in both his feet (2 Sam. 4:4). The second mention takes place when, years later, as David sought out Jonathan's heirs so that he could "show kindness" to them, he was brought into David's court. That invitation brought Mephibosheth into David's family, where he was cared for and protected (2 Samuel 9). His name comes up a third time the night of David's flight from Absalom when Ziba, Mephibosheth's guardian, tells David that Mephibosheth has turned traitor—that in the confusion and anarchy of the Absalom rebellion he was counting on the old Saul loyalists to come into power and make him king (2 Sam. 16:1–4).

And now a fourth appearance. As Mephibosheth meets David, he certainly does not look as if he has been anticipating a personal coronation—beard ragged and clothes looking as if they have been slept in. David, with Ziba's accusation in mind, questions his loyalty. Mephibosheth claims that

Ziba betrayed him—left him stranded in the city without a mount on the night of Absalom's coup; otherwise he would certainly have been with David in his flight.

So who is telling the truth, Ziba or Mephibosheth? Most readers side with Mephibosheth. But there is a deliberate withholding of a verdict by the narrator of this story, in order to give emphasis to David's response. David believed Ziba's accusation when he first heard it. As he now listens to Mephibosheth, he knows that both stories cannot be true. Here the narrative takes us into new territory: David doesn't *care* who is telling the truth. There is no cross-examination, no calling in of witnesses. David accepts both men, Ziba and Mephibosheth, back into his city. His love is large enough, expansive enough, to handle faithlessness, fecklessness, lies, and hypocrisy. David does not insist on having a "pure church."

This is the characteristic Davidic note, the anticipation of gospel. David first sought out Mephibosheth from a position of strength. He used his strength to love generously, *covenantally*. He treated Mephibosheth with the same love with which God had saved David.

In this final act of love to Mephibosheth, David is fatigued from battle, having barely survived the worst rejection and betrayal of his life; he is grieving the terrible death of his son and abandonment by many of his trusted friends. And now Mephibosheth stands before him with Ziba's accusation of betrayal (16:3) hanging over his head. There has been so much treachery in the past few days, so many faithless—is Mephibosheth one more who has betrayed his love? If David has been betrayed by his own son, why wouldn't Mephibosheth, with a legitimate (as Saul's grandson) claim on the throne, also betray him?

It does not matter. David does not have to know. He takes Mephibosheth's story (vv. 26–28) at face value and keeps faith with him. David in weakness, his kingdom in fragments about him, is as strong as ever in his commitments.

Every step David takes on his return as king is also a step in recovery of the kingdom: The followers of Absalom are brought around by Amasa; the old loyalist followers of Saul are brought on board by Ziba, Shimei, and Mephibosheth. The flight from Jerusalem when the kingdom was disintegrating in slow motion, piece by piece falling away (Shimei, Ahithophel, Mephibosheth), is now put back together piece by piece (Shimei, Ziba, Mephibosheth) and restored into wholeness.

The final name in the chronicle of the return is a friend David made while in exile, Barzillai the Gileadite.

19:31 Now Barzillai the Gileadite had come down . . . to escort him over the Jordan. [32] Barzillai was a very aged man, eighty years old. . . . [39] Then all the people crossed over the Jordan, and the king crossed over; the king kissed Barzillai and blessed him, and he returned to his own home. . . .

The last person mentioned in David's return, as the king recovers his kingdom, is Barzillai. Every conversation and encounter that takes place in the course of David's return is strategically charged with either political or personal implications. But not Barzillai. Barzillai wants nothing from David, needs nothing from David.

Barzillai, along with Shobi and Machir, was David's host in Gilead when he arrived in flight from Absalom (2 Sam. 17:27–29). He gave him sanctuary and food, much-needed protection, and lavish provisions in bed and board. Fifteen hundred years later, Benedict made it a rule in the monasteries he directed that every person who knocked at the door of the monastery was to be received as if she or he were Christ—a Christ-guest. Benedict cited Jesus as a precedent: "I was a stranger and you welcomed me" (Matt 25:35); he could as well have invoked Barzillai as patron in his practice of hospitality.

David quite naturally wants to reciprocate Barzillai's hospitality with hospitality of his own, now that he is in the position to give it; he invites him to make his home with him in Jerusalem. But Barzillai declines. Barzillai is there that day simply to say goodbye.

Barzillai owes nothing to David and has nothing to gain from him. Virtually everyone in this parade of people, not least David himself, has something at stake in how things will develop from this day forward. But not Barzillai. Barzillai's presence in David's company this day is sheer blessing. He is with David to bless him and be blessed by him. This is a rare instance of friendship without self-interest. Barzillai's age and wealth serve to detach him from the drives of ambition and acquisition. David is not for him a person to use to fulfill his own needs—whether his political and social needs, or the much more common "need to be needed." And he himself will not be used by David. If David thought that bringing back Barzillai to Jerusalem would serve as a trophy of the allegiance of East Jordan, he was disappointed. Age and wealth do not always provide such detachment and freedom. Plenty of people only get more cranky and grabby as they add years to their lives and money to their accounts. But Barzillai exhibits the combination of old age and great wealth at its finest: a freedom from need that is employed in freeing another— Barzillai goes with David to the Jordan with the express purpose of "sending him off" free of obligation, free to be king with no strings attached.

Thus, the last person to escort David on his return across the Jordan is there only to send David on his way freely. What we see in Barzillai, standing with David at the banks of the Jordan that day, is the courtesy of a host saying goodbye to his guest.

And David, poised now for his final ascent to Jerusalem, where he will resume his kingdom work, up to his neck with people in need and people whom he needs, accepts Barzillai's gift of hospitality as gift and responds with a kiss and a blessing. He doesn't try to hold on to this precious host, but lets him go in affectionate blessing, releasing him with God's benediction. The single sign of continuity between the hospitality in Gilead and the return to responsibilities in Jerusalem is Barzillai's son, Chimham, who will now make his home in David's court.

It is fitting that Barzillai, blessing and being blessed, provides the last entry in the story of David's return. In the murk and tangle of mixed motives and negotiated advantages that have clustered at the Jordan, this scene gives the last word to free generosity, to the grace of hospitality—a rare moment in David's life, and all the more to be treasured in that everything in David's world is soon to disintegrate again into rivalry and self-seeking and violence. Frame this moment! Treasure it—we are not to see the like of it again in this story.

> 19:40 **The king went on to Gilgal, and Chimham went on with him; all the people of Judah, and also half the people of Israel, brought the king on his way.**
>
> [41] **Then all the people of Israel came to the king, and said to him, "Why have our kindred the people of Judah stolen you away, and brought the king and his household over the Jordan . . . ?"** [42] **All the people of Judah answered . . . , "Because the king is near of kin to us. . . . "** [43] **But the people of Israel answered the people of Judah, "We have ten shares in the king, and in David also we have more than you. . . . Were we not the first to speak of bringing back our king?" But the words of the people of Judah were fiercer than the words of the people of Israel.**

David does not even make it back home to Jerusalem before the bickering starts up. Everybody wants David back as king, but not everyone wants what goes with him, namely, a unified kingdom. The disruption of the Absalom rebellion gave the old Saul loyalist party hope that they might come to power; David has seemingly brought them back into line. But now a not-unrelated but deeper fissure appears: the old North-South division.

The twelve tribes never did have an easy time of it with one another; each had always retained a good measure of individual autonomy. The ten tribes of the north (Israel) had a somewhat common identity, as over against the two tribes of the south (Judah). Worship of God, earlier at Shiloh and then at Jerusalem, had been their single unifying act. But when they insisted on having a king "like the other nations," they became a politically unified nation. Saul made a beginning at getting the twelve tribes functioning as a single nation, and David had finished the job. But even though the imposed unity seemed to function smoothly under David's rule, it now appears that it did not go very deep. The people still identified themselves as "northerners" (Israel) and "southerners" (Judah). And now, with David's return, they become rivals in claiming him as "their" king, bickering among themselves, each side claiming to have an insider's advantage.

The squabbling that broke out that day in Gilgal, as the people brought David back to be their sovereign in Jerusalem, continues to be reproduced in Christian communities. We are all agreed that we want Jesus to save us from our sins and rule over us from the "right hand of the Father," but then we break up into factions, each group claiming precedent or privilege in being "first." Eastern Orthodox and Roman Catholic, Baptist and Presbyterian, Evangelicals and Pentecostal, Anglican and Methodist, Mennonite and Quaker—and so many others: 287 denominations in North America alone at last count!—each insisting on the exclusive honor of returning Jesus to the throne from which he has been chased by an Absalomic world in revolt. Everyone, it seems, wants Jesus as sovereign but doesn't want to mingle too intimately with the various peoples over whom he exercises his sovereignty.

David is not pleased. He has been through a lot. He has recovered from the loss of Absalom, negotiating step by step the recovery of his kingdom, dealing with complex emotional and political details. He has been blessed and sent on his way across the Jordan with the affection and hospitality of the old man Barzillai. He set out on the ascent to his city and throne triumphant in the company of an exuberant people—a glorious moment. He has hardly, though, taken the first step when the crowd of people who have come to accompany him on the victory parade split into camps "North" and "South," wrangling over who has the better claim on David as king. It is not an edifying sight. The contrast between what they are there for (to welcome David), and what they in fact are doing (fighting among themselves over who will be the chief welcomer), could not be more stark.

At first, the southerners (Judah) seem to be getting the best of it, their voices louder and angrier than the northerners (Israel). Then one man

silences the cacophony with a blast from his ram's-horn trumpet (the sho-
far) and calls to his fellow Israelites (the "northerners") to walk away from
the inaugural parade and secede from David's rule. In effect he says, "If we
can't be equal with you in this government, we won't be part of it at all.
We won't be second-class citizens. We have our northern pride and aren't
going to put up with humiliations from you. Go ahead, take David as your
king; we're going our own way!"

A SECOND REVOLT: SHEBA (20:1–26)

20:1 Now a scoundrel named Sheba son of Bichri, a Benjaminite, happened
to be there. He sounded the trumpet and cried out,
   "We have no portion in David,
   no share in the son of Jesse!
   Everyone to your tents, O Israel!"
So all the people of Israel withdrew from David and followed Sheba son
of Bichri; but the people of Judah followed their king steadfastly from the
Jordan to Jerusalem.

The emotional climate created by the coming together of two "weather
systems," David's charismatic presence, and the people's emotional wrangling was such that Sheba the Bichrite's demagogic speech sparked a storm
of secession. The northerners walked away from Gilgal, insulted and angry: "If you want David so badly, you can have him; we're leaving." And
they left and went home (to their "tents").

The southerners now have David all to themselves and lead him to Jerusalem. But Sheba the Bichrite had "rained" on the parade. The long and
careful work of bringing the north and south together, which had been one
of David's major earlier achievements, was in ruins.

The only thing we know about Sheba the son of Bichri is that he is a
Benjaminite, that is, a northerner of the tribe of Saul. That puts him in the
camp of the Saul loyalist party that was never quite integrated into David's
kingdom.

Back in Jerusalem, but with the northern tier of his kingdom broken
away, David does two things, one symbolic and the other military: He puts
away the concubines and he dispatches Amasa to pursue the rebel leader,
Sheba the Bichrite.

The action regarding the concubines is a matter of public relations,
"making a statement" that sets David above partisan politics.

20:3 David came to his house at Jerusalem; and the king took the ten concubines whom he had left to look after the house, and put them in a house under guard, and provided for them, but did not go in to them. So they were shut up until the day of their death, living as if in widowhood.

This is the third time that the "ten concubines" are mentioned. First, as David flees from Absalom he leaves them behind to take care of his household (2 Sam. 15:16). Next, we learn that Absalom makes a public show of taking the concubines as his own, exhibiting his royal power through his sexual virility. And now David, in his first act on returning to power, sequesters the ten concubines. He gives them protection, a place to live, and food to eat, but he no longer has anything to do with them sexually. They live out their lives "as if in widowhood."

What does this mean? The concubines are part of the cultural landscape of David's world that we know little about. The three references in the story to the concubines emphasize the cultural chasm between us and David. One thing that we do know is that concubines were part of the trappings of royalty in the ancient East, and by having them David was doing what all the other kings did.

But why does he put them away? We can only speculate on the significance of David's action: Did his experience during the Absalom rebellion chasten and purify his concept of what it means to be king? Absalom took one feature of David's kingship, the concubines, and exploited it to make himself appear greater than David. Whereas Absalom took and used the concubines to show off his power, David now sets the concubines aside to divest himself of anything that hints of prideful glamour—he is God's king, not the people's king. He has come back not to "out-Absalom Absalom," but to humbly represent God's sovereignty.

Perhaps David's taking on of concubines in the first place was a thoughtless going along with what kings in general did in those days. But now that Absalom has so conspicuously used the concubines to embellish his charisma, David counters that image-building publicity stunt by refusing to use these women at all. He will excise manipulative sex and power from his conduct as king. It has been a long time coming, but "better late than never." By putting away the concubines, he sends a signal to his people: "This is a chastened king you are dealing with now; suffering has done some good work here; I'm not the same old king." We cannot know for sure, but the matter of the concubines may have such significance.

Ignorant as we are of the social and cultural nuances involved with royal concubines, we cannot venture very far into interpretation here. But the triple repetition of the concubines is evidence that the storyteller senses something important is going on. Storytellers often write more than they know; truths emerge in the process of narration of which the narrator is not fully aware.

Perhaps there is something of that here: Could it be that we are enabled to see in David's putting away of the concubines a seed of sensitivity to women's dignity that would take millennia to germinate? The concubine is the archetypal "used" woman—useful only for her ability to perform. None of the ten concubines is named; they are not persons, they are de-personalized functions. In their first mention in the story, they are used by David to take care of the household, a domestic function; in the second mention, they are used by Absalom to demonstrate his royal virility, a sexual function; in the third mention, David pulls them out of the world of function and role entirely—they will never again be "used." They live the rest of their lives without function—they simply *are*; the Hebrew phrase translated "living as if in widowhood" is ambiguous; it can also be rendered, "as widows, but fully alive women."

It is common for commentators to feel sorry for these women in their defunctionalized life. Since they are now *use*less, certainly they must now feel useless. But could it not be that they would now, for the first time since their concubinage, feel truly themselves, their sheer being and being-there adequate reason for being there? What might the ten concubines do with themselves now that they had no sexual or domestic use? Maybe they prayed. It is not past imagining to see these ten concubines as a primitive community of cloistered nuns, withdrawn from the sexual and domestic impositions of the culture, and free for a vigorous life of adoration of God. Maybe the storyteller subliminally senses something in David's treatment of the concubines that could hardly be explicitly imagined in that culture, but that would later, much later, germinate from the soil of the biblical story in freeing women (and others) from culture-imposed roles.

20:4 **Then the king said to Amasa, "Call the men of Judah together to me within three days, and be here yourself."** [5] **So Amasa went to summon Judah; but he delayed beyond the set time that had been appointed him.** [6] **David said to Abishai, "Now Sheba son of Bichri will do us more harm than Absalom; take your lord's servants and pursue him. . . .** [7] **Joab's men went out after him. . . .** [8] **When they were at the large stone that is in Gibeon, Amasa came to meet them. . . .** [9] **Joab said to Amasa, "Is it well with you, my brother?" And Joab took Amasa by the beard with his right hand to kiss him.**

[10] But Amasa did not notice the sword in Joab's hand; Joab struck him in the belly . . . and he died. . . .
    Then Joab and his brother Abishai pursued Sheba son of Bichri.

Having taken care of the concubines, David turns his attention to the rebel Sheba, a threat to his kingdom every bit as serious as Absalom's. He orders Amasa, his newly appointed commander of the military, to round up the troops and be ready in three days to go after Sheba. Amasa does not show up on time, whether out of incompetence or insubordination we do not know. David cannot wait, and puts Abishai in charge.

And now Joab's name reappears in the text (v. 7). After his insubordinate murder of Absalom, he was summarily dismissed from his post and replaced by Amasa. Now, as Abishai takes over from the delinquent Amasa, Joab, like a bad penny, shows up.

Joab and his men set out after Sheba. They are only six miles out of Jerusalem (at Gibeon) in their pursuit of Sheba when Amasa catches up with them. Joab goes to greet Amasa, acting like an old friend (they are cousins, remember); with one hand, he grabs him by the beard, a gesture of "old boy" affection, and leans in to kiss him; but he has a sword in his other hand, and at the same time that he kisses Amasa he stabs him in the belly. Murdered Amasa is left on the road, disemboweled in a pool of blood. The gory remains of Amasa stop traffic until someone pulls the mutilated corpse off the road and covers it.

This is Joab's fourth murder of which we have an account: Abner, Uriah, Absalom, and now Amasa—each of them an act of treachery.

20:14 Sheba passed through all the tribes of Israel to Abel. . . . [15] Joab's forces came and besieged him in Abel. . . . Joab's forces were battering the wall to break it down. [16] Then a wise woman called from the city, "Listen! Listen! Tell Joab, 'Come here, I want to speak to you.'" [17] He came near her; and the woman said, . . . [18] . . . "They used to say in the old days, 'Let them inquire at Abel'; and so they would settle a matter. [19] I am one of those who are peaceable and faithful in Israel; you seek to destroy a city that is a mother in Israel. . . . " [20] Joab answered, "Far be it from me. . . . [21] That is not the case! But a man . . . , called Sheba son of Bichri, has lifted up his hand against King David; give him up alone, and I will withdraw from the city." The woman said to Joab, "His head shall be thrown over the wall to you." [22] Then the woman went to all the people with her wise plan. And they cut off the head of Sheba son of Bichri, and threw it out to Joab . . . , and all went to their homes, while Joab returned to Jerusalem to the king.

The pursuit of Sheba resumes with Joab in charge. Amasa is dead; Abishai, whom David appointed, is not mentioned again; Joab has taken over. It is a long pursuit, far into the north country to the city of Abel. Sheba and his troops have taken refuge within the city walls, and Joab goes to work to knock the walls down. Joab is good at this kind of thing—he knows the craft of war.

But the destruction of the city is deflected in a surprising way—a "wise woman" (v. 16) confers with Joab. This is the second time that Joab and a "wise woman" appear together in the David story. Earlier (14:1–3) Joab sent to Tekoa for a "wise woman"; now a wise woman of Abel sends for Joab. She negotiates a deal: She will give up Sheba in exchange for Joab's withdrawal from the city. Joab agrees. Sheba's head is thrown over the city wall, and Joab leaves.

This is the final episode in the story of David's return to power and the recovery of his kingdom. It is a complex story, with many characters playing their parts, giving voice to various motives, as the God-blessed, God-promised sovereignty of David is assured. But throughout, the behavior and voice of Joab have disturbed the peace. Repeatedly he has helped David, but in the wrong way. In this final episode, it looks as if Joab has the decisive role again; but it is not to be so—a "wise woman" upstages him and puts in the last word.

Joab took over in the early stage of the Sheba revolt and made his mark in his characteristic way—violent and treacherous in the murder of Amasa. And then he meets the wise woman of Abel, who diverts him from his hell-bent strategy of destruction and saves her city. Walter Brueggemann notices the striking contrast between Joab's murderous ruthlessness and the woman's peaceable wisdom. Wisdom is pitted against violence, and wisdom wins. "The wise are those not trapped in conventional perceptions. They are those who can think of an alternative way around the present set of circumstances. In this case the only option seems to be Joab versus Sheba to the death. The city is sure to be destroyed in the process . . . [but] a woman speaks the word that breaks the threat of the king, a woman who stands outside the seduction of politics and militarism and can imagine another way. She prevails even against arms and anger. . . . Wise words override ruthless policy. At the end, not only the woman and the city are saved; something of David's dignity and self-respect are also rescued from Joab's mad, obedient intent" (Brueggemann, *First and Second Samuel*, 332).

20:23 Now Joab was in command of all the army of Israel; Benaiah son of Jehoiada was in command of the Cherethites and the Pelethites; 24 Adoram

was in charge of the forced labor; Jehoshaphat son of Ahilud was the
recorder; [25] Sheva was secretary; Zadok and Abiathar were priests; [26] and Ira
the Jairite was also David's priest.

Earlier in the story of David's reign, we were given a list of his leaders (2
Sam. 8:15–18); this is a similar list, the two lists framing the story of David.
In this second list, there is one additional officer, Adoram, in charge of
"forced labor"; there is one replacement, Sheva for Seraiah as secretary;
David's sons are deleted as priests, and Ira the Jairite put in their place. It
is an unemotional, matter-of-fact ending to an emotional, transcendence-
charged story, like the credits listed at the end of a film.

In reflecting on what we have just read, we realize that this is not the
kind of narrative we are used to reading in a religious book. We are used
to "moral lessons" and "theological truths." But this story, while it is both
moral and theological, cannot be boxed into either of those categories.
This is a story of God's ways with men and women the way they are, not
the way they are supposed to be. God, as the story is told, is not separate
from the story in such a way as to be generalized into "truths." The *way*
God works, patiently and behind the scenes, "slow to anger and abound-
ing in steadfast love" (Psalm 103:8), establishes divine sovereignty by using flawed, rebellious, out-of-the-way men and women to do it. It is the
kind of storywriting (story*telling*) that will surface a thousand years later in
the four Gospels of Matthew, Mark, Luke, and John. This narrative trains
us in perceiving and responding to God as God is, not as we would wish
or fear is the case—unforced, attentive to details, ever-present but mostly
hidden, sure . . . and sovereign. As this narrative is reread and reheard, generation after generation, it continues to release subtleties and intricacies of
"Presence" that continue to shape and reshape our lives.

21. David in Retrospect
2 Samuel 21–24

The book of 2 Samuel concludes with a symmetrical wrap-up of David's life. At first glance, these acts and words look as if they are a sort of appendix of miscellaneous materials. But a closer look discerns design: Seemingly unrelated materials are put together in such a way as to provide a coherent conclusion to the book.

Chronologically, this is not the end of the David story, for the account of David's actual last days extends into 1 Kings 1–2. But this part of the narration is given the "sense of an ending" by means of a symmetrical arrangement of summarizing acts and words. Two stories bracket this section (21:1–14 and 24:1–25). Two lists are set within the brackets (21:15–22 and 23:8–39). And placed in the center are two poems (22:1–51 and 23:1–7). The stories give witness to the troubled historical world in which David worked and lived; the lists provide names of some of the key people associated with David and the work to which they were assigned, anchoring the drama in the prose of daily work; and the poems at the center express David's relationship with God. The sequence is from outside in—from historical events to personal, workday relationships to God and the soul; and then from inside back out again—from God to persons to events. The poems of God and the soul at the center show David at his most intense and intimate. But it is not an isolated center: Events and names lead up to the God-center, and names and events develop from it.

Once we realize how and why these materials are put together, that is, discern the deliberate literary design involved in the writing, we will not look for a chronological sequence. These stories, people, and poems are gathered from various times and circumstances in David's life and arranged in this way as a kind of summing up.

FIRST STORY: THE FAMINE AND RIZPAH (21:1–14)

21:1 Now there was a famine in the days of David for three years; . . . and David inquired of the LORD. The LORD said, "There is bloodguilt on Saul and on his house, because he put the Gibeonites to death." ² So the king called the Gibeonites and spoke to them. . . . ³ David said to the Gibeonites, " . . . How shall I make expiation, that you may bless the heritage of the LORD?" ⁴ The Gibeonites said . . . ⁵ . . . , "The man who consumed us and planned to destroy us . . . ⁶ let seven of his sons be handed over to us, and we will impale them before the LORD at Gibeon. . . . " The king said, "I will hand them over."

⁷ But the king spared Mephibosheth, the son of Saul's son Jonathan. . . . ⁸ The king took the two sons of Rizpah . . . and the five sons of Merab. . . . ; ⁹ he gave them into the hands of the Gibeonites, and they impaled them on the mountain before the LORD. . . . They were put to death . . . at the beginning of barley harvest.

¹⁰ Then Rizpah . . . took sackcloth, and spread it on a rock for herself, from the beginning of harvest until rain fell . . . ; she did not allow the birds of the air to come on the bodies by day, or the wild animals by night. ¹¹ When David was told what Rizpah . . . had done, ¹² David went and took the bones of Saul and . . . of his son Jonathan from the people of Jabesh-gilead . . . ¹³ . . . and they gathered the bones of those who had been impaled. ¹⁴ They buried the bones of Saul and . . . Jonathan in the land of Benjamin . . . in the tomb of his father Kish. . . . After that, God heeded supplications for the land.

Emotionally and dramatically, Rizpah commands the center of this story. Rizpah wild in grief; Rizpah stubbornly protecting the unburied, exposed bodies of her two sons from violation by carrion vultures and snarling jackals; Rizpah helpless before the royal decree that ordered the death of her sons, yet steadfast in her vigil over their corpses as she guards them day and night for weeks (maybe months) from further mutilation and shame; Rizpah, an enduring witness of personal and intimate love against impersonal government and an abstract justice.

Rizpah is a hard-used woman, who refuses to be reduced to the harsh conditions of her culture. Her defiance of convention sets her apart from and above the world in which she suffers.

Rizpah's luminous and tender protest against the violation of her sons takes place in a dark and brutal time. There is a famine in the land, which has gone on for three years. King David prays for guidance. He learns that the famine is a punishing consequence of an evil act by King Saul. At some unspecified time during his reign, Saul had massacred Gibeonites, violating a solemn peace treaty that Joshua had made with them, and that sin now infected the land in the form of famine.

The story of the Gibeon-Israel pact is told in Joshua, chapter 9. Joshua had just led the people of Israel into the promised land of Canaan, capturing cities and conquering the opposition left and right. He appears unstoppable. Most of the Canaanite kings get together to fight for their lives, but one group, the Gibeonites, use cunning instead of swords. They dress in ragged clothes and worn-out sandals, get together some moldy bread and torn wineskins and present themselves to Joshua as travelers from a far country who have come because they had heard of Israel's God; they want to be in on what God is doing: "Make a treaty with us," they said, "let us be part of what God is doing in this land."

And Joshua did it—made a peace treaty with them, guaranteeing their lives. Three days later, Joshua learns that he was tricked by the Gibeonites; he punishes them by assigning them slave-servant status in the work of worship—"hewers of wood and drawers of water for the house of my God" (Josh. 9:23)—but he keeps the peace treaty. No Gibeonites are to be killed, ever, in Israel. And then Saul violated the peace treaty by ordering a massacre of Gibeonites. Joshua's peace pact with the Gibeonites, repudiated by Saul's massacre, has now resulted in the three-year famine. Natural disaster is traced back to a moral evil.

It is not our habit today to account for famines and floods and epidemics of disease by tracing them to evil acts. But even if we count ourselves fortunate to know far more about meteorology and disease than our ancestors, we would do well not to be overly condescending to their sense of the deep interconnectedness of all things. The moral and the physical are not confined separately in airtight categories. Sin cannot be contained; guilt cannot be quarantined. One of the most influential and sophisticated poems of the twentieth century, T. S. Eliot's "The Waste Land," is built on just that premise: The spiritual condition of a society is at the root of everything else that takes place—moral corruption results in a cultural wasteland. Maybe there is a more intimate interconnection between the way people live and the kind of world they live in than we commonly suppose.

David, having discerned the connection between the violation of the treaty and the famine in the land, wants to do something about it. Curiously, though he does start out to pray, he does not ask God what to do. Instead he asks the Gibeonites what he should do. They tell him to hand over seven sons of Saul, the man who ordered the massacre, so that they can ritually sacrifice them. Their position is that the sacrifice of the sons, guilty by descent, will wipe out the moral wrong and the famine will end.

That the Gibeonites would propose such a solution is understandable—they have been smarting under Saul's violation of the Joshua peace covenant. But that David should have listened to them is odd. Since when does God's king take spiritual counsel from outsiders to the law of God? Human sacrifice was not Israel's way of doing things. But David did what they asked. Included among the seven to be sacrificed were the two sons of Rizpah.

Rizpah was introduced into the David story back in 2 Samuel 3:7, as Saul's concubine. After Saul's death, Abner, commander of the army, took her as his own, provoking the angry outrage of Saul's son, Ishbaal. But Abner bullied Ishbaal into submission. Rizpah had no voice in that incident—she was a trophy, a prize, a *thing* to be fought over. Concubines aren't consulted; they are used.

The Gibeonite sacrifice of Rizpah's two sons (the other five were Saul's grandsons by his daughter Merab) probably took place in that general time period, that is, early in David's reign. Rizpah reenters the story now not as a sexual conquest but as a morally sensitive, emotionally alive *mother*, unwilling to dumbly acquiesce to the David-sanctioned Gibeonite killing of her sons.

She could not prevent the sacrificial killing of her sons, but she is able to prevent the indignities visited by birds and animals on their exposed bodies. Rizpah is brought into the story magnificent in her lament, spreading her prayer rug of sackcloth on the bare rock beside the bodies of her sons and keeping watch, waiting for the rain that will end the famine.

But there is more: Rizpah is not only magnificent in her compassionate, mothering humanity, she has influence. This woman who is voiceless and powerless, this victimized woman, influences David. And it is what David does under her influence that ends the famine.

David hears of Rizpah's lonely vigil out on the mountain and is moved to a like compassion for the remains of Saul and Jonathan, whose bodies had also been violated. David sends for their remains ("the bones") and gives them a decent and dignified burial in the family tomb of their father and grandfather, Kish.

It is "after that," that is, after David's recovery and burial of Saul and Jonathan, which was triggered by Rizpah's bold and compassionate vigil for her sons, that "God heeded supplications for the land" (v. 14). In other words, the storyteller makes us understand that it is not the Gibeonite sacrifices that break the famine, but Rizpah's prayerful vigil and David's compassionate burial.

And that is why Rizpah's story finds its place in this summarizing cluster of material on David: Rizpah brought David to his theological senses, demonstrating that it is not sacrifice that God wants, but mercy; it is not by taking life that we expiate sin, but by honoring it, not by inhuman cruelties, but by human compassion (see Micah 6:7–8). It is conceivable that Rizpah plays a role in what is articulated in the David tradition in prayers such as "Sacrifice and offerings you do not desire, but . . . " (Psalm 40:6) and "You have no delight in sacrifice" (Psalm 51:16).

The Greeks have a similar story, the story of Antigone and her state-executed brother, Polynices. Antigone, like Rizpah, poured out her grief and courageously expressed her loyalty in defiance of the conventions of justice and the order of society. Antigone and Rizpah witness the power of female courage and female initiative—the exquisitely *personal*, the prayer-ful, in contrast to and defiance of the lumbering machinery of convention and institution. They both give dignity to death, to the *person*. They are women of morality and mercy. Unlike Rizpah, Antigone had no influence with King Creon, who had ordered the execution of her brother and then ordered her death. Antigone dies tragically; Rizpah does not—Rizpah's action enters salvation history.

FIRST LIST: DAVID'S GIANT KILLERS (21:15–22)

21:15 **The Philistines went to war again with Israel, and David went down together with his servants. . . .** [16] **Ishbibenob, one of the descendants of the giants, . . . said he would kill David.** [17] **But Abishai son of Zeruiah came to his aid, . . . and killed him. . . .**
   [18] **After this a battle took place with the Philistines, at Gob; then Sibbecai the Hushathite killed Saph, who was one of the descendants of the giants.** [19] **Then there was another battle with the Philistines at Gob; and Elhanan . . . killed Goliath the Gittite. . . .** [20] **There was again war at Gath, where there was a man of great size, who had six fingers on each hand, and six toes on each foot . . . ; he too was descended from the giants.** [21] **When he taunted Israel, Jonathan son of David's brother Shimei, killed him.** [22] **These four were descended from the giants in Gath; they fell by the hands of David and his servants.**

Interestingly and significantly, this section is not about David in strength, but David in weakness. David needed friends and had them. David, for all his charisma and achievement, was not self-sufficient.

Four fierce and formidable giants are listed, all associated with the Philistine stronghold of Gath: Ishbibenob (wonderful name for a giant!), Saph, Goliath (already famous from the story in 1 Samuel 17), and an unnamed giant with six fingers and six toes. And four giant killers are listed: Abishai, Sibbecai, Elhanan, and Jonathan. Of the four, two (Abishai and Jonathan) are David's nephews. The nephews are worth noting, for while David suffered many family troubles, he also benefited from considerable family loyalty. The odd name in the list is Elhanan, named as the killer of Goliath. Backed by the strong tradition that it was David himself who killed Goliath (1 Samuel 17), a later historical account tells us that it was actually Goliath's *brother* who was killed by Elhanan (see 1 Chron. 20:5).

John Bunyan picked up the imagery that comes from this and other "giant" stories in the Bible, and Percy Dearmer later adapted it, to make the great hymn we know: "Who so beset him round/With dismal stories/Do but themselves confound—/His strength the more is./No foes shall stay his might;/Though he with giants fight,/He will make good his right/To be a pilgrim."

FIRST POEM: "THE LORD IS MY ROCK" (22:1–51)

Abruptly, there is a shift of voice. Until now the story has been told *about* David; David now speaks in his own voice. It is a voice, characteristically, in prayer. David prays.

Readers of the story of David have for many generations now inserted psalms of David at appropriate places in the narrative, suggesting the kind of praying that David engaged in through the various circumstances of his life. Here is the precedent for such practice: The original storyteller selects a psalm and sets it into the story at this summing-up moment in David's life, a valedictory psalm. Psalm 18 is selected, and enters the David story as 2 Samuel 22.

This is a most exuberant prayer. Nothing David prayed gathers more of his life together in one place than does this psalm. Von Balthasar quotes one of the Christian church's early pastors, Irenaeus, as saying that "the glory of God is a fully alive human being" (von Balthasar, *The Glory of the Lord*, 75). David fits Irenaeus's model.

22:1 David spoke to the LORD the words of this song on the day when the LORD delivered him from the hand of all his enemies, and from the hand of Saul.

God has spoken to and through David; now David speaks to God, which is to say that David prays. All our words to God presuppose a context, a world, which God speaks into being and in which God speaks; the speech is revelation. The context is particularized here in the phrase "delivered . . . from the hand of all his enemies, and from the hand of Saul." The word "delivered" is a key word in David's prayer: "delivered" and its synonym "saved" occur fourteen times (either as a noun or as a verb) in our reading/praying of it. "Deliver" and "save" deeply root David's prayer in God's gracious action. It is common to suppose that first we pray and then God acts; the sequence is reversed here: God acts and then David prays. Both sequences are possible, but this one deserves more prominence than we often give it.

> 22:2 **He said:**
> **The LORD is my rock, my fortress, and my deliverer,**
> 3 **my God, my rock, in whom I take refuge,**
> **my shield and the horn of my salvation,**
> **my stronghold and my refuge,**
> **my savior; you save me from violence.**
> 4 **I call upon the LORD, who is worthy to be praised,**
> **and I am saved from my enemies.**
>
> 5 **For the waves of death encompassed me,**
> **the torrents of perdition assailed me;**
> 6 **the cords of Sheol entangled me,**
> **the snares of death confronted me.**
> 7 **In my distress I called upon the LORD;**
> **to my God I called.**
> **From his temple he heard my voice,**
> **and my cry came to his ears.**

The single most characteristic thing about David is his relationship to God. David believes in God, thinks about God, imagines God, addresses God, and prays to God. He also forgets God, disobeys God, sins against God, and ignores God. But God is the reality that accounts for and defines all that David does and says. The largest part of David's existence is not David, it is God.

The evidence for David's pervasive, saturated awareness of God is in his profusion of metaphor: rock, fortress, deliverer, refuge, shield, horn of salvation, stronghold, savior. David is immersed in God. Every visibility reveals an invisibility. David names God by metaphor. Metaphor is the witness of language that there is a comprehensive interconnectedness to life invisible and visible, that is, "heaven and earth." Everything seen and heard, tasted, touched, and experienced, if only followed far enough and deeply enough, brings us into the presence of God. Even rocks. *Rock* is the lead-off metaphor as this prayer begins. It is frequent in David's praying vocabulary, arguably his favorite metaphor for God (it will occur five more times in this prayer). But a rock is the farthest thing possible from God. Is there anything lower on the scale of creation than rock? Yet the extreme unlikeness provokes in David an awareness of likeness. David notices what is everywhere around him, and the more he notices, the more he notices *God.* David is a poet, a theological poet—a God noticer, a God namer of the best kind, noticing and naming God in the immediacy of revelation and experience.

And virtually everything David notices and names about God, he prays. Nothing in or about God is left on the shelf to be considered at a later time and brought up for discussion when there is leisure for it. God is personal and present and requires *response.* The first person pronouns "my" and "I" are spoken twenty-one times in this opening salvo of prayer. There is not much that David knows of God that he does not pray.

In long retrospect over the Jewish and Christian centuries, it is no exaggeration to say that anything we know about God that is not prayed soon turns bad. The name of God without prayer to God is the stuff of blasphemy. So-called theologians, whether amateur or professional, who do not pray are in league with the devil. Indeed, the devil can be defined as that species of theologian who knows everything about God but will have nothing to do with him.

David prays. David prays the metaphors, prays the experience, prays the revelation. Everything that happens to him becomes, through prayer, God's salvation within him.

22:8   **Then the earth reeled and rocked;**
       the foundations of the heavens trembled
       and quaked, because he was angry.
   9 **Smoke went up from his nostrils,**
       and devouring fire from his mouth;
       glowing coals flamed forth from him.
 10 **He bowed the heavens, and came down;**
       thick darkness was under his feet.
 11 **He rode on a cherub, and flew;**
       he was seen upon the wings of the wind.
 12 **He made darkness around him a canopy,**
       thick clouds, a gathering of water.
 13 **Out of the brightness before him**
       coals of fire flamed forth.

14 **The LORD thundered from heaven;**
   the Most High uttered his voice.
15 **He sent out arrows, and scattered them**
   —lightning, and routed them.
16 **Then the channels of the sea were seen,**
   the foundations of the world were laid bare
   at the rebuke of the LORD,
   at the blast of the breath of his nostrils.

17 **He reached from on high, he took me,**
   he drew me out of mighty waters.
18 **He delivered me from my strong enemy,**
   from those who hated me;
   for they were too mighty for me.
19 **They came upon me in the day of my calamity,**
   but the LORD was my stay.
20 **He brought me out into a broad place;**
   he delivered me, because he delighted in me.

We are not many lines into this prayer before we recognize the revelational substratum on which it is being built. It is a recasting of the story of God's people being rescued from Egypt and worshiping at Sinai, God's Red Sea salvation of the chosen people from Egyptian slavery and the Sinai covenant, making with them a life of freedom. We have read these stories in Exodus, but where does David come up with all these details? We never read *these* in Exodus. David is not content merely to quote the Moses passages. He does not simply reference them in order to ground himself in authority; he *imagines* the scenes of the split-asunder sea and the thunder-rocked mountain. He enters the stories not to look for information but in order to become a participant. He isn't making things up; he is making himself "at home" in the story. David is showing us how to read the Bible.

The many psalms that come out of the David tradition, and this psalm in particular, show us a David who characteristically uses words magnificently. He uses words to sing and pray. He uses words to mint reality, fresh and shining. David is a poet—which is to say that he uses words to *make* something, not just talk about something. (The Greek word, *poieo*, root of our word "poet," means "make".)

God does not go to all the trouble of revealing reality so that we can stand around as spectators and look at it. The revelation is provided so that we can enter and become at home in it. Language is a primary way in which we come to be "at home." As we learn language, we are finding out not so much what is there but where we are. We are learning the neighborhood and finding the words that connect us with what and who is there. Imagination supplies the connections, the continuities, the relationships that are there but not visible. Imagination fills in the blanks, reads between the lines. In learning and using language, all of us start out as poets. We *make* sense of the world with words; we *make* our way with words; we *make* present with words what is absent; we *make* known with words what is unknown. Make, make, make . . . with words. Poets.

Poetry and prayer are natural allies. It is no accident that they are fused in the person of David, poet and pray-er. Prayer is practiced from the perception that the reality of God is immediate and personal; and poetry is the use of language most immediate and personal. The recovery of poetry in our lives goes hand in hand with the recovery of prayer. The fact that David is a practicing poet is as significant as that he practiced prayer.

David's prayer and poetry come together in his realization that he himself is included in the revelation of God: "He reached from on high, he took me. . . ./He brought me out into a broad place;/he delivered me, because he delighted in me" (vv. 17, 20). God's action in the past (Egypt and Sinai) does not remain in the past; it becomes present. David is in on it. There is no gap between Moses and David. By faith and prayer the two become contemporaries.

22:21 The LORD rewarded me according to my righteousness;
          according to the cleanness of my hands he recompensed me.
  22   For I have kept the ways of the LORD,
          and have not wickedly departed from my God.
  23   For all his ordinances were before me,
          and from his statutes I did not turn aside.
  24   I was blameless before him,
          and I kept myself from guilt.
  25   Therefore the LORD has recompensed me according to my righteousness,
          according to my cleanness in his sight.

Verse 21 introduces an abrupt change of mood and rhythm. From the cascade of metaphor that witnesses the action of a saving God, the poem slows to a meditative, ruminative eddy. Out of context, this reflective passage would mislead—the tone of mature and achieved assurance, even of arrival, verges on a complacency that could be interpreted as self-righteousness. But held firmly between David's participation in God's action, which begins his prayer (vv. 1–20), and his continuing witness to God's action, which completes it (vv. 29–51), this passage will not be misused as a text for self-congratulating piety.

Nearly all of the essential action in the biblical story has to do with God. But there *are* things we do that make a difference. Character develops, decisions are made, habits are nurtured, attention is trained, commandments are obeyed, and sins are confessed. These are not the largest part of the Christian life—*who God is* and *what God does* make up by far the largest part of the story. But what we do is still part of it. With the God-context firmly and thoroughly established, what David did (what *we* do) is given a nod.

Human behavior appropriate to the large God-context is now distilled into five gnomic aphorisms—morally balanced, wisely observed couplets:

> 22:26 **With the loyal you show yourself loyal;**
> **with the blameless you show yourself blameless;**
> 27 **with the pure you show yourself pure,**
> **and with the crooked you show yourself perverse.**
> 28 **You deliver a humble people,**
> **but your eyes are upon the haughty to bring them down.**

There is nothing uniquely Davidic (or Jewish/Christian) about these moral observations. It would not surprise us to come across these lines in an old Babylonian or Egyptian archive. But even if they are not distinctively biblical, they are still immensely important: They describe a *moral* world in which the way we live affects (and is affected by) who we are. How we behave and how we think matters. God's grace does not exempt us from living in common courtesy. God's initiative does not relieve us of the responsibility of getting out of bed in the morning. A bad person does not see the same tree that a good person sees. A bad life incapacitates us for real life. There is a vast accumulation of aphorism and insight from every century and civilization that articulates this moral truth. Moral wisdom is no less true for not being at the heart of our humanity. The heart of our humanity (as of this prayer as a whole) is God. But moral appendages, like fingers and toes, cannot be dismissed because they are not the heart. David's prayer also includes this richly textured moral wisdom that is common to humankind.

But the reflective interlude is soon over and David is at it again, with his somersaulting, cartwheeling exuberance that prays from the center of God's action in his life:

> 22:29 **Indeed, you are my lamp, O LORD,**
> **the LORD lightens my darkness.**

^{30} By you I can crush a troop,
   and by my God I can leap over a wall.
^{31} This God—his way is perfect;
   the promise of the LORD proves true;
   he is a shield for all who take refuge in him.

^{32} For who is God, but the LORD?
   And who is a rock, except our God?
^{33} The God who has girded me with strength
   has opened wide my path.
^{34} He made my feet like the feet of deer,
   and set me secure on the heights.
^{35} He trains my hands for war,
   so that my arms can bend a bow of bronze.
^{36} You have given me the shield of your salvation,
   and your help has made me great.
^{37} You have made me stride freely,
   and my feet do not slip;
^{38} I pursued my enemies and destroyed them,
   and did not turn back until they were consumed.
^{39} I consumed them; I struck them down, so that they did not rise;
   they fell under my feet.
^{40} For you girded me with strength for the battle;
   you made my assailants sink under me.
^{41} You made my enemies turn their backs to me,
   those who hated me, and I destroyed them.
^{42} They looked, but there was no one to save them;
   they cried to the LORD, but he did not answer them.
^{43} I beat them fine like the dust of the earth,
   I crushed them and stamped them down like the mire of the
      streets.

^{44} You delivered me from strife with the peoples;
   you kept me as the head of the nations;
   people whom I had not known served me.
^{45} Foreigners came cringing to me;
   as soon as they heard of me, they obeyed me.
^{46} Foreigners lost heart,
   and came trembling out of their strongholds.

David's prayer now becomes a witness to how God equips him to do God's work—David in action, David infused with the energy of God, David doing the work of God.

But when we look at the actual work that David describes, we are apt to be shocked: David's primary work is war. Most of the work that David exults in doing because God makes it possible for him to do it involves killing people. His work world features weapons and fighting.

Christian readers of the text are faced with a hard challenge: How do we handle the paradox of this wonderfully human life served up to us immersed in such dehumanizing conditions and with David a willing—yes, enthusiastic—participant in the dehumanizing, the killing?

We make a start by acknowledging and accepting the conditions in which life, and even more emphatically the Christian life, is conducted. Conditions: weather, soil, money, racial feelings and class rivalries, tribal traditions and social customs, technology and sex, the kinds of music played and the way language is used, and the sorts of stories told. The conditions, for must of us, become assumptions. We absorb these conditions with our mother's milk and rarely, if ever, think about them. Sometimes the conditions are favorable, sometimes unfavorable to being formed in the image of God, but they are always *there*. We do not live the Christian life in a social or cultural or political vacuum.

Charles Williams, in a brilliant exposition of the coming into being of the Christian community, wrote that Jesus was born under three conditions: Roman power, Greek culture, and human sin (Williams, *The Descent of the Dove*, 4). Williams convincingly insists that the Holy Spirit, who gives exposition to the life of Jesus through the shifting conditions of the centuries of the church's life, is *always* at work in conditions. It is not that the conditions limit the Spirit's work; rather, our Lord the Spirit chooses to work within the limits. By working within these limits, the Spirit does not baptize the conditions. Not many Christians look on first-century Palestine, for example, as a golden age. What we understand here is twofold: there are virtually no conditions that preclude the Spirit's work, and the Spirit never works apart from the conditions. God uses any conditions at hand in the making of the Kingdom, and that includes David stamping down his enemies "like the mire of the streets" (v. 43).

The conditions in which David's life is lived and narrated, and in which he is now praying, were made up in large part of Philistine culture and Canaanite morality—which is to say, violence and sex. The Philistine beer mugs and Canaanite fertility goddesses that archaeologists dig up from old ruins symbolize the two cultures. It is hard to imagine a more uncongenial time or more unlikely conditions for living a convincingly articulated life to the glory of God—unless, perhaps, "under Pontius Pilate."

And yet, here it is: David—born, living, and dying in Iron Age violence and sex, not exempt from their influence but not confined to it either—in quite incredible ways transcending the conditions so that it is possible, and common, for us to read the story and hardly notice the conditions. But we *must* notice them, for we live under conditions that are equally, and similarly, unfavorable. The cultural embodiments of violence and sex, war and promiscuity, don't seem to have changed that much. And because they are *human* conditions, they are the only conditions in which a holy life can be lived.

22:47 **The LORD lives! Blessed be my rock,**
       and exalted be my God, the rock of my salvation,
   48 **the God who gave me vengeance**
       and brought down peoples under me,
   49 **who brought me out from my enemies;**
       you exalted me above my adversaries,
       you delivered me from the violent.

   50 **For this I will extol you, O LORD, among the nations,**
       and sing praises to your name.
   51 **He is a tower of salvation for his king,**
       and shows steadfast love to his anointed,
       to David and his descendants forever.

There is not much of life that is left unexplored or unattended by David. And always—or at least eventually—the largest part of life for him was God. That is the witness of this great poem-prayer.

If we are not adoring, believing, and obeying, we miss out on most of what is right before our eyes. Ignoring or denying God does not, first of all, make us bad; it makes us small—puny and stringy, like the sculptures Giacometti gave to the twentieth century to show what a century of secularizing godlessness has done to men and women.

David's life, in contrast, was a God-affirming and God-affirmed life, large and expansive, what Jesus named as having "life . . . abundantly" (John 10:10), and what Paul calls "the immeasurable greatness of his power for us who believe" (Eph. 1:19).

David, with all his rough edges, never gets around to loving his enemies the way his descendant Jesus would do it, and his morals and manners leave a lot to be desired. These do not come across in the story, though, as disfiguring blemishes so much as simply the conditions in which we all must work. Nor is there any danger that David's failures and sins will be used to legitimize bad behavior; we read them, rather, as evidence that we don't first become good and then get God. First we get God—and then over a patient lifetime are trained in God's ways.

SECOND POEM: "THE LAST WORDS OF DAVID" (23:1–7)

"Last words" are words to be held on to, savored, and pondered. Last words are not trivial words, "throwaway" words. Last words can be tested for authenticity against an entire life now available to examination: If they pass the test, they acquire authority. Tested against life, they can be judged true or false by that life. If the person's life falsifies the words, we forget them. But if the person's life is foundational to the words, we hold them dear. Christians prize Jesus' seven last words from the cross as distilled gospel. We honor David's last words as a true epitaph to his life.

(These are not, of course, David's literal "last" words. The last words he spoke are recorded in 1 Kings 2, and strike us not as a fulfillment of his life but as a deviation from it—neither typical nor edifying!)

The "last words" are given in the form of a finely crafted poem (David was a good poet!) in three stanzas: David's messianic identity (v. 1), David's kingly work (vv. 2–4), David's covenant legacy (vv. 5–7).

> 23:1 Now these are the last words of David:
> The oracle of David, son of Jesse,
>   the oracle of the man whom God exalted,
> the anointed of the God of Jacob,
>   the favorite of the Strong One of Israel:

First, David's messianic identity. David understood himself as God-defined. This messianic identity is built up in four phrases. First, he was "son of Jesse." Spirituality begins in biology. There is nothing unique about David; he is one of eight sons born to a farmer in Bethlehem. The first phrase is followed by a second. He is not *only* Jesse's son; he is "anointed of the God of Jacob"—biology is only the first word, not the definitive last word on human life. "Anointed" is the same word that comes into English as "messiah." The day Samuel poured oil over David's head and the "spirit of the LORD came mightily upon David" (1 Sam. 16:13), marking him as God's choice as king, David's identity is God-formed. This God-formed identity is then elaborated in two more phrases, "God exalted" and "favorite of the Strong One of Israel." (In earlier translations the final phrase has been translated "sweet psalmist of Israel," but most scholars today are convinced that the Hebrew phrase is more accurately rendered as "favorite of the Strong One of Israel.") Following the proportions of the text, David's identity is made up of one part Jesse to three parts God.

23:2 **The spirit of the LORD speaks through me,**
      his word is upon my tongue.
   3 **The God of Israel has spoken,**
      the Rock of Israel has said to me:
   One who rules over people justly,
      ruling in the fear of God,
   4 **is like the light of morning,**
      like the sun rising on a cloudless morning,
      gleaming from the rain on the grassy land.

Next, David's kingly work. David's identity is vocational. It is not only who he is but also what he does: He is a king. His kingly work is described under two aspects, speaking and ruling. David is aware that God's "word is upon my tongue" and that he is the person "who rules over people justly." There is a sense in which speaking and ruling are one. David is a poet-king. He uses words skillfully and reverently; he occupies his throne justly and reverently. *God's* words and *God's* rule provide precedent and foundation to David's kingly work.

David's life is not separated into private and public, into personal and political, into spiritual and secular. He carries his God-identity into his God-work. What David does is who David is.

David understands his lifework (or work life) as shaped by "the fear of God" and, as such, a rule that brings goodness to people. Using images that combine light ("sun rising") and fertility ("rain on the grassy land"), David portrays a rule characterized as welcome and fruitful, which is to say that it is not oppressive, mean, exploitative, or tyrannical. David's work in ruling Israel is a playing out of God's work of ruling humankind.

23:5 **Is not my house like this with God?**
      For he has made with me an everlasting covenant,
      ordered in all things and secure.
   Will he not cause to prosper
      all my help and my desire?
   6 **But the godless are all like thorns that are thrown away;**
      for they cannot be picked up with the hand;
   7 **to touch them one uses an iron bar**
      or the shaft of a spear.
   And they are entirely consumed in fire on the spot.

Finally, David's covenant legacy. "Everlasting covenant" sets who David is and what David does in a context far larger than David. God's word and work in creation and salvation are far, far larger than anything that David says or does—a world both immense and intricate. David is conscious that all his life he has been a participant in God's sovereignty, but he is also quite aware that he has not been the sovereign, the one running things. He has never been indispensable to God's purposes. "Covenant" is one of the huge words threaded through the biblical revelation in which we can trace God's intentions and faithfulness, God's initiative and steadfast love, and God's inventive grace and imaginative mercy. Covenant means that God has made all the critical decisions and that God will follow through on them. Covenant means that we are pulled into what God has done and is doing (we do not desperately pull God into what we are doing). In the presence of covenant, we are prevented from isolating ourselves in the cramped quarters of our feelings and experience. Because of covenant we live in hope: "Will he not cause to prosper/all my help and my desire?"

The nontheological word that we use for arrangements between two parties is "contract." Contract is superficially something like covenant, but with God left out. Humans make contracts; God makes a covenant. Contracts are the way in which we try to work out fair and just arrangements between people who have conflicting self-interests. We use contracts across a wide spectrum of relations: political, business, educational, and marital. But necessary as they are, they don't work very well. The evidence that they don't work very well is that through the centuries we have developed a huge and sprawling legal and judicial system to deal with the consequences of dishonored or failed contracts. We human beings do not seem to be very good at keeping contracts—we are not honest enough, not steadfast enough.

But unlike a contract, covenant is initiated and guaranteed by God. Covenant lasts. Covenant is an arrangement that includes us but that is not dependent for its validity on us. Covenant is God's sovereignty expressed in such a way that it includes our participation. Covenant is a binding freedom. Covenant is a grand and freeing word. When David looks back over his life, he understands it in terms of God's covenant: "Is not my house like this with God?" (v. 5).

The metaphor used to describe those who refuse to live in covenant ("the godless") is thorns—useless and impossible to work with, the sooner burned up the better. The contrast with the earlier image of sun and rain (v. 4) could not be stronger or easier to imagine. There are many ambiguities in life, difficult-to-make decisions regarding what to say and do, but this is not one of them. The difference between a life in God's covenant and a perpetual round of negotiated contracts is like the difference between letting the sun rise on you on a cloudless morning and an endless round of picking up thorns with your bare hands. No contest.

When we test these words against David's life, questions arise: Is this an idealized, romantic cover-up of what actually happened? Is this an attempt to make David look far better than he ever was?

These questions are answerable. First of all, there has been no attempt throughout the David story to idealize him. All his sins and failures have been dragged out into the light of day for public scrutiny. Second, even though the primary story line has been about God's choice of David as king and his providence worked through David's rule, it has also been easy to "read" the underlying tensions between political factions throughout. The considerable political scheming that has gone on between the Saul party and the David party has not been suppressed. We are not being given an impersonal and objective "history" of David—the bias toward presenting David as the legitimate king and Solomon as his successor has been quite out in the open.

And so, given the frankness and honesty in which the story has been told, we can hardly suppose that these "last words" are intended to "theologize" or "spiritualize" David in death into something that he was not in life (like the embarrassing eulogies that are sometimes delivered at funerals).

Rather, what we are given in this poem is "last" words in the sense of "final"—the essence of David, the heart of the story in which David figures so prominently. Read in this way, David is exhibited with great clarity as an everyman—this is what the newspaper obituaries don't report, what family members have long forgotten, and what the psychologists never were able to see: *God* in this person, in me, in you—in David. The Christian community, reading the David story retrospectively from the Jesus story, reads "into" the Christian life what in these "last words" of David is foundational to the Christian life: messianic (Christ) identity, kingly (Holy Spirit–directed) work, and a covenant (God-sovereign) context.

SECOND LIST: "THE NAMES OF THE WARRIORS" (23:8–39)

23:8 **These are the names of the warriors whom David had . . .** [39] **. . . — thirty-seven in all.**

This list of warriors in David's service, analogous to the list of giant killers in 21:15–22, is full of interest to those who search for clues to the composition of David's company. Scholars comb the list and find much that throws light on the variety of men who served David.

The listing is illuminated at the center by a vivid and representative anecdote from David's fugitive days at the cave of Adullam before he became king (vv. 13–17). The story relates the high-risk exploit of three unnamed men who brought water to David from the "well of Bethlehem." They had overheard David speak nostalgically of how he would love to have a drink from that old well in his hometown. When they brought it to him, having wormed themselves through treacherous ranks of Philistines, David, instead of drinking it, poured it out as a kind of sacramental offering in honor of the men's loyalty. It was water that was too good, too holy, to be merely drunk. There must have been hundreds of such stories about David floating around from the "old days" but not included in the main story. A few hundred years later, this particular story is picked up and integrated into the "official" narrative of the Davidic dynasty as told in the book of Chronicles (see 1 Chron. 11:15–19).

Two names from David's roster of warriors call for special comment, one by its placing, the other by its omission. Uriah the Hittite is placed as the final name in the list, where it must be noticed. The unadorned name triggers memories of David at one of his worst moments; Uriah is the epitome of the obediently loyal servant betrayed by his master in an attempt to save his own skin. Uriah's name at the end of the list is an eloquent reminder that David cannot be elevated past criticism, idealized into transcendence, or used as a moral model. Whenever that happens in sermon or Sunday school lesson, someone needs to step up and simply say, "Uriah the Hittite."

The omitted name is Joab. Joab was the single most important man in David's company. From a strictly historical point of view, it is unthinkable that Joab's name be omitted from the listing of David's warriors. It is hardly conceivable that David could have either achieved the throne or held on to it without Joab. Undeterred by moral scruples, the ruthless strongman Joab did what had to be done to bring David to power and keep him there. So why is he not in the list? Was someone not paying attention? Did the writer inadvertently forget? Joab's name could not have been accidentally omitted; it was *deleted*. And it was deleted in order to say, in effect: "Joab is not necessary to this story; you may think that David could not have been God's king without Joab's ungodly help. Joab certainly thought he was necessary. David probably thought he was necessary. But he was not necessary. God uses people like Joab, but he does not need them. No. This story can be read whole and complete without Joab's name being mentioned." For a secular historian who deals exclusively with human motives and actions, pulling the name of Joab out of the account would be like removing every third or fourth stud from the walls of a building, resulting in the collapse of the entire narrative structure—Joab was the single most important person holding things together both militarily and politically. For a theological historian, who believes that God is present and at work in everything that men and women do, pulling the name of Joab out of the account is more like taking a piece of siding off an exterior wall—you notice the blank spot but it doesn't threaten the structure. And so the writer of Samuel, in compiling this final list of the people who count most in David's kingdom, quietly omits Joab. And we do not even miss him. Joab was only self-important. He was not David-important, and certainly not God-important.

SECOND STORY: THE PESTILENCE AND ARAUNAH (24:1–25)

The first story in this concluding mosaic of David materials (21:1–14) featured a disaster (famine) and a named person (Rizpah) who was involved in the recovery; this second matches it with another disaster (pestilence) and a named person (Araunah) involved in the recovery. And, of course, David is centrally involved in each story. Like the famine/Rizpah story, this plague/Araunah story involves a sin that has consequences in natural disaster, a disaster that ends when David acts appropriately. But there are also differences.

> 24:1 **Again the anger of the LORD was kindled against Israel, and he incited David against them, saying, "Go, count the people of Israel and Judah."**

This first sentence has two statements in it that set this story at odds with our modern, Enlightenment-trained ways of thinking: "The anger of the LORD was kindled" and "[The LORD] incited David [to sin]." God is angry for no reason; God incites David to commit a sin. Faced with a God who gets angry irrationally and a God who seduces his anointed king to do something disastrous, we ask, "What's going on here?" Later in the episode we will meet up with the destroying angel (vv. 16–17). None of these elements "make sense" to us. For people who like their religion tidy and explanatory, this does not make for a good ending. Our questions (Why is God angry? What kind of God is this who tricks David into sinning? What business do angels have destroying people—I thought they were around to help?) make it difficult to get beyond the first sentence.

But the story isn't concerned with answering our questions. The story comes out of a world where God is beyond (but not beneath) our understanding and does not feel compelled to account for what he does or the way he does it. God, while never irrational, cannot be reduced to rational explanations. God exceeds our understanding; we cannot confine God to what we can figure out about him. God is sovereign mystery. When Job tried to get answers to questions like this, God put him in his place with a volley of questions of his own, beginning with, "Who is this that darkens counsel by words without knowledge?" and "Where were you when I laid the foundation of the earth?" (Job 38:2, 4).

All the same, this story is disturbingly awkward theologically: God angry without cause; God seducing David to sin. The awkwardness, though, turns out to be useful, for it prevents us from reducing God to what we expect or understand of God. It keeps us alert and receptive to divine mystery. It shakes us out of our cultural preconceptions. It stands in the way of distilling the Bible into predictable moralizing anecdotes. God will not fit into our idea of how we think God should act. But if we stay with the story long enough (all the way to Jesus!) we find that God is more, not less, better, not worse than what we expect. Truth that is larger than ourselves, whether scientific or theological, is always at first baffling. It is painful to be torn away from the womblike security of accepted concepts. Honest readers of the Bible spend much of their time scratching their heads. And those who teach others to read the Bible do well not to be too ready to cook up explanations that eliminate the difficulties. When we submit ourselves to the story itself, we find that from the impenetrable dark clouds of divine sovereignty and human sin, shafts of sunlight break through—prayer, mercy, forgiveness, promise.

In this large context of God's sovereign mystery, David does three things: He takes a census (vv. 2–9), he listens to his heart and Gad, God's prophet (vv. 10–17), and he buys Araunah's threshing floor and builds an altar on it (vv. 18–25).

> 24:2 **So the king said to Joab . . . , "Go through all the tribes of Israel, from Dan to Beer-sheba, and take a census of the people. . . . "** [4] **. . . So Joab and the commanders of the army went out . . . to take a census of the people of Israel. . . .** [9] **Joab reported to the king the number of those who had been recorded: in Israel there were eight hundred thousand soldiers able to draw the sword, and those of Judah were five hundred thousand.**

It becomes obvious as this story is told that the census taking is a flagrant sin. Even Joab, who is not noted for spiritual and moral sensitivities, objects. But David persists. The sin-nature of the census is not explained, but students of this text are agreed that it involves a radical departure from living by faith—counting soldiers is the opposite of trusting in God; census taking stands in contrast to the kind of praying we find in Psalm 20: "Some take pride in chariots, and some in horses,/but our pride is in the name of the LORD our God" (Psalm 20:7). A census provides the basis for conscripting soldiers (explicit in our story, v. 9) and assessing taxes, two primary features of depersonalized and tyrannizing state power. David's government, which is intended to represent a personal God, now moves into faceless bureaucracy. Somewhere along the line, David has become more interested in numbers than in names.

The plague that follows is a dramatic rendition of what usually follows more slowly and subtly. Sin has social consequences. The king sins and the people get sick. The act of sin is not always public, attention-getting, and reported in the newspapers. More often it is disguised in routines and only afterward, sometimes a long time afterward, is found to be killing people all over the place. Wendell Berry, Kentucky farmer and American prophet, is blunt: "It is easy to assume that we do not participate in what we are not in the presence of. But if we are members of a society, we participate, willy-nilly, in its evils" (Berry, *What Are People For?* 81).

The devil's work is abstraction, turning people into statistics, turning local conditions into generalized ideas. The evil with David was not in the "numbering" itself, but the replacement of names by numbers. The practice and habit of using numbers to account for reality is at the root of many evils in society: the horror of war masked by "body counts"; the dumping grounds of poverty disinfected by the "percentage of unemployed"; the rapaciousness of greed hidden behind "net worth" and "annual profits." The moment these accounting procedures dominate the life of church and community and government, great evils run rampant and undetected.

24:10 But afterward, David was stricken to the heart because he had numbered the people. David said to the LORD, "I have sinned greatly in what I have done. But now, O LORD, I pray you, take away the guilt of your servant; for I have done very foolishly." [11] When David rose in the morning, the word of the LORD came to the prophet Gad, David's seer, saying, [12] "Go and say to David: Thus says the LORD . . . [13] . . . "Shall three years of famine come to you on your land? Or will you flee three months before your foes while they pursue you? Or shall there be three days' pestilence in your land?" . . . [14] Then David said to Gad, " . . . let us fall into the hand of the LORD, for his mercy is great; but let me not fall into human hands."

> [15] So the LORD·sent a pestilence on Israel . . . and seventy thousand of the people died. . . . [16] But when the angel stretched out his hand toward Jerusalem to destroy it, the LORD relented concerning the evil, and said to the angel who was bringing destruction among the people, "It is enough; now stay your hand." The angel of the LORD was by then by the threshing floor of Araunah the Jebusite. [17] When David saw the angel who was destroying the people, he said to the LORD, "I alone have sinned, and I alone have done wickedly; but these sheep, what have they done? Let your hand, I pray, be against me and against my father's house."

David's sin results in a plague that kills seventy thousand people. David responds by taking responsibility and praying for mercy. Prayer brackets the plague (vv. 10 and 17). After his census taking, a prideful act in the service of ambition and power, David finds himself dealing with God. The seer (or prophet) Gad brings God's word to him (Nathan did this work on earlier occasions), and David quickly finds himself dealing not with his own plans but with God's. David prays. His first prayer is one of repentance (v. 10). His second prayer is intercession (v. 17). He knows he has done wrong and admits it. He accepts responsibility and intercedes for those who are suffering because of his sin. We are not told how he comes to this realization, but he does—and his first response to his sin is to pray. David deals with God. His second response is to pray for those who are caught in the consequences of his sin. David does not always obey God, but he always *deals* with God. David is not always sensitive to God, but he always ends up calling on God. David is not always prayerful, but he always ends up praying. This final David story has, fittingly, David praying, confessing his sins and caring for the people, prayer personal and for the people. The psalms, so many of which are ascribed to David, remember David primarily as a person of prayer. This concluding story in Samuel shows David in the act of prayer.

"Stricken to the heart," David repents his venture into numbering the people and returns to the far more personal language of "these sheep" (v. 17). It is the same image that Jesus later employs to emphasize his particular attention to and personal care for every soul (Luke 15:3–7; John 10:1–18).

> 24:18 That day Gad came to David and said to him, "Go up and erect an altar to the LORD on the threshing floor of Araunah the Jebusite." [19] Following Gad's instructions, David went up . . . [24] . . . [and] bought the threshing floor and the oxen for fifty shekels of silver. [25] David built there an altar to the LORD, and offered burnt offerings and offerings of well-being. So the LORD answered his supplication for the land, and the plague was averted from Israel.

David's third action is to buy Araunah's threshing floor and build an altar on it. Araunah is identified as a Jebusite, that is, a survivor of David's earlier capture of Jerusalem. Araunah is eager to give the threshing floor to David, but David insists on paying. He will not use his position as king or the desperate conditions of the plague to shortcut his own responsibilities: "I will not offer burnt offerings to the LORD that cost me nothing" (v. 24).

Previous to this incident (this story is undated, but obviously pulled out of its chronological sequence), David had captured Jerusalem (2 Sam. 5:6–10). The Jebusites, who lived there, were defeated, and David made the city the capital of the United Kingdom (Judah and Israel). The first thing he did was build a palace from which to rule (2 Sam. 5:11–12); he followed this up by bringing the ark of the covenant to Jerusalem in order to establish a central place of worship for the United Kingdom (2 Samuel 6). And then David moved to what seemed like the climax to this sequence of actions: He announced that he would build a temple of God for the ark of the covenant. He would provide a flourishing final architectural focus on *God* the King, ruling and saving. David's pastor, Nathan, approved the plan, but after a night of prayer, withdrew his approval. He told David that God would not permit him to build God's temple. David's son would build a house of God, but not David. David prayerfully and obediently accepted the interruption in his plans to do something great for God, and submitted himself to letting God do what still needed to be done by God for David (2 Samuel 7). Many students of this text see this as the most important thing David ever did, this sovereign not-doing that cleared the ground for God to express his sovereignty first of all in a "house not made with hands" (2 Cor. 5:1).

A rehearsal of this background is necessary for understanding the significance of David's purchasing the threshing floor of Araunah. For this very threshing floor would later become the site for the Temple of God that Solomon eventually built. We learn this from the later retelling of the David story in 1 Chronicles 21–22 (where Araunah is spelled Ornan). This link between Araunah's threshing floor and the site of Solomon's Temple would, of course, have been known to the first hearers and readers of the story without its being spelled out.

And so this final story in Samuel shows us David providing the foundation for the temple that he was not permitted to build. It was a foundation that came not from David's achievements but from his forgiven sin, not from what David did for God, but for what God did for him, listening to his prayers and having mercy on the people. It is also significant that it is a foundation that David acquired peaceably and not by violence; he paid Araunah a fair price for it.

In the final story in this David summation (chapters 21–24), David sins and God forgives, David prays and God listens, David builds an altar and worships and God delivers. At the site where David worships, there will soon be a temple built (by Solomon) that will give focus and structure to the worship of God's people for the next five hundred years.

There is a great temptation in making a conclusion to make it tidy and neat. And when theological and moral issues are involved, the temptation is especially strong. But tidiness does violence to both scripture and life.

An old Sufi story about a folk figure named Nasrudin exposes the violence involved in tidiness. Nasrudin found a falcon sitting on a windowsill. He had never seen a bird of this kind before. "You poor thing," he said, "how were you ever allowed to get into such a state?" He clipped the falcon's talons, cut its beak straight, and trimmed its feathers. "Now you look more like a bird," said Nasrudin.

It is noteworthy that this is not the kind of conclusion we are given in the David story. We are given a conclusion, but not a manicured conclusion.

The six episodes of chapters 21–24, pulled out of various contexts and times and artfully arranged, provide a comprehensive sense of ending without domesticating the David story into something morally manageable and theologically tame. The art is impressive: two stories, two lists, and two poems arranged concentrically: story one, list one, poem one, and then poem two, list two, and story two, in reverse order. The stories provide the large, comprehensive context; the lists assert the conditions in which it all takes place; the poems form a center where God is encountered. There is symmetry here, but a restrained symmetry. God does not make codes or diagrams, he makes creatures. The David story is full of odd angles, unexplained mysteries, awkward moments—the conclusion honors the hiddenness of God in all of this.

The two bracketing stories give us the essential David. Story is the primary literary form in the Bible as a whole, and in the books of Samuel. By means of story, David is presented to us as personal and particular—he is not generalized into a "truth," but put before us in a great diversity of settings and relationships. These two final stories are representative in that they pull marginal people, Rizpah and Araunah, into the plot. Rizpah, an abused and powerless woman, and Araunah, a non-Israelite survivor of David's Jerusalem campaign, are treated with dignity—named and necessary to David. In both of these stories David is flawed and failed and on his knees seeking help. David is central to the story, but he is not sufficient. He is not a hero who dominates and throws everyone else into the shadows. Outsiders like Rizpah and Araunah are essential to the David story. God does not work with the "best and brightest."

The two lists provide stark evidence of the workaday culture in which David lived and did his work. It was a warring culture made up of warriors. God's holy revelation is put forth and God's holy people are formed in conditions that are decidedly unholy. The social world in which this story has taken place is coarse and crude—the sexual practices and warring traditions that David more or less took for granted were shaped far more by Canaanite mythologies than by Mosaic commands. There are some who cynically read the David story exclusively in terms of his environment. The cynic reduces David to a bloody barbarian chieftain with a minor talent for poetry. But while the culture defines the world in which David lived, it does not define David. Neither does it obliterate the salvation work of God. Culture, whether tenth century B.C. Canaanite or twenty-first century A.D. North American, is the straw used to make the bricks of the city of God. The two lists stand as a quiet rebuke to any who attempt to avoid culture and construct a holy place in which God can do his work (or to do God's work for God) uncorrupted and uncontaminated by the godless world's ways.

The two poems at the center are, respectively, a prayer and an oracle. Prayer is our speech addressed *to* God: petition and praise. Oracle is our speech as it derives *from* God: proclamation and witness. Poetry is our most intense and intimate use of words. The two poems present David at his most intense and most intimate. David is a poet using words to *make* and not just to say. Words, the primary means of God's revelation, making the world and the world's Savior, are taken up by David. David uses words to speak to God (the prayer) and to speak from God (the oracle).

These three elements (stories, lists, poems), each doubled so that we get it right, are all necessary to receive this narrative rightly: the diverse humanity of David told in the stories; the barbaric culture of which David was a part represented in the lists; and the soul of David developed and expressed in the poems.

Insofar as this is also the story of every man and woman, we see ourselves led through the concentric circles, affirmed in our basic humanness, confronted with the inescapable conditions of our culture, and from time to time finding our true voice at the center, speaking to and for God.

Works Cited

Auerbach, Erich. *Mimesis.* Trans. Willard Trask. Princeton, N.J.: Princeton University Press, 1953.

Barth, Karl. *Church Dogmatics.* Trans. G. T. Thompson. Edinburgh: T. & T. Clark, 1936.

Berry, Wendell. *What Are People For?* San Francisco: North Point Press, 1990.

John Bright. *The Kingdom of God.* Nashville: Abingdon Press, 1958.

———. *A History of Israel.* Philadelphia: Westminster Press, 1959.

Brueggemann, Walter. *First and Second Samuel.* Interpretation: A Bible Commentary for Teaching and Preaching. Louisville, Ky.: John Knox Press, 1990.

Butterfield, Herbert. *International Conflict in the Twentieth Century.* New York: Harper & Brothers, 1960.

Calvin, John. *Commentary on the Book of Psalms.* Trans. James Anderson. Grand Rapids: Wm. B. Eerdmans Publishing Co., 1949.

Chesterton, G. K. *George Bernard Shaw.* New York: Hill & Wang, 1956.

Hertzberg, Hans Wilhelm. *I & II Samuel.* The Old Testament Library. Philadelphia: Westminster Press, 1964.

Heschel, Abraham. *The Prophets.* New York: Harper & Row, 1962.

Lewis, C. S. *The Four Loves.* London: Geoffrey Bles, 1960.

McCarter, P. Kyle, Jr. *II Samuel.* The Anchor Bible. Vol. 9. Garden City, N.Y.: Doubleday & Co., 1984.

Miskotte, Kornelis H. *When the Gods Are Silent.* Trans. John W. Doberstein. London: William Collins Sons, 1967.

Noth, Martin. *The History of Israel.* London: A. & C. Black, 1958.

von Balthasar, Hans Urs. *The Glory of the Lord.* Vol. 2. San Francisco: Ignatius Press, 1984.

von Hugel, Baron Friedrich. *Essays & Addresses on the Philosophy of Religion, Second Series.* London: J. M. Dent & Sons, 1963.

von Rad, Gerhard. *Old Testament Theology*. Vol. 1. New York: Harper & Row, 1962.

Whyte, Alexander. *Bible Characters*. Vol. 1. London: Oliphants Ltd., 1952.

Williams, Charles. *The Descent of the Dove*. London: Longmans, Green & Co., 1939.

Hymns Cited

The hymn "Come, Thou Fount of Every Blessing" is by Robert Robinson, 1758, and is no. 356 in *The Presbyterian Hymnal*. Louisville, Ky.: Westminster/John Knox Press, 1990.

The hymn "Let All the World in Every Corner Sing" is by George Herbert, 1633, and is no. 468 in *The Presbyterian Hymnal*. Louisville, Ky.: Westminster/John Knox Press, 1990.

The hymn "He Who Would Valiant Be," by John Bunyan, 1684, was adapted by Percy Dearmer, 1906, and is no. 414 in *The Worshipbook*. Philadelphia: Westminster Press, 1970.

For Further Reading

Bright, John. *The Kingdom of God*. Nashville: Abingdon Press. 1953.

Brueggemann, Walter. *First and Second Samuel*. Interpretation: A Bible Commentary for Teaching and Preaching. Louisville, Ky.: John Knox Press, 1990.

Hertzberg, Hans. *I & II Samuel*. Philadelphia: Westminster Press, 1964.

Sternberg, Meir. *The Poetics of Biblical Narrative*. Bloomington, Ind.: Indiana University Press, 1985.

LaVergne, TN USA
18 January 2010
170355LV00003B/9/A